Discipleship Essentials

A GUIDE TO BUILDING YOUR LIFE IN CHRIST

EXPANDED EDITION

Greg Ogden

IVP Connect

An imprint of InterVarsity Press
Downers Grove, Illinois

InterVarsity Press
P.O. Box 1400, Downers Grove, IL 60515-1426
World Wide Web: www.ivpress.com
E-mail: email@ivpress.com

1st edition ©1998 by Greg Ogden

Expanded edition ©2007 by Greg Ogden

InterVarsity Press® is the book-publishing division of InterVarsity Christian Fellowship/USA®, a student movement active on campus at hundreds of universities, colleges and schools of nursing in the United States of America, and a member movement of the International Fellowship of Evangelical Students. For information about local and regional activities, write Public Relations Dept., InterVarsity Christian Fellowship/USA, 6400 Schroeder Rd., P.O. Box 7895, Madison, WI 53707-7895, or visit the IVCF website at <www.intervarsity.org>.

All Scripture quotations, unless otherwise indicated, are taken from the Holy Bible, New International Version®. NIV®. *Copyright ©1973, 1978, 1984 by International Bible Society. Used by permission of Zondervan Publishing House. All rights reserved.*

The readings "Demands My All" (chap. 2), "Handling the Trauma of Holiness" (chap. 6) and " The Intimate Presence" (chap. 14) are used by permission of Darrell Johnson.

The reading "If Quiet Time Is New to You" (chap. 3), adapted from Lord of the Universe, Lord of My Life, *is used by permission.*

Design: Cindy Kiple

Images: Anatoliy Zavodskov/iStockphoto

ISBN 978-0-8308-1087-1

Printed in the United States of America ∞

Library of Congress Cataloging-in-Publication Data

Ogden, Greg.
  Discipleship essentials: a guide to building your life in Christ/
  Greg Ogden.—Expanded ed.
    p. cm.
  Includes bibliographical references.
  ISBN-13: 978-0-8308-1087-1 (pbk.: alk. paper)
  1. Christian life—Study and teaching. I. Title.
  BV4511.O33 2007
  248.4017—dc22

                                                                                    2007031446

| P | 24 | 23 | 22 | 21 | 20 | 19 | 18 | 17 | 16 | 15 | 14 | 13 | 12 | 11 | 10 | 9 | 8 | 7 | 6 | 5 |
| Y | 28 | 27 | 26 | 25 | 24 | 23 | 22 | 21 | 20 | 19 | 18 | 17 | 16 | 15 | 14 | 13 | 12 | 11 | 10 | 09 |

To Eric
a dear brother who in his dying
radiated the presence
of the living Christ.

Contents

A Word from the Author

Since the first release of *Discipleship Essentials*, it has been quite gratifying to see that this tool has been used in such a variety of settings to assist the growth and multiplication of disciples of Jesus. The response to *Discipleship Essentials,* though, is simply an indicator of a broadly felt need. Discipleship or spiritual formation appears to be a theme that is coming into focus as a vital necessity.

Dietrich Bonhoeffer chided the church two generations ago because we were settling for what he called "cheap grace." He said that we were practicing a brand of Christianity without a cross. This was *easy believism*. In many circles it would seem that all that is necessary is to embrace certain creedal tenets, such as justification by faith alone. The ability to affirm right doctrine signifies that we are in the club. Dallas Willard has dubbed this as "bar code" Christianity. If we can be rung up by the great scanner in the sky, then eternal life is assured. With this understanding of the Christian life, what is the need to have a transformed life?

Michael Wilkins comes at the same issue from a different angle. In his survey of Christian groups, people will readily identify themselves as "Christians," but be quite reluctant to call themselves "disciples." Why might this be? Being a Christian is easy. The only thing required is that we acknowledge our need of a savior and to receive a gift that I cannot earn nor deserve. But if I identify myself as a disciple, then I am making a statement about the quality of my followership. Being a Christian is a statement about what Christ has done for me; being a disciple is a statement about what I am doing for Christ. X

Our problem is that we have made peace with an unbiblical distinction. Christian leaders have sent the message that it is alright to be a Christian without being a disciple of Christ. We expect that only a small percentage of Christians will "graduate" into the category of discipleship. We are reaping the results of the false notion that we have sown. It is broadly being acknowledged today by Christian leaders that we have done a miserable job of making disciples. George Barna and George Gallup consistently tell us that their polling demonstrates that in terms of moral values and lifestyle choices there is little distinction between Christian and non-Christian. We are compromised at the core.

We must reaffirm that biblically that there is no distinction between embracing God's grace as a forgiven sinner and following Jesus as the primary shaping influence over our life. Christian and disciple are interchangeable as we read in Acts, "The disciples were called Christians first at Antioch" (Acts 11:26). Therefore we must recalibrate where we set the bar of discipleship.

Discipleship Essentials was conceived for this very purpose. What are the basics that a follower of Jesus needs to *practice as spiritual disciplines* (part 1), *comprehend as core biblical and theological truth* (part 2), *become in terms of character and lifestyle* (part 3), and *do to engage the church and the world* (part 4)? This is the content, but what is the context? One of the key issues here is—how are disciples made? The church has settled for a program approach. Pastors stand up in front of their congregations announcing the latest enrichment opportunities while the same 20 percent show up. "You all come!" we shout. They stay away in droves.

Disciples, though, are made in relationships through personal, eyeball-to-eyeball invitation. How different this is from our normal approach to the program church! When I begin a new discipleship group of three or four, I approach a potential participant only after having prayed for a sense of call to this person. I say to them something like, "I have been praying about who to ask to join with me and a couple of others on a journey together as we grow to be followers of Christ. The Lord has put you on my heart. Would you come along with me as we grow together over the next year to live more fully into what it means to be a disciple of Jesus Christ?" Oh, how different it feels to be issued a personal call rather than a mass invitation!

I said at the outset of my book *Transforming Discipleship* that transformation in these small, reproducible groups of three or four has been the "ah-ha!" of my ministry. Almost every week for the last twenty-two years, I have had at least one of these groups in my schedule and it is always the highlight of my life. To the see these same people then reproduce by discipling others so that there is growth of a multi-generational tree—wow! It doesn't get any better than this!

To all those who have written to me with their stories of transformation, I have been blessed through them to know that the call to write this material has been met with hungry hearts who have taken the task of making disciples seriously is most fulfilling! Thank you from the bottom of my heart.

I can only hope and pray that a century from now (if Christ has not returned) when church historians study the time in which we live that it will be called an *age of discipleship*.

Greg Ogden
April 2007

Getting the Most from
Discipleship Essentials

What would happen to the church of Jesus Christ if a majority of those who claim to follow Christ were nurtured to maturity through intimate, accountable relationships centered on the essentials of God's word? Self-initiating, reproducing disciples of Jesus would be the result.

Discipleship Essentials is specifically designed to implement small, reproducible discipleship units. The vision that stands behind this tool is an ever-expanding, multi-generational discipling network. This tool brings together three elements which creates the climate for the Holy Spirit to bring about accelerated growth.

The first element is the unchanging truth of God's Word. We have moved into a post-Christian era in the Western world. Previously, when Christendom reigned, it was generally assumed that there was such a thing as a "revealed" truth or at least scientific, objective truth that was true for all. But now in these post-Christian times relativism prevails, especially in the realm of morals and lifestyles. "Live and let live" is the byword that reflects today's highest value—*tolerance*. It is assumed that all lifestyles and moral convictions are equal, because all truth is personal. In the midst of this morass of relativism, each of these twenty-four chapters is built around a "core truth" that is true for all, because the source of this truth is a God who is the same for all.

For many, the Christian life seems like a mishmash of disconnected tiles. We have pieces of truth collected from sermons, private study, the wisdom of fellow believers, insightful books and so on. Yet we have not put them together so that they together tell a coherent story. One person who used this material in a discipleship group said it was like seeing the empty spaces of a mosaic being filled in, so that she could now see the complete picture of the Christian life and message. The lessons are sequentially laid out so that there is logical flow and tiles are connected.

Yet for the truth of God's Word to be released in its transforming power, it must be pursued in the context of trusting, intimate and lasting relationships.

The second element in the Holy Spirit's laboratory is transparent relationships. The individual has replaced the family or community as the basic unit of our society. Serial and discarded relationships mark our era. The prevailing philosophy is personal fulfillment based upon what feels good or right for me now. Many have not even witnessed the health of long-term, loving commitment. At the core of every human being is the desire for deep and satisfying relationships because we are created in the image of God. God made us for relationship with himself and with one another. A small discipleship group is a place to learn how to intimate and self-revealing in a safe

to love & be loved.

place over time. What we will ultimately have when all is said and done is the people we love.
Transformation occurs when we grapple with the truth of God's Word in the context of transparent relationships. It is a biblical axiom that the Holy Spirit will have free sway in our lives to the extent to which we open ourselves up to one another. Honesty with God is not sufficient. We give God permission to reshape our lives when we risk self-revelation and confession to others. We can't grow in Christ by ourselves. We are people made for community.

There is *a third element that creates the climate for transformation—mutual accountability.* Accountability is taking the relational context of discipleship to another level. Accountability means giving your discipling partners authority to call you to keep the commitments you have made to one another. You will convene your discipling relationship around a mutual covenant (see p.14). A covenant is a shared agreement whereby you clearly state your mutual expectations. In so doing you are giving each other permission to hold you to your agreement.

In summary, when the truth of God's Word is at the heart of self-revealing, intimate relationships rooted in mutual accountability, you have the ingredients for Spirit-motivated transformation. This tool provides the structure for these three elements to come together. Add to this discipling unit a vision for equipping followers of Jesus to pass on the faith from one generation to the next, and you have the components to renew a ministry from the bottom up.

CONTEXTS FOR DISCIPLING

Discipling in the minds of many has become associated with a one-on-one, teacher-student relationship. In writing *Discipleship Essentials* I experimented with this material in a number of contexts. Up to that point my discipling paradigm had also been one-on-one. In addition to this traditional approach I led a threesome called a *triad* and a discipleship group of ten. I was startled by the difference in dynamics. I have come to see groups of three or four as the optimum setting for making disciples.

Why do I believe that a triad or quad to be superior to one-on-one? (1) The one-on-one sets up a teacher-student dynamic. The pressure is upon the discipler to be the answer person or the fountain of all wisdom and insight. When a third person is added, the dynamic shifts to a group process. The discipler can more naturally make his or her contribution in the dynamic of group interchange. (2) Triad discipling shifts the model from hierarchical to relational. The greatest factor inhibiting those who are being discipled to disciple others (multiplication) is the dependency fostered by one-on-one relationsips. The triad/quad, on the other hand, views discipleship as a come-alongside relationship of mutual journey toward maturity in Christ. The hierarchical dimension is minimized. (3) The most startling difference between one-on-one and threes or fours is the sense of "groupness." The sense of the Holy Spirit's being present in our midst occurred much more often in the group versus the one-on-one. (4) There is wisdom in numbers. The group approach multiplies the perspectives on Scripture and application to life issues, whereas one-on-one limits the models and experience. By adding at least a third person there is another perspective brought to the learning process. The group members serve as teachers of one another. (5) Finally, and not to be minimized, by adding a third or fourth person who is being equipped to disciple others, the multiplication process is geometrically increased.

You might ask, if three is better than two, why isn't ten better than three? The larger the group, the more you water down the essential elements that make for transformation. (1) *Truth*—Learning occurs in direct proportion to the ability to interact with the truth, which becomes more difficult with an increased number of voices contributing. It also becomes increasingly difficult to tailor the rate of learning to the individual, the larger the size of the group. (2) *Transparent relationships*—Self-disclosure is integral to transformation, and openness becomes increasingly difficult in direct proportion to the size of the group. If we are not free to divulge our struggles, then the Spirit will not be able to use the group members to effectively minister at the point of need. (3) *Mutual accountability*—The larger the group, the easier it is to hide. Accountability requires the ability to check to see if assignments were completed, or commitments to obedience were maintained. Greater numbers decrease access to a person's life.

ROLE OF THE DISCIPLER

Discipleship Essentials can be used in a number of contexts (personal study, one-on-one, one-with-two or a discipleship group of ten), but whatever the context the key person is the discipler. Tools don't make disciples. God works through disciples to model life in Christ for those who desire maturity. Simply covering the content violates the intent of this tool. The tool is a vehicle which helps create the context and provide content for disciplers who want to invest themselves in love and commitment to growing disciples. The tool raises the issues of discipleship, but the discipler embodies the principles in life patterns and convictions. Modeling will be where the real instruction occurs. Remember Jesus' words, "Everyone when he is fully taught will be *like* his teacher" (Luke 6:40 RSV).

The most recent studies in secular education reveal that modeling is still the most significant learning dynamic. Neither coercion nor rewards shape human behavior as much as a "motivated attempt to resemble a specific person."[1] The lowest level of learning is compliance when one individual has control over another. The second level is identification. Influence is maintained because of a desire to remain in a satisfying relationship. Internalization is the third and highest step, for the desired behavior has become intrinsically rewarding. Modeling creates an atmosphere that affects values, attitudes and behavior.

Some of the specific roles a discipler will carry out are as follows:

1. The first and key role of the discipler is to issue an "invitation to accountable relationship."

The commitment is described and the covenant is signed (see p. 14 for "The Disciple's Covenant"). The discipler becomes the "keeper of the covenant." The discipling process should not commence until the invited disciple has prayed over and signed the covenant of commitment. Without the covenant there are no mutually agreed-upon standards for accountability.

The action pages in *Discipleship Essentials* are the tools for facilitating this accountability role. After lessons eight (p. 80) and sixteen (p. 146) you are asked to review the original covenant and re-covenant together. An action page after lesson twenty (p. 184) asks you to prayerfully consider who will be your discipleship partners for the next leg of journey in order to continue the discipleship chain.

2. Initially, the discipler is the group convener and guide. The lessons are laid out in such a way that the discipler simply walks the partners through the discussion format. Approximately one-quarter to one-third of the way through the discipling process, the members rotate the task of guiding the weekly format, as a way to equip and prepare for leadership of the next generation.

3. The discipler prepares the assignments of *Discipleship Essentials* just as the disciples do. Even though the discipling appointment will be guided by questions asked by the discipler, the guide shares his or her own responses to the discovery questions in the natural flow of conversation.

4. The discipler models transparency by sharing personal struggles, prayer concerns and confession of sin. The discipler does not need to have all the answers to biblical and theological questions. Feel free to say, "I don't know, but I'll try to find the answer or let's research this together." (The power of modeling is not dependent upon a false perfectionism. The discipler will gain as much insight into Scripture and the Christian life as those who are being discipled for the first time.)

SUGGESTED STUDY FORMAT

Though *Discipleship Essentials* is twenty-five sessions, I would not expect that you could cover the assignment in twenty-five weeks. The relationship is always primary. Just plowing through the lessons would violate the spirit of this type of group. Every group will vary in length according to your style of learning, the depth of personal matters you are sharing at any given time and the detours you take to pursue issues raised by the study. Remember that the idea behind a small, tailored discipleship group is to proceed at the pace that is comfortable for the participants. Don't feel obligated to cover every question, but use this book as a menu from which to select, especially if some of the material is familiar and already incorporated in your life.

The assignments are to be completed individually in their entirety prior to the discipling appointment. Each lesson contains discussion guides specifically designed for each of the following elements:

Core Truth—The core truth serves as the nugget around which each lesson is built. The rest of the chapter is designed to further clarify the central focus. Begin each lesson with a review of the core truth's question and answer.

Memory Verse—When we commit the Bible to memory, God's viewpoint on life slowly becomes ours. The psalmist writes, "I have hidden your word in my heart that I might not sin against you" (Psalm 119:11). This discipline helps us grow to be more like Christ as we are grounded in his truth, encourage other believers with God's Word, and share our faith with others. These verses should be reviewed approximately every sixth lesson.

Inductive Bible Study—The place to discover reality from the only perspective that counts is the Bible. We are not interested in stowing away truth as if we were simply trying to acquire more knowledge. The object of this Bible study is to encounter reality and then through X God's power bring our lives in line with it. Larry Richards has summarized well the reality structure of God's Word: "That is, in the Word of God the Spirit of God has revealed the true nature of the world we live in, the true nature of man and of God, the ultimate consummation of history, the pattern of relationships, and response to God and to life which corresponds with 'the way things really are.'"[2]

Reading—Each lesson concludes with a teaching printed in the guide. This reading is intended to provide a contemporary discussion of the eternal core truth that will challenge our lifestyle and stimulate our thinking. The follow-up questions will help make the learning concrete. X

Weave prayer through all that you do. Begin by acknowledging Christ's presence through the   Holy Spirit, and open your lives to what he may desire to do in you. As you deepen your life together through personal sharing, prayer is a response to the burdens you unload or the blessings God gives. Finally, intercede for one another that you can make the changes in thought, word and deed that the Lord has brought to your attention.

---

[1]*The Study of Identification Through Interpersonal Perception,* quoted in Lawrence O. Richards, *A Theology of Christian Education* (Grand Rapids: Zondervan, 1975), p. 83.
[2]Lawrence O. Richards, *Youth Ministry* (Grand Rapids: Zondervan, 1972), p. 29.

A Disciple's Covenant

In order to grow toward maturity in Christ and complete *Discipleship Essentials,* I commit myself to the following standards:

1. Complete all assignments on a weekly basis prior to my discipleship appointment in order to contribute fully (see "Suggested Study Format").

2. Meet weekly with my discipleship partners for approximately one and one-half hours to dialogue over the content of the assignments.

3. Offer myself fully to the Lord with the anticipation that I am entering a time of accelerated transformation during this discipleship period.

4. Contribute to a climate of honesty, trust and personal vulnerability in a spirit of mutual up-building.

5. Give serious consideration to continuing the discipling chain by committing myself to invest in at least two other people for the year following the initial completion of *Discipleship Essentials.*

    Signed_____

    Dated_____

(The above commitments are the minimum standards of accountability, which are reviewed and renewed after lessons eight and sixteen. Feel free to add any other elements to your covenant.)

Part One

GROWING UP IN CHRIST

Welcome to a relational discipleship journey that promises a time of accelerated spiritual growth. X This intimate, highly invested experience brings together three ingredients that the Holy Spirit will use to form Christ in you: vulnerability, truth and accountability. *Vulnerability* happens when you open your life in a self-revealing way to other believers, giving permission for the Spirit to work in you. The more honest and transparent you are with others, the more you are entrusting your life to the Lord. The *truth* of Scripture serves as the cutting edge for growth. Since the material in this study is laid out in a sequential and systematic way, you will enjoy seeing the truth take shape before you eyes. Finally, *accountability* involves entering into a mutual covenant with others in which you are giving each other authority to hold one another to your commitments. The combination of these three elements serves as the mold that God uses to give his shape to your life.

Making disciples is the theme of chapter one. Solid foundations will be laid in your life, and a part of spiritual maturity is the desire to pass on that faith to others. May God so take hold of you that you are equipped to invest in others and to make it a commitment for life.

Being a disciple (chapter two) is serious business. The only way to be molded into the person God wants you to be is to abandon self in obedience to Christ.

Chapters three to six focus on the disciplines of faith, what God uses in our lives to help us grow up into Christlikeness. The word *discipline* sometimes carries with it a certain heaviness or weightiness, but the idea of discipline in this book is thought of in the way Richard Foster speaks of it in his *Celebration of Discipline.* He says that spiritual disciplines are those practices that put us in the presence of God where we can have an intimate relationship with him.

Quiet time, the subject of chapter three, introduces the practice of a daily routine of meeting with the Lord. A quiet time can become a safe place where you experience the Lord as your fortress and protector as well as your closest friend. It can be the place in your day where you freely pour out your heart in an unedited fashion and where God can speak back to you through his Word and Spirit.

Bible study is a key ingredient in a quiet time. This book teaches the inductive method, an investigative study where you discover the meaning of a biblical text through a series of discovery questions. This method is used throughout these studies to guide the unearthing of God's truth.

Prayer is another key ingredient of a quiet time. A simple guide for prayer is provided in chapter five to give structure to the dialogue of prayer.

Finally, in chapter six we focus on *worship*. Whether private or public, worship is the activity that will characterize our eternity in heaven, and we can experience a bit of that awe and wonder even now.

PREPARING FOR THE TASK AHEAD

The best way to prepare for your discipling session is to take a little time each day to work through the material. It is much better to spend twenty minutes each day than to do it all in one evening.

Discipline takes practice to incorporate into our daily routine. It has been shown that new habits take approximately three weeks to become comfortable and another three weeks to become a part of one's way of doing things. Pray that these disciplines will become second nature to your life and your partners'.

You have a wonderful, painful, delightful, challenging adventure ahead. God bless you as you grow up into him.

1 / Making Disciples

LOOKING AHEAD

MEMORY VERSE: Matthew 28:18-20
BIBLE STUDY: Luke 6:12-16; 9:1-6, 10
READING: A Biblical Call to Making Disciples

 ## Core Truth

What is discipling?

Discipling is an intentional relationship in which we walk alongside other disciples in order to encourage, equip and challenge one another in love to grow toward maturity in Christ. This includes equipping the disciple to teach others as well.

1. Identify key words or phrases in the question and answer above, and state their meaning in your own words.

2. Restate the core truth in your own words.

3. What questions or issues does the core truth raise for you?

Memory Verse Study Guide

Jesus' mission statement for the church is to make disciples. These pivotal verses (Matthew 28:18-20) are commonly referred to as the Great Commission.

1. *Putting it in context:* Read Matthew 28. What key events precede Jesus' giving the Great Commission, and how would this have affected the disciples?

2. The memory verses are *Matthew 28:18-20.* Copy these verses verbatim.

3. What do these verses teach us about Jesus?

4. Why does Jesus stress his authority (v. 18) as a backdrop to his command to "make disciples"?

5. How is disciplemaking to be carried out?

6. When is a disciple made?

7. How have these verses spoken to you this week?

Inductive Bible Study Guide

Jesus always lived with a view to the end of his earthly ministry. The preparation of a few who would carry on his ministry after he ascended to the Father was ever before him. This Bible study focuses on the training and transference of ministry to his selected disciples.

1. *Read Luke 6:12-16; 9:1-6, 10.* What do you suppose Jesus included in his all-night prayer? (See the reading on page 20 for some ideas.)

2. What can you learn about Jesus' strategic purpose for the selection of the Twelve from 9:1-6?

3. What power and authority was given to the disciples? What power and authority can we expect to receive from Jesus today?

4. What was Jesus' role with the disciples after their return (9:10)?

5. What questions do these passages raise for you?

6. What verse or verses have particularly impacted you? Rewrite key verses in your own words.

Reading: A Biblical Call to Making Disciples

When Jesus commanded his disciples to "go and make disciples of all nations" (Matthew 28:19), he spoke the mission statement for the church. Jesus told his disciples to do what he had done during his three years of ministry. Jesus made disciples by selecting a few into whom he poured his life.

JESUS' METHOD OF DISCIPLEMAKING

What was the strategic advantage of having twelve men who would "be with him" (Mark 3:14)? There are many reasons, but two seem most relevant.

Internalization. By focusing on a few Jesus was able to ensure the lasting nature of his mission. We might wonder why Jesus would risk others' jealousy by publicly selecting twelve from a larger group of disciples (Luke 6:13). Why didn't Jesus simply continue to expand his growing entourage and create a mass movement? The apostle John captures Jesus' caution when people clamored to him because of the marvelous signs: "But Jesus on his part would not entrust himself to them, because he knew all people and needed no one to testify about anyone; for he himself knew what was in everyone" (John 2:24-25 NRSV).

Though Jesus ministered to the needs of the crowds, he knew they were fickle. The same ones who shouted "Hosanna" on Palm Sunday were shouting "Crucify him" five days later on Good Friday. Knowing the whims of the throng, Jesus built his ministry on a select few who would form the superstructure of his future kingdom. Disciples cannot be mass produced but are the product of intimate and personal investment. A. B. Bruce summarizes this point: "The careful, painstaking education of

the disciples secured that the Teacher's influence on the world should be permanent, that His Kingdom should be founded on deep and indestructible convictions in the minds of a few, not on the shifting sands of superficial impressions on the minds of many."[1]

Multiplication. Just because Jesus focused much of his attention on a few does not mean that he did not want to reach the multitudes. Just the opposite. Eugene Peterson puts this truth cleverly: "Jesus, it must be remembered, restricted nine-tenths of His ministry to twelve Jews, because it was the only way to reach all Americans."[2]

Jesus had enough vision to think small. Focusing did not limit his influence—it expanded it. When Jesus ascended to the Father, he knew that there were at least eleven who could minister under the authority of his name, an elevenfold multiplication of his ministry. Robert Coleman captures the heart of Jesus' methodology when he writes, "[Jesus'] concern was not with programs to reach the multitudes but with men the multitudes would follow."

PAUL'S APPROACH TO DISCIPLEMAKING

We see that the apostle Paul adopted the same goal and methodology in his ministry that Jesus modeled. Paul's version of the Great Commission is his personal mission statement. "We proclaim him, admonishing and teaching everyone with all wisdom, so that we may present everyone perfect in Christ. To this end I labor, struggling with all his energy, which so powerfully works within me" (Colossians 1:28-29). Paul is so passionate about making disciples that he compares his agony over the maturity of the flock to the labor pains of a woman giving birth: "My dear children, for whom I am again in the pains of childbirth until Christ is formed in you" (Galatians 4:19).

Following Jesus' method, Paul invested in individuals to make disciples. He too had his sights on the multitudes, but he knew that solid transmission of the faith would not occur as readily through speaking to an audience. Paul encouraged Timothy to use a personal style to link the gospel to future generations when he exhorted him, ("What you have heard from me through many witnesses entrust to *faithful* people who will be able to *teach others* as well" (2 Timothy 2:2) NRSV, emphasis added). Paul envisioned an intergenerational chain of disciples linked together through personal investment. Contained in this verse are generations in the discipling network, creating the following path: Paul → Timothy → faithful people → teach others.

We know Paul lived out this admonition, for his letters are filled with the names of those to whom he gave himself. Paul replaced himself in the battle with soldiers like Timothy, Titus, Silas (Silvanus), Euodia, Syntyche, Epaphroditus, Priscilla and Aquila. They accompanied Paul on his missionary journeys, were entrusted with ministry responsibility and became colaborers in the gospel. Paul attributed the change in their lives to the impact of the message of Christ in his life on them.

The Bible teaches us not only the message of our faith but also the method by which that faith is to be passed on to future generations. We are called to do God's work in God's way. The manner in which the Lord works is incarnational: life rubs up against life. We pass on Christlikeness through intimate modeling.

Paul said, "I urge you to imitate me" (1 Corinthians 4:16) and "You became imitators of us and of the Lord" (1 Thessalonians 1:6).

DISCIPLEMAKING TODAY

Disciplemaking ensures that the gospel is embedded deeply in the lives of mature believers who serve as links to the future. (Discipling then is a relationship where we intentionally walk alongside a growing disciple or disciples in order to encourage, correct and challenge them in love to grow toward maturity in Christ.)

This book brings together three ingredients necessary to produce maturity in Christ. *Relational vulnerability* means honest, self-disclosing and confessional relationships that give the Holy Spirit permission to remake us. Second, *the centrality of truth* is emphasized when people open their lives to one another around the truth of God's Word and the Lord begins to rebuild their lives from the inside out. And third, *mutual accountability* is authority given to others to hold us accountable to mutually agreeable standards—"iron sharpening iron."

We will not make disciples through methods of mass production that attempt shortcuts to maturity. Robert Coleman clarifies the challenge: ("One must decide where he wants his ministry to count—in the momentary applause of popular recognition or the reproduction of his life in a few chosen men who will carry on his work after he has gone."[4]) The irony is that focusing on a few takes a long-range view by multiplying the number of disciples and therefore expands a church's leadership base. (Though adult education programs and small group ministries are good tools to produce maturity, without the focus of small discipling units a solid foundation is difficult to build.) Keith Phillips's chart compares the numeric difference between one person a day coming to Christ and one person a year being discipled to maturity.[5]

Year	Evangelist	Discipler
1	365	2
2	730	4
3	1095	8
4	1460	16
5	1825	32
6	2190	64
7	2555	128
8	2920	256
9	3285	512
10	3650	1,024
11	4015	2,048
12	4380	4,096
13	4745	8,192
14	5110	16,384
15	5475	32,768
16	5840	65,536

Catch the vision and invest yourself now!

[1]A. B. Bruce, *The Training of the Twelve* (Grand Rapids: Kregel, 1971), p. 13.
[2]Eugene Peterson, *Traveling Light* (Downers Grove, Ill.: InterVarsity Press, 1982), p. 182.
[3]Robert E. Coleman, *The Master Plan of Evangelism* (Old Tappan, N.J.: Revell, 1964), p. 21.
[4]Ibid., p. 37.
[5]Keith Philips, *The Making of a Disciple* (Old Tappan, N.J.: Revell, 1981), p. 23.

Reading Study Guide

1. What were Jesus' reasons for choosing twelve to be with him?

What can we learn from this about how to bring people to maturity in Christ?

2. How did Paul emulate Jesus' methodology?

3. Paul wrote in 1 Corinthians, "I urge you to imitate me" (4:16). Can you see yourself saying or living that? Why or why not?

4. What ingredients are necessary for an effective discipling relationship?

5. What questions do you have about the reading?

6. Does the reading convict, challenge or comfort you? Why?

Going Deeper

Coleman, Robert E. *The Master Plan of Evangelism*. Old Tappan, N.J.: Revell, 1964. Summarize the eight-step process outlined in this classic.

2 / Being a Disciple

LOOKING AHEAD

MEMORY VERSE: Luke 9:23-24
BIBLE STUDY: Luke 5:1-11
READING: Demands My All

 Core Truth

Who is a disciple?

A disciple is one who responds in faith and obedience to the gracious call to follow Jesus Christ. Being a disciple is a lifelong process of dying to self while allowing Jesus Christ to come alive in us.

1. Identify key words or phrases in the question and answer above, and state their meaning in your own words.

2. Restate the core truth in your own words.

3. What questions or issues does the core truth raise for you?

Memory Verse Study Guide

Jesus never enticed someone to be a disciple under false pretenses or promises. He clearly laid out the conditions and benefits of being one of his followers.

1. *Putting it in context:* Read Luke 9:18-27. What is the setting for Jesus' call to discipleship?

2. The memory verses are *Luke 9:23-24.* Copy these verses verbatim.

3. What does it mean to deny self?

4. Illustrate ways from your own experience that you attempt to save your life.

5. Why does losing your life for Jesus actually save it?

6. How have these verses spoken to you this week?

Inductive Bible Study Guide

The magnetism and power of the person of Jesus is at the heart of our faith. Note how the following incident portrays the compelling draw as well as the frightening impact of Christ on Peter's life.

1. *Read Luke 5:1-11.* Describe the setting as a backdrop for the dramatic catch of fish (vv. 1-3).

2. What was Jesus trying to demonstrate about himself with the command "Put out into deep water, and let down the nets for a catch" (v. 4)?

3. Notice Peter's conflicted reaction to the large catch of fish (v. 8). Why does he respond in this way?

4. What does it mean to catch people (v. 10)?

5. In verse 11 Luke tells us that the disciples "left everything and followed him." What did they give up? (Notice that this happened immediately after a great business success.)

6. How would you describe the power of the person of Jesus?

7. What questions does this passage raise for you?

8. What verse or verses have particularly impacted you? Rewrite key verses in your own words.

Reading: Demands My All

Darrell Johnson *

"Life is difficult." That is the way M. Scott Peck begins his very helpful book *The Road Less Traveled.*[1]

Most people do not see this truth. Most people believe that life should be easy. The road most traveled is the road of moaning and grumbling about life's difficulties. The road less traveled is the road of accepting life's difficulties and meeting them head-on.

What Peck says about life in general is even more true about life with Jesus Christ. Discipleship is difficult. Following Jesus Christ is costly. In his Sermon on the Mount Jesus made it very clear that living with him meant walking a road less traveled. "Enter through the narrow gate," he said, "for wide is the gate and broad is the road that leads to destruction, and many enter through it. But small is the gate and narrow the road that leads to life, and only a few find it" (Matthew 7:13-14).

Jesus promises to give anyone who will follow him abundant life (John 10:10), but he makes it very clear from the beginning that to follow him is difficult and costly. He calls us to follow him on the road less traveled.

JESUS' TRUE IDENTITY

Mark 8:27-35 may be the hardest of the hard sayings of Jesus. Jesus and his disciples were traveling through the villages around Caesarea Philippi, a city north of the Sea of Galilee. Caesarea Philippi was a pluralistic city, a city of rich and diverse religious and philosophic heritage. Up to this point in his ministry Jesus had done and said things that had stimulated the question "Who is this man?" In Caesarea Philippi Jesus asked his disciples, "Who do people say I am?" After receiving various answers, Jesus then asked the disciples, "Who do you say I am?" Peter, speaking for the Twelve, said, "You are the Christ" (v. 29; Matthew 16:16).

Jesus accepted their answer, but he immediately began to fill those terms—Messiah and Son of God—with unexpected meaning. "The Son of Man," Jesus' favorite way of referring to himself, "must suffer many things and be rejected by the elders, chief priests and teachers of the law, and that he must be killed and after three days rise again" (v. 31). Jesus knew he *must* leave Caesarea Philippi and make his way to Jerusalem. And he knew that in Jerusalem he *must* suffer. And not only suffer but be rejected. And not only be rejected but be killed, crucified. And then be raised.

Peter could not handle Jesus' words. "Never, Lord!" he said. "This shall never happen to you!" (Matthew 16:22). Suffering and death did not fit Peter's concept of the Messiah. The Messiah comes in glory and power.

Peter also knew the implication for himself of Jesus' concept of Messiahship. Just as there would be no resurrection for Jesus without crucifixion, so there would be no resurrection for the disciples without crucifixion. Peter had become the mouthpiece of the tempter, repeating the temptation Jesus had resisted in the wilderness.

*Some of the readings were written by Darrell Johnson, associate professor of pastoral theology, Regent College, Vancouver, B.C.

JESUS' DIFFICULT ROAD LESS TRAVELED

From that day Jesus walked and taught the road less traveled, the road that leads to Easter but that goes right through the cross. There are all kinds of forks in the road offering another way, a way around the cross, but each of them eventually ends in a cul-de-sac. There is only one road to life. This road ends on the other side of the empty tomb, and we do not get there except through the cross.

Jesus gave this hard saying not only to his disciples but also to the multitudes. William Barclay rightly observed, "No one could ever say that he was induced to follow Jesus by false pretenses. Jesus never tried to bribe men by the offer of an easy way."[2] Jesus was up-front with any would-be follower: "If anyone would follow me—and I hope you will because I can give life abundantly—this is what you are in for" (see Mark 8:34-35).

Notice he uses the word *if*. That *if* reflects Jesus' acknowledging our freedom to choose. A certain rich man heard Jesus' call to discipleship, and he walked away (Mark 10:17-22). He heard what he was in for and judged it too costly. Mark tells us that Jesus looked at the man and loved him (v. 21), still knowing what his choice would be. But Jesus did not run after him or change the terms of the call. Jesus said, "Estimate the cost" (Luke 14:28). "You call Me Messiah, Christ. You wish to follow Me? If so, you should realize quite clearly where I am going, and understand that by following Me, you will be going there too."

Jesus uses three vivid phrases to describe the road less traveled: deny yourself, take up your cross, and lose your life for my sake.

Deny yourself. This is probably one of the most misunderstood and misapplied commands of our Lord. The word Mark uses in 8:34 means "to resist," "to reject" or "to refuse," in short, to say no.

The phrase *deny yourself* is used in a number of important New Testament texts. For example, in Mark 14:71 Jesus had been arrested, and Peter was standing outside the courtroom warming himself by a fire. Peter was confronted three times and accused of having known Jesus. He began to curse and swear, saying, "I don't know this man you're talking about." Peter denied that he even knew who Jesus was.

To deny yourself is to say, "I do not know the person."

Denying yourself may involve denying things, but this is not what Jesus is getting at. Neither does it mean denying your self-worth. Denying yourself does not mean denying your feelings. And although some would say if you are enjoying following Jesus, something must be wrong, in truth it is not about denying yourself happiness. Finally, denying yourself does not mean deny your brains.

To deny yourself means to deny your self-lordship. It means saying no to the god who is me, to reject the demands of the god who is me, to refuse to obey the claims of the god who is me. A decisive no—"I do not know Lord Me—I do not bow down to him or her anymore." Jesus calls us to say no to ourselves so we can say yes to him.[4]

Take up your cross. This phrase has also been misunderstood and misapplied. Many people use it to refer to enduring an illness or disability, a negative experience or bothersome relationship: "This is the cross I must bear." But Jesus' words mean much more. "Jesus' statement must have sounded repugnant to the crowd and the disciples alike."[5] The phrase would evoke the picture of a criminal forced to carry a cross beam upon which he was to be publicly executed.

A criminal picked up his cross only after receiving the death sentence. When a criminal carried his cross through the streets, for all practical purposes he was a dead man. His life had ended. A man on his way to public crucifixion "was compelled to abandon all earthly hopes and ambitions."[6] Jesus calls his followers to think of ourselves as already dead, to bury all our earthly hopes and dreams, to bury the plans and agendas we made for ourselves. He will either resurrect our dreams or replace them with dreams and plans of his own.

This is a hard saying, but a liberating saying as well. Human bondage in all its forms is the result of being our own gods. Freedom comes when we lay down the ill-gotten, false crown, when we say no, when we live as though the gods who are us have already died.

Lose your life for my sake. Herein lies the paradox of the road less traveled: we finally find ourselves when we lose ourselves for Jesus' sake. And how do we lose our lives for him? By investing all that we are and have for him and his gospel. By saying to him, "Here is my home, my checkbook, my talents and gifts, my brain, my heart, my hands, my feet, my mouth. Here—it's all yours. Use it all to glorify yourself and further your purpose on earth."

This a risky thing to say according to the world's wisdom. But in the end, when history is completed, what will really matter? Nothing except the kingdom of God. The only investments that pay off in the end are the investments made in the kingdom now. Those who walk the road less traveled, the road of losing everything for Jesus' sake, end up gaining everything that finally matters. Jim

Elliot summarized it well: "He is no fool who gives what he cannot keep to gain what he cannot lose."

That is why Paul told the Philippians, with great joy,

> Whatever was to my profit I now consider loss for the sake of Christ. . . . I consider everything a loss compared to the surpassing greatness of knowing Christ Jesus my Lord, for whose sake I have lost all things. I consider them rubbish, that I may gain Christ. . . . I want to know Christ and the power of his resurrection and the fellowship of sharing in his sufferings, becoming like him in his death, and so, somehow, to attain to the resurrection from the dead. (Philippians 3:7-11)

ACCEPTING THE CHALLENGE

What are some of the signs that we have not yet met Jesus' challenge head-on? The signs abound in churches today and manifest themselves as jealousy—not having what others have; competition—trying to achieve more than the next person; argumentative spirits—needing to have our own way; oversensitivity—becoming resentful when not recognized for our work or wanting it to be noticed that we've lost it all for Christ. We believe that we deserve the things we have—the nice homes and new cars. We plan our future without reference to the kingdom of God and spend the resources we have to improve our own kingdom. We use the gifts of God to advance our own name, our own reputation.

But "unless a kernel of wheat falls to the ground and dies, it remains only a single seed. But if it dies, it produces many seeds" (John 12:24). The road to Easter goes through Good

Friday. The road to new life goes through the death of the old. The road to resurrection goes through crucifixion. Jesus calls us to walk that road, the road he walked.

[1]M. Scott Peck, *The Road Less Traveled* (New York: Simon & Schuster, 1978), p. 15.
[2]William Barclay, *The Gospel of Mark* (Philadelphia: Westminster Press, 1954), p. 201.
[3]F. F. Bruce, *The Hard Sayings of Jesus* (Downers Grove, Ill.: InterVarsity Press, 1983), p. 151.
[4]Bill Lane, *The Gospel According to Mark* (Grand Rapids: Eerdmans, 1974), p. 307.
[5]Ibid., p. 207.
[6]Bruce, *Hard Sayings*, p. 150.

Reading Study Guide

1. Do you agree or disagree with the following statement from Peck: "Life is difficult. . . . Once we truly see this truth, we transcend it"? Why?

2. Why was it difficult for Peter to accept that Jesus must die at the hands of the religious leaders?

   Why is this still difficult to accept?

3. The reading identifies a number of things that denying yourself does not mean. Which speak to you and why?

4. According to the author, to "take up our cross" means that our life is already finished. What does this mean, and how do you react to it?

5. How do we find our lives in losing them?

6. The reading concludes by identifying some signs that we have not met Jesus' radical claims head-on. Which of these are issues for you?

7. What questions do you have about the reading?

8. Does the reading convict, challenge or comfort you? Why?

Going Deeper

Hall, Bill. "Biblical Foundations of Discipleship." Chapter 1 of *The Complete Book of Discipleship*. Colorado Springs: NavPress, 2006.

3 / Quiet Time

LOOKING AHEAD

MEMORY VERSE: Psalm 1:1-3
BIBLE STUDY: John 15:1-11
READING: If Quiet Time Is New to You

 **Core Truth**

How does a disciple grow in Christ on a daily basis?

Just as Jesus went to a "solitary place" to meet with his Father (Mark 1:35), so a disciple should daily pull away from the busyness of life for a quiet time, a personal rendezvous with the Lord and Savior.

1. Identify key words or phrases in the question and answer above, and state their meaning in your own words.

2. Restate the core truth in your own words.

3. What questions or issues does the core truth raise for you?

Memory Verse Study Guide

Healthy fruit in our lives is the byproduct of well-nourished and cultivated roots. If we sink our inner life deep into the truth of God's Word, life will blossom in us.

1. *Putting it in context:* Read Psalm 1. In what ways are the wicked contrasted with the righteous?

2. The memory verses are *Psalm 1:1-3*. Copy these verses verbatim.

3. The blessed man is first defined by what he does not do. What is the blessed man to avoid?

4. What does it mean to delight in the law of the Lord?

5. What comparison is made in verse 3?

   What does this image teach us about how fruit grows and is nurtured in our lives?

6. How would you define *prospers* (v. 3)?

7. How have these verses spoken to you this week?

Inductive Bible Study Guide

Jesus also selects an organic image to describe the kind of relationship that we are to have with him if we are to bear fruit. Jesus says that he is the vine and we are the branches (John 15:5).

1. *Read John 15:1-11.* The word *remain* defines the connection between the vine and the branches (vv. 4, 5, 6, 7, 9, 10). According to these verses, what does it mean to remain?

2. What do we do to remain in the vine?

3. Our purpose, according to Jesus, is to bear fruit (v. 8). What is the nature of the fruit that is to be produced through our lives?

4. Pruning is a necessary process in order to produce more fruit (v. 2). What does the Lord use to prune us of the "dead" branches in our lives?

5. Jesus issues a warning that those branches that do not remain are cut off, thrown into the fire and burned (vv. 2, 6). What does Jesus mean by this?

6. What does Jesus mean when he says, "Apart from me you can do nothing" (v. 5)?

7. Jesus states in verse 11 that the intent of these instructions is to implant his joy in us and bring it to completion. What was the joy of Jesus that he wanted us to have?

8. What verse or verses have particularly impacted you? Rewrite key verses in your own words.

Reading: If Quiet Time Is New to You

Adapted from Lord of the Universe, Lord of My Life.[1]

A daily quiet time is a private meeting each day between a disciple and the Lord Jesus Christ. It should not be impromptu. We can commune with the Lord on a spur-of-the-moment basis many times each day, but a quiet time is a period of time we set aside in advance for the sole purpose of a personal meeting with our Savior and Lord.

A daily quiet time consists of at least three components.

- Reading the Bible with the intent not just to study but to meet Christ through the written Word.

- Meditating on what we have read so that biblical truth begins to saturate our minds, emotions and wills. "Meditate on [the Book of the Law] day and night" (Joshua 1:8).

- Praying to (communing with) God: praising, thanking and adoring him as well as confessing our sins, asking him to supply our needs and interceding for others.

WHY IS IT IMPORTANT?

Why should we have a daily quiet time? There are at least three reasons.

It pleases the Lord. Even if there were no other consequences, this would be sufficient reason for private daily communion with God.

Of all the Old Testament sacrifices there was only one that was daily—the continual burnt offering. What was its purpose? Not to atone for sin but to provide pleasure (a sweet-smelling aroma) to the Lord. The New Testament directs us to continually offer up a sacrifice of praise to God, "the fruit of lips that confess his name"

(Hebrews 13:15). It may astonish us to realize that God is seeking people who will do just that: "They are the kind of worshipers the Father seeks" (John 4:23). One indicator of the depth of our relationship with the Lord is our willingness to spend time alone with him not primarily for what we get out of it but for what it means to him as well.

We receive benefits. The psalmist had this in mind when he wrote, "As the deer pants for streams of water, so my soul pants for you, O God. My soul thirsts for God, for the living God" (Psalm 42:1-2). We benefit from a quiet time in several ways.

- *Information.* We learn about Christ and his truths when we spend time with him and his Word. Before we can obey him we need to know what he commands. Before we can understand what life is all about we need to know what he has taught.

- *Encouragement.* At times we get discouraged. There is no better source for inspiration than the Lord Jesus Christ.

- *Power.* Even when we know what we should be and do we lack the strength to be that kind of person and do those kinds of works. Christ is the source of power, and meeting with him is essential to our receiving it.

- *Pleasure.* Being alone with the person we love is enjoyable, and as we spend time with Christ we experience a joy unavailable anywhere else.

Jesus had a quiet time. "Very early in the morning, while it was still dark, Jesus got up, left the house and went off to a solitary place, where he prayed" (Mark 1:35). If our Lord found it necessary to meet privately with his Father, surely his example gives us a good reason to do likewise.

The question is whether we will be mediocre Christians or growing Christians. A major factor in determining the answer is whether or not we develop the discipline of a daily quiet time.

HOW TO BEGIN

Once you desire to begin a daily quiet time, what can you do to start?

First, remember the principle of self-discipline: do what you should do when you should, the way you should, where you should and for the correct reasons. In other words, self-discipline is the wise use of your personal resources (such as time and energy).

Second, set aside time in advance for your quiet time. A daily quiet time should take place each day at the time when you are most alert. For some this will be in the morning, perhaps before breakfast; for others it will be another time of the day or evening. Though it is not a hard and fast rule, the morning is a preferable time since it begins before the rush of thoughts and activities of the day. An orchestra does not tune its instruments after the concert.

How much time should you spend? This will vary from person to person, but a good plan to follow is to start with ten minutes a day and build up to approximately thirty minutes. This regularly scheduled chunk of time can be a major factor in strengthening self-discipline. Here's a suggestion: pause while reading this and make a decision—now—about when and for how long, beginning tomorrow, you will meet the Lord Jesus Christ for a daily quiet time.

Third, plan ahead. Go to bed early enough so that you can awaken in a refreshed condition to meet Christ. The battle for the daily quiet time is often lost the night before. Staying up too late hampers our alertness, making us bleary-eyed and numb as we meet the Lord, or else we oversleep and skip the quiet time altogether.

Fourth, make your quiet time truly a quiet time. Psalm 46:10 speaks to this: "Be still, and know that I am God." Turn off your radio or television. Find as quiet a place as possible and make sure your location and position are conducive to alertness. Get out of bed. Sit erect. If you are stretched out in bed or reclining in a chair that is too comfortable you might be lulled into drowsiness.

Fifth, pray as you start your time with God. Ask the Holy Spirit to control your investment of time and to guide your praising, confessing, thanking, adoring, interceding, petitioning and meditating, as well as to help you get into the Bible. Open your mind and heart to Scripture.

Sixth, keep a notebook handy. Write down ideas you want to remember and questions you can't answer. (Expression deepens impression—and writing is a good mode of expression.)

Last, share your plans and goals with a friend. Tell him or her you are trying to develop the discipline of a daily quiet time. Request his or her prayer that God will enable you to succeed with your objectives.

WHEN PROBLEMS ARISE

Following are some common problems that are often encountered along the way.

I know I ought to have a daily quiet time, but I don't want to. Solution: Ask the Holy Spirit to plant within you the desire to have a daily quiet time. Nobody else can do this for you. You cannot generate the desire, and no other person can produce it for you.

I don't feel like having a daily quiet time today. Solution: Have your quiet time anyway and honestly admit to Christ that you don't feel like meeting him but that you know he nevertheless is worth the investment of your time. Ask him to improve your feelings and try to figure out why you feel this way. Then work on the factors that produce such failings.

My mind wanders. Solution: Ask the Holy Spirit to give you strength to set your mind on Christ and his Word. Use your self-discipline to direct your mind so that it wanders less and less. If you are in a quiet place, singing, praying and reading out loud will give a sense of dialogue. Your mind will wander less when you write things down, like making an outline for prayer or study notes while reading the Bible.

I miss too many quiet times. Solution: Ask the Lord to strengthen your desire and to give you power to discipline your use of time. Share with another Christian friend your desire to have a daily quiet time and allow your friend to hold you accountable for it. Don't let an overactive conscience or the accusations of the devil play on your guilt. Confess that you have failed to keep your appointment with Jesus, ask his forgiveness and renew your relationship.

My daily quiet time is a drag. Solution: Pray that the joy of the Lord would be restored to your private meeting with Christ (Psalm 51:12). Put some variety into your approach. Sing a hymn for a change, or try a different form of Bible study.

There are two major reasons it is so difficult to develop the discipline of a daily quiet time. First is the influence of the flesh. Keep in mind that your old nature is opposed to daily quiet time (and to every other discipline that would please Christ; see Galatians 5:16-17). Pray that the Holy Spirit will enable your new nature to overcome your old nature in this battle.

The second reason is resistance by Satan. The devil opposes your every effort to please Christ. His strategy is to rob you of daily quiet time joy, to complicate your time schedule by keeping you up late at night and making it hard for you to get up in the morning, to make you drowsy during your time with the Lord, to make your mind wander, and otherwise to disrupt your meeting with Christ. Ask the Holy Spirit to restrain the devil.

Do It Now!

Plan now for your daily quiet time tomorrow—and every tomorrow. If you miss a morning, do not quit. Deny the devil the pleasure of defeating you. Ask the Lord to forgive you for missing the meeting and to help you make it next time. You will doubtless miss several times, and it will take repeated beginnings before you succeed in developing this discipline. Indeed, it takes some people months to mature to the point where they develop the habit of a daily quiet time. For some it is a lifelong battle. In any case, don't quit when you miss. With God's help determine that you will grow to be a committed disciple who meets Christ regularly in meaningful daily quiet times.

---

[1]*Lord of the Universe, Lord of My Life* (Downers Grove, Ill.: InterVarsity Press, 1973), pp. 7-12.

Reading Study Guide

1. What is a quiet time, and what elements should be included?

2. Of the three reasons listed for a quiet time, which is the most compelling to you?

3. Of the practical suggestions listed, which ones give you the most difficulty? Which do you find helpful?

4. Which of the problems have you experienced? Are the suggestions helpful?

5. What questions do you have about the reading?

6. Does this reading convict, challenge or comfort you?

Going Deeper

Foster, Richard. "The Spiritual Disciplines: Door to Liberation." Introduction to *Celebration of Discipline*. 20th anniversary edition. San Francisco: HarperSanFrancisco, 1998.
Munger, Robert Boyd. *My Heart—Christ's Home*. Downers Grove, Ill.: InterVarsity Press, 1954.

4 / Bible Study

LOOKING AHEAD

MEMORY VERSE: 2 Timothy 3:16-17
BIBLE STUDY: Psalm 119:1-16
READING: Inductive Bible Study

 ## Core Truth

What place should the Bible have in a disciple's daily quiet time?

Because the Scriptures of the Old and New Testament are the uniquely inspired revelation of God and the standard of truth in all matters of faith and practice, a portion of each day should be set aside to read, study and meditate on God's Word. The Bible is to the spirit what food is to the body.

1. Identify key words or phrases in the question and answer above, and state their meaning in your own words.

2. Restate the core truth in your own words.

3. What questions or issues does the core truth raise for you?

Memory Verse Study Guide

These verses are part of a classic New Testament passage that conveys both the source and the value of the Bible.

1. *Putting it in context:* Read 2 Timothy 3. How is Paul's instruction about the nature of Scripture a contrast to the nonbelieving world that Paul describes?

2. The memory verses are *2 Timothy 3:16-17.* Copy the verses verbatim.

3. Paul says that "all Scripture is God-breathed," or inspired. How is the inspiration of Scripture different from an "inspired" speech or writing?

4. How is Scripture useful in these ways?

   Teaching

   Rebuking

   Correcting

   Training

5. How does Scripture equip us for every good work?

6. Studying Scripture can simply increase our information. How do we move from information to transformation?

7. How have these verses spoken to you this week?

Inductive Bible Study Guide

Psalm 119 is the longest of the psalms and is a celebration of God's law. The value of God's law is stated succinctly: "Your word is a lamp to my feet and a light for my path" (v. 105). By reading the first sixteen verses we will see what our attitude should be toward God's Word and its place in our lives.

1. *Read Psalm 119:1-16.* What are the different words and phrases for the law of God?

2. What are we to do regarding the law of God?

3. What will be the results in our lives if we do these things?

4. Verse 11 gives one reason for memorizing Scripture. What is the reason stated here, and what other reasons come to mind?

5. What questions do you have about this passage?

6. What verse or verses have particularly impacted you? Rewrite key verses in your own words.

Reading: Inductive Bible Study

Inductive Bible study uses the scientific method of investigation. We start with the data in the biblical text and from that draw conclusions about meaning and application. The process of study begins with the six investigative questions that a good reporter would use in gathering information to write a story—Who? What? Where? When? How? Why? Once the truth has been found, its meaning can be explored and application to our lives is possible. The following outline provides much detail—more than you could ever follow in one study—but gives a good overview of the three-step study process. See page 44 for a sample study using this outline.

HOW TO PREPARE

First of all, pray, asking the Lord to quiet your heart and to make you receptive to the truth that you will hear.

I. **Observation (What does it say?)** If we take obedience to God seriously then we must find out what God is saying. The first step is to observe exactly what is in the text before we jump to our own preconceived ideas.

   A. Overview
      1. Skim material with a view to its main themes.
      2. Note context of passage and background if necessary.
      3. Reread in a different translation and look for differences.
      4. Look for main thought divisions—read the passage in paragraphs.

   B. Ask Six Investigative Questions
      1. *Who* are the main characters, and how are they described?

      a. Notice a description of God, Jesus and/or the Holy Spirit.
      b. Consider how (or if) the character or personality of the author relates to the passage.
      c. Notice any supernatural beings mentioned.
      d. Notice any human characters mentioned.
      2. *What* is happening?
      List key verbs, commands given by and to whom, promises, conditions implied in text or context, local customs mentioned, flow of conversation.
      3. *Where* do the events occur?
      How many miles from one place to another? Is this place significant for other events?
      4. *When* do the events occur?
         a. How long does each event take?
         b. What can be learned from the mention of rulers, ages of characters, lapse of time, genealogies, cultural differences?
         c. Are there clues about the historical background or season of year?
      5. *Why* do the events occur?
      6. *How* do the events happen?

   C. Summary
      1. Write down the main thrust of the passage. This may become the main thought that you want to develop.
      2. Make notes on unsolved problems as you go through the text. These may be solved in the process of understanding, or you may have to consult reference works such as commentaries, study Bibles, dictionaries or atlases.

II. Interpretation (What does it mean?)

The aim of interpretation is to bring out the meaning of the passage for the people to whom it was written and for us today.

A. Definitions
   1. What do the terms, phrases and sentences mean?
   2. What are modern equivalents?
   3. List any surprising terms used, as well as figures of speech—similes, metaphors, puns, plays on words, hyperbole.

B. Relationships
   1. Why this phrase, word or idea?
   2. Why did the author say it here?
   3. What relationship does one thought have to another?

C. Implications
   1. What is the full significance of the statements?
   2. Beware of spiritualizing or allegorizing.

III. Application (What does it mean to me?)

A. Cultivate a voice of the Spirit.
B. Apply the main point to your life.
   1. What has already been a part of my thinking? What is new to me?
   2. What requires a change of thought? How can I make that change?
   3. Where do I need a change in my behavior?
   4. What can I do now?
      Set long- and short-range goals for behavior. Have a plan. Break down your change of behavior or things you want to know into steps. For example: get counseling, get suggestions for reading, set goals in behavior change, ask someone to hold you accountable.

C. Assert your will.
D. What principles are relevant if the historical situation is no longer relevant?
E. Apply your knowledge to particular areas.
   1. Attitude and obedience to God; attitude toward self.
   2. Situations and relationships in family life.
   3. Coworkers, employers, subordinates, fellow students.
   4. Teaching, practices, relationships in your home church and in other churches, missionary work.
   5. National, political, sociological and economic questions.

Sample Bible Study

Luke 18:1-8

Observe	Interpret	Apply
What does it say?	What does it mean?	What does it mean to me?
(who, what, when, where, why how)		

Observe

Who are the main characters, and how are they described?

1. Judge
   - did not fear God
   - did not care about people
   - was unjust
2. Widow
   - kept bothering the judge to render justice
3. God
   - brings about justice to his chosen ones
   - listens to those who cry out to him
   - renders justice quickly

What is happening?

1. List key words or phrases.
   - parable, pray, not lose heart, justice, faith
2. Promise
   - God will bring justice quickly to those who cry out to him
3. Flow of conversation
   - widow keeps coming to the judge
   - judge refuses to give justice
   - she keeps bothering him, and he finally renders justice because he is getting worn out

Why is this story told?

1. To show us that
   - we should always pray and not lose heart
   - God is eager to grant justice to those who cry out to him
2. It makes us think: Will the Son of Man find faith when he returns?

Interpret

Raise appropriate questions and draw conclusions about the meaning of the text.

1. *Why does Jesus choose an unjust judge to make a point about the justice of God? Is the unjust judge being compared to or contrasted with God?* It appears that the point is that if even an unjust judge will render justice because of the persistence of the widow, how much more will a God who cares.

2. *Why does Jesus choose a widow as the protagonist?* Widows were powerless. All they had was the power of persistence, no other leverage.

3. *What is the main point of the parable?* To pray and not lose heart. To remain in faithful prayer to the end, until Jesus returns.

4. *What is the point that Jesus wants us to learn about God?* God is eager to render justice and he hears the cries of his people.

Apply

Confession—I too easily lose my focus of attention when I am praying for people to come to Christ who have been resistant for a long time.

Attitude of obedience—Prayerful intercession over long-term needs. Pray for my sister daily for the relief of her chronic back pain.

Reading Study Guide

1. What is the inductive method?

2. Why is it considered a scientific method?

3. What is the difference between observation, interpretation and application?

4. This method can be greatly simplified for daily use. What do you notice from this study method that could be helpful in getting the most from a passage of Scripture?

5. Practice this method by creating your own three-column guide on Luke 11:5-13. Review the instructions to see the items that you will want to draw from the text. Share your findings with your partner(s). What issues did this raise for you?

Going Deeper

Watson, David. "The Word of God." Chap. 7 in *Called and Committed: World-Changing Discipleship*. Wheaton, Ill.: Harold Shaw, 2000.

5 / Prayer

Looking Ahead

MEMORY VERSES: Matthew 6:9-13
BIBLE STUDY: Luke 11:5-13; 18:1-8
READING: How Do We Pray?

 Core Truth

What is prayer, and how can a disciple pray effectively?

Prayer is transparent dialogue. It is a conversation with God in which we address him and in quiet are addressed by him. There are four types of prayer, which are summarized by the acronym ACTS.

Adoration: appreciating God for who he is apart from what he has done for us.

Confession: acknowledging to God our specific sin and seeking his pardon.

Thanksgiving: appreciating God for his benefit to us.

Supplication: interceding for ourselves or others according to God's will.

1. Identify key words or phrases in the question and answer above and state their meaning in your own words.

2. Restate the core truth in your own words.

3. What questions or issues does the core truth raise for you?

Memory Verse Study Guide

There is no better place to begin to learn how to pray than to study the prayer that was a response to Jesus' disciple's request, "Lord, teach us to pray" (Luke 11:1).

1. *Putting it in context:* The Lord's Prayer is set in Matthew 6, where Jesus contrasts true and false ways of showing devotion to God. How is the Lord's Prayer an expression of true love for God?

2. The memory verses are *Matthew 6:9-13.* Copy these verses verbatim.

3. The first petition is that the Father's name be hallowed. Why does Jesus start here?

4. What scope of subjects does the Lord's Prayer cover?

5. Notice the different types of prayer in the Lord's Prayer. What seems to be missing from the types listed?

6. Why is this a helpful model for prayer?

7. How have these verses spoken to you this week?

Inductive Bible Study Guide

These two passages of Scripture help to interpret one another. This study weaves them together, so be ready to flip back and forth between them. We will discover how Luke 11 helps explain Jesus' unusual comparison of God to an unrighteous judge in Luke 18.

1. *Read Luke 11:5-13; 18:1-8.* What is the point of Jesus' stories about prayer in 11:5-8 and 18:1-5? How do the widow and the friend illustrate this point?

2. What position do the friend and the widow have in relationship to their "benefactors"? What does this teach us about the posture of prayer?

3. What do these passages teach us about God? Is God a reluctant giver who must be cajoled? Use these passages to show that God is generous.

4. What attitude of prayer is Jesus calling us to have in 11:9 and 18:1, 8?

5. Why does God want us to ask him for things when he already knows our needs?

6. Can God's actions be influenced by our prayers? Why or why not?

7. What questions do you have about this passage?

8. What verse or verses have particularly impacted you? Rewrite key verses in your own words.

👓 Reading: How Do We Pray?

Prayer is transparent dialogue. It is the way we have an intimate conversation with the Creator of the universe and the Redeemer of our lives, who is wild about spending time with us. Prayer represents the place of greatest safety where we can pour out our hearts in an unedited fashion, much like we would to a dear friend who accepts us as we are, warts and all.

Though the following poem is about friendship, it expresses our experience of prayer as well.

> Oh, the comfort—the inexpressible
> comfort of feeling safe with a person,
> Having neither to weigh thoughts,
> Nor measure words—but pouring them
> All right out—just as they are—
> Chaff and grain together—
> Certain that a faithful hand will
> Take and sift them—
> Keep what is worth keeping—
> And with the breath of kindness
> Blow the rest away.[1]

Prayer is a come-as-you-are affair. It is God's welcome into his heart. Richard Foster begins his wonderful book *Prayer: Finding Your Heart's True Home* with this winsome invitation:

> The Lord is inviting you—and me—to come home, to come home to where we belong, to come home to that for which we were created. His arms are stretched out wide to receive us. His heart is enlarged to take us in. For too long we have been in the far country: a country of noise and hurry and crowds, a country of climb and push and shove, a country of frustration and fear and intimidation. And he welcomes us home: home to serenity and peace and joy, home to friend-

ship and fellowship and openness, home to intimacy and acceptance and affirmation.[2]

Prayer is a relationship with the One who has already declared us his beloved children and who wants to be close to us. So what should we talk about in prayer? Just as conversations with close friends have topics, so there is a dialogue we can have with our Lord. It is the subject matter of prayer, the parts of the conversation, that we will examine here. Using the acronym ACTS introduced earlier, we'll discuss the four basic parts of prayer: adoration, confession, thanksgiving and supplication.

ADORATION

The first movement of the heart in prayer is adoration. It is helpful to distinguish adoration from thanksgiving. Adoration is appreciating who God is himself, whereas thanks-giving is appreciating God for what he has done for us. Ole Hallesby captures this nuance. "When I give thanks, my thoughts circle about myself to some extent. But in praise my soul ascends to self-forgetting adoration, seeing and praising only the majesty and power of God, His grace and redemption."[3]

Adoration lifts us out of ourselves to behold the wonder and beauty of God. The psalms, the worship book of the Bible, are effusive and demonstrative in their praise.

> I will exalt you, my God the King,
>   I will praise your name for ever and
>   ever.
> Every day I will praise you
>   and extol your name for ever and ever.
> Great is the LORD and most worthy of
>   praise;

his greatness no one can fathom.
(Psalm 145:1-3)

One way to practice adoration is to select an attribute of God and write in your journal the fruits of your imagination. For example, some ideas might include: God is sovereign—that means that not one molecule in the universe is out of God's control; God is omniscient—never will God have to slap his forehead and say, "Oh boy, I forgot all about that"; God is immanent—like air, God is the very breath in which we live and move and have our being.

Isn't it rather egocentric of the Lord to want us to fill our minds and hearts with thoughts of him? If we see praise only as giving God compliments, then we miss the everyday nature of praise. Enjoyment spontaneously overflows in praise. We go to an enjoyable movie and speak its praises. When my wife and I take a Sunday-afternoon drive on a spectacular day, we keep saying to each other, "Look at that." Praise not only expresses our joy, it also completes it.

Why does God want us to praise him? Not only because he deserves it, but for what we get out of it. What is the greatest thing God can give us? More of himself. "Praise is the sweet echo of his own excellence in the hearts of his people."[4]

CONFESSION

When we fill our hearts with the glory of God and pray as Jesus taught us, "Hallowed be your name," the natural movement of our hearts is to see the darkness of our lives in light of his radiance. In our former house the walls were painted "antique" white, which to my eyes looked pretty white until pure white was placed next to it. It was only then that I could see how tainted was the antique white. When we measure our lives against God's moral per-

fection, we begin to see how contaminated our hearts are.

In Greek, *confess* means "to agree with." In confessing to God we are agreeing with God about what he sees. By making confession a regular part of our conversation with the Lord we are giving him permission to show us our lives through his eyes. Our prayer is "Lord, let me see me as you see me."

Confession is the courageous and honest admission that we have violated God's holy law and are in desperate need of forgiveness. King David ran from God for almost a year after his adulterous affair with Bathsheba and his treacherous abuse of power in having her husband killed. Finally the prophet Nathan unmasked David's deceit and said, "You are the man" (2 Samuel 12:7). That is when David came clean. Psalm 51 records his penitence.

Have mercy on me, O God,
    according to your unfailing love;
according to your great compassion
    blot out my transgressions. . . .
For I know my transgressions,
    and my sin is always before me.
Against you, you only, have I sinned
    and done what is evil in your sight.
(Psalm 51:1, 3-4)

The idea of confession brings to mind a confusing issue. How do we distinguish between Satan's accusations and God's conviction? We often forget that we have an enemy who is called the "accuser of the brethren" and who wants us to wallow in our guilt. This enemy has plenty of ammunition with which to work. His objective is to discourage us about the progress we are making in our relationship with Christ, perhaps through nagging messages such as "You call yourself a Christian yet you are still dealing with the same things. Come on, who are you kidding?" We begin to draw the conclusion that we are unworthy to be God's child. These weights of discouragement are not of God but are the enemy's ways of taking us out of the battle.

Yet God's convicting Spirit is incisive, focused and piercing. The searchlight of the Holy Spirit unmasks specific sins, and we are then led to godly sorrow and grief over how we violated our relationship with the God who claimed our heart. From there we are led to repentance, which means a change of behavior. And finally—and immediately—the Lord cleanses our spirit so that inwardly we feel fresh and renewed like the air after the first rains of spring.

Satan causes us to wallow in unnamed guilt, but God's conviction is focused and meant to lead us to restoration. Any demeaning messages and put-downs are not from the Lord but are from our overactive conscience or the one who wants us to believe lies about ourselves. There is no condemnation for those who are in Christ Jesus.

THANKSGIVING

When we truly understand the rescue that God has performed in snatching us from the guilt and condemnation of our sin, then we will realize that the fundamental motive of Christian living is thanksgiving. One of the signs of the filling of the Holy Spirit, says Paul, is "always giving thanks to God the Father for everything, in the name of our Lord Jesus Christ" (Ephesians 5:20).

An old man walks alone on a Florida beach carrying a bucket of shrimp. He makes his way to the end of the pier, and soon a mass of dancing dots fills the sky. The evening silence gives way to screeching birds. For half an hour the man stands surrounded by the birds until the bucket is empty. But even when the food is gone, the gulls perch on his hat and linger. This weekly offering to the sea gulls was his way of giving thanks.

The man is Eddie Rickenbacker. In October 1942 he was flying in his B-17 on a mission to deliver a message to General Douglas MacArthur when he went down in the Pacific. All eight crew members escaped into life rafts. After eight days, all their rations were gone. All means of survival had been exhausted. In a weakened state, the men shared in an afternoon devotional service and then tried to rest. As Rickenbacker was dozing with his hat over his eyes, he felt something land on his head. He knew it was a sea gull, which meant food. The crew survived. God had sent a sea gull hundreds of miles from shore to their rescue. Rickenbacker never forgot to say thanks.

We so easily lose our sense of gratitude and forget the good things the Lord has done for us. Thanksgiving is the cultivation of a memory. It is prayerfully listing the good that is in our life.

SUPPLICATION

Supplication means to ask with intensity, earnestness and perseverance, to ask and keep on asking. In the context of prayer Jesus says, "Ask and it will be given to you; seek and you will find; knock and the door will be opened to you" (Luke 11:9). Supplication can be broken down into intercession for others and petitions for ourselves.

Intercession is to stand between two parties and plead the case of one to another. In this case it is to stand between God and another and plead to God on the other's behalf. Intercession is perhaps the most unselfish act of love, because the person who is blessed by God seldom knows who has been praying for him or her. God has given us the great privilege of bringing others into his presence through prayer, just as the four friends carried the paralytic into the presence of Jesus in Mark 2:1-12.

And how should we pray intercessory prayers? As a point of comparison we can place the content of our prayers against Paul's intercession in Ephesians 1:16-19, 3:16-19, and Colossians 1:9-12. While we often focus on material needs such as healing, job problems or financial matters, Paul was concerned that God would be found sufficient, that the knowledge of God's will would fill our lives, that we would be surrounded and inundated by the love of God.

Our failure to ask is a failure to know Jesus well. Jesus said to the Samaritan woman at the well, "If you knew the gift of God and who it is that asks you for a drink, you would have asked him and he would have given you living water"

(John 4:10). John Piper says that a prayerless Christian is like a bus driver trying to push his bus out of a rut by himself because he doesn't know that Clark Kent is on board. If we knew, we would ask.[5]

This leads us back to where we began. Prayer is an invitation into the heart of the Father. Jesus says that even evil fathers give good gifts to their children when they ask. Would a father give a scorpion to a son who asks for a fish? "How much more will your Father in heaven give the Holy Spirit to those who ask him" (Luke 11:13). Prayer needs no special religious language. We are invited to know and carry on a transparent conversation with the One who accepts us as we are. Let your conversation be marked by adoration, confession, thanksgiving and supplication.

[1]Dinah Maria Mulock Craik, "Friendship."
[2]Richard Foster, *Prayer: Finding the Hearts' True Home* (San Francisco: HarperSanFrancisco, 1992), p. 1.
[3]Ole Hallesby, *Prayer* (Minneapolis: Augsburg, 1959), p. 141.
[4]John Piper, *Desiring God* (Portland, Ore.: Multnomah Press, 1986), p. 41.
[5]Ibid., p. 133.

Reading Study Guide

1. What is adoration?

2. What makes God worthy of worship?

3. What is confession?

Why does it follow adoration?

4. What is the connection between thanksgiving and remembering?

5. What is the biblical definition of intercessory prayer?

How does this contrast with how we often pray for one another?

6. Why is prayer so difficult?

7. What questions do you have about this reading?

8. Does this reading convict, challenge or comfort you? Why?

Going Deeper

Foster, Richard. "Prayer." Chap. 3 in *Celebration of Discipline.* 20th anniversary ed. San Francisco: HarperSanFrancisco, 1998.

6 / Worship

LOOKING AHEAD

MEMORY VERSE: Revelation 4:11
BIBLE STUDY: Revelation 4—5
READING: Handling the Trauma of Holiness

 **Core Truth**

What activity defines the primary purpose of the church?

The functions of the church have been variously defined as teaching, fellowship, outreach and worship (see Acts 2:42-47). Of these important functions, honoring God through worship is the church's primary purpose, because it is our eternal vocation.

1. Identify key words or phrases in the question and answer above, and state their meaning in your own words.

2. Restate the core truth in your own words.

3. What questions or issues does the core truth raise for you?

Memory Verse Study Guide

In Revelation 4 we are brought into the throne room of God. His throne blazes with glory and beauty and is surrounded by creatures who continually praise the Lord, saying, "Holy, holy, holy is the Lord God Almighty" (v. 8).

1. *Putting it in context:* Beginning with Revelation 4:1, note the elements of worship in this heavenly scene.

2. The memory verse is *Revelation 4:11.* Copy the verse verbatim.

3. Why is God declared worthy?

4. What does it mean that God is worthy?

5. What does it mean for God to *receive* glory and honor and power?

6. What do you think are the benefits to us when we worship God?

7. How has this verse spoken to you this week?

Inductive Bible Study Guide

Revelation 4—5 opens a window on the continuous activity around the throne of God. Through this window we get a glimpse of our eternal vocation.

1. *Read Revelation 4—5.* Describe your impressions of the heavenly scene around the throne of God (4:1-11).

2. What characteristics are ascribed to God (4:1-11)?

3. What images are used in chapter 5 to describe Jesus?

    What do you make of the sudden shift of images for Jesus from "the Lion of the tribe of Judah" (5:5) to "the Lamb looking as if it had been slain" (5:6)?

4. Why is Jesus considered worthy to open the scroll (5:9-10, 12)?

5. What do these chapters teach us about the worship of God?

6. What questions do you have about this passage?

7. What verse or verses have particularly impacted you? Rewrite key verses in your own words.

Reading: Handling the Trauma of Holiness
The Key to Authentic Worship of the Living God
Darrell Johnson

The church is a caring community—a serving, studying, praying, healing community. But what is the fundamental purpose of the church? If it is true that "the chief end of man is to glorify God and enjoy Him forever" (Westminster Shorter Catechism), then fundamentally the church is a worshiping community.

Isaiah's experience in the year of King Uzziah's death brings us to the heart of authentic worship. Two factors make for vital worship of God: the presence of God and the God who is present. The awareness that God is present and a recognition of who this God is make for meaningful worship. In other words, authentic worship of God is a function of our affirmation that he is here and our understanding of who he is. The vitality and relevance of our worship is directly related to our view of God.

The depth and authenticity of our worship of God flows automatically from our concept of God—from who we think he is. That seems straightforward enough, doesn't it? All we need to do is think correctly about the God who is here with us. However, two "laws of the soul" militate against knowing God as he really is.

WE THINK GOD LOOKS LIKE WE DO

First, we tend to form our own conceptions of God. All too often we create a god who is simply the projection of the God we wish existed. We tend to create God in our own image.

A number of years ago Spencer Marsh wrote a delightful book entitled *God, Man and Archie Bunker.*[1] The author shows how Archie Bunker's God acts and feels very much like Archie, a white racist, acts and feels. Marsh recounts a

classic example of this. The one occasion that George Jefferson, Archie's black neighbor, had dinner at Archie's, Archie asks him, "Are you an atheist?"

George: "No, I believe in God."

Archie: "That's nice . . . Interestin', too. I mean how the black people went from worshiping snakes and beads and wooden idols . . . all the way up to our God."

George: "What do you mean, your God?"

Archie: "Well, he's a white man's God, ain't he?"

George: "That ain't necessarily so. What makes you think God isn't black?"

Archie: "Because God created man in his own image, and you'll note I ain't black."

George: "Well, don't complain to me about that."

Archie: "Look, you seen the pictures of God, ain't you? That Dago artist painted him on the ceiling in Rome . . . remember?"

George: "You mean that white Dago artist painted him."

Archie: "Ev'ry picture I ever seen of God, he was white."

George: "Maybe you were looking at the negatives."

Every human being has that same tendency—to form our own conceptions of who God is.

Fortunately for us, God desires that we come to know him as he really is. Out of that desire to be known, God has revealed himself—in creation, in the life and history of Israel, in Scripture and most completely in Jesus Christ. This leads us, however, to the second tendency of our hearts: we often suppress God's revelation of himself.

WE REFUSE TO LOOK AT GOD

When God does reveal himself as he really is, we either ignore what we see or repress it. We do this because of what God reveals about himself. What we discover about him is too much to handle. The writer of the book of Hebrews says, "It is a dreadful thing to fall into the hands of the living God" (Hebrews 10:31). This was Isaiah's experience. He was brought face to face with God in his essence—and he trembled to the bone, crying out, "Woe to me! . . . I am ruined!" (Isaiah 6:5).

Throughout Scripture God reveals different dimensions of his character, what we call the attributes of God. A. W. Tozer defines an attribute of God as "whatever God has in any way revealed as being true about Himself."[2] Scripture speaks of many of God's attributes: his self-existence, self-sufficiency, eternality, wisdom, transcendence, faithfulness, goodness, justice, mercy, grace, love and sovereignty, to name only some. But the one underlying, overarching, all-encompassing attribute of God that he reveals is his holiness. Holy is what God is in his very essence.

> In the year that King Uzziah died, I saw the Lord seated on a throne, high and exalted, and the train of his robe filled the temple. Above him were seraphs, . . . calling to one another: "Holy, holy, holy, is the LORD Almighty; the whole earth is full of his glory." (Isaiah 6:1-3)

From the beginning to the end of time that song continues to rise from the angelic choir and the voices of the saints. Not "Love, love, love"; not "Mercy, mercy, mercy"; not "Truth, truth, truth"; but "Holy, holy, holy is the Lord God Almighty, who was, and is, and is to come"

(Revelation 4:8).

To encounter the living God in his holiness is a deeply frightening experience, as Isaiah shows us. The holy God constitutes a threat to humans. We either deal with that threat in all its trauma or ignore or suppress it, and unfortunately most people do the latter. It is the way our psyche deals with trauma, and therefore we live with a less than adequate view of God. It is psychologically easier to live with a lie than with such shocking truth. Karl Barth once said that religion is not the fruit of humanity's pursuit of God but the product of our repression of the trauma caused by the holiness of God. Adam hid from God—and people since have continued to do so.

Why is the holiness of God such a threat? The answer hinges on the meaning of the word *holy*. Two basic ideas are contained in that word. The first is separateness, being totally other; the second is purity, having absolute perfection. The first constitutes a threat to our autonomy or self-lordship; the second constitutes a threat to our moral integrity. We can better understand each of these threats by looking at the prophet Isaiah's response to them.

SELF-RULE CRUMBLES BEFORE HIS HOLINESS

The root of the word *holy* is related to a word that means "divide." *Holy* therefore comes to mean something totally unique, separated from the normal. When God reveals himself as holy, he is saying he is the Wholly Other. He is totally and wholly other than anything else. In Isaiah's words God is "high and exalted" (Isaiah 6:1). Emil Brunner expresses it well.

> Holiness is the Nature of God, that which distinguishes Him from everything else. . . . Holiness is not a quality

which God possesses in common with other beings; on the contrary, it is that which distinguishes Him clearly and absolutely from everything else.[3]

Through Jesus Christ we discover that God is personal, that he is our friend, that he cares for us, that he watches over us. But we must never lose sight of his essential character—he alone is God. There exists between him and us an infinite quantum leap.

Notice that Isaiah's first response to God is terror. "Woe to me, . . . I am ruined! For I am a man of unclean lips" (Isaiah 6:5). Isaiah, a mere man, in the very presence of God! He trembles to the bone. So did Job: "I am unworthy" (Job 40:4). So did Habakkuk: "I heard and my heart pounded, my lips quivered at the sound; decay crept into my bones, and my legs trembled" (Habakkuk 3:16). In the presence of the holy God, humans cannot but feel the gulf that separates us from God.

Meeting the holy, living God smashes the myths of autonomy, the myth that human beings are the final authority, our own lords. In the presence of God we are but dust and ashes. Every breath we breathe is a gift of his grace. When a person refuses to bow in humility before the holy Creator, he or she represses the truth about God in order to function (Romans 1:18-23).

A PURITY THAT TOLERATES NO UNCLEANNESS

There is a second meaning to the word *holy*. Holiness, by its very nature, must burn away sin.

Isaiah's response to God's self-revelation is therefore to be expected. When he said, "Woe is me. . . . For I am a man of unclean lips" (Isaiah 6:5), he confessed that what came from his lips manifested what was deep in his heart—sin. In the presence of the fire of purity Isaiah

trembled, for he knew he rightly should die in the flames of holiness.

We ignore this attribute of God because we want to feel that we are good people, yet in the presence of such absolute purity our claims of moral excellence are shallow. We must either own up to our sinfulness before God or change our concept of him to remove the shame we feel. We construct a morally neutral God who doesn't really care about anything.

Notice that the Lord said nothing to Isaiah about his sin. Yet holiness by its very nature exposes uncleanness. Authentic worship will always have two expressions—awe before the Wholly Other and shame before the Absolutely Pure.

But fortunately that is not the whole story.

THE PARADOX OF GOD'S HOLINESS

Though Isaiah was terrified in the presence of God, he also desired to remain in it. "Woe is me," he cries out, but he doesn't run away. Perhaps he knew that he could never flee God's presence. Or perhaps there is something about God in his holiness that is irresistible.

The holy Lord draws us to himself even in our fear and shame. Is it that we were made for him? Even though we feel that threat to our existence—that threat to our supposed virtue, wisdom and righteousness—even though we know he could annihilate us because of our sin, we still need him. He is what we have thirsted for all our lives.

Like Isaiah, we are caught in a dangerous tension. Isaiah senses his nothingness, both as a human and as a sinner, yet he desires to sing with the hosts of heaven, "Holy, holy, holy." But how can he? How can he remain before the Holy God as a sinner? We recognize the very center of God's heart when Isaiah writes,

Then one of the seraphs flew to me with

a live coal in his hand, which he had taken with tongs from the altar. With it he touched my mouth and said, "See, this has touched your lips; your guilt is taken away and your sin atoned for." (Isaiah 6:6-7)

The tension is resolved by grace. The solution to Isaiah's dilemma (and ours) is atonement. "But here the atonement does not come from man's side by an offering of sacrifice. It comes from God's side, God Himself effecting it through the seraph by means of a coal."[4] This is a beautiful foreshadowing of the cross of Jesus Christ. On the cross God himself effects the final remedy for sin. We can take refuge from God's awesome holiness in the wounds of Jesus Christ—wounds that touch not only our lips but our very being with forgiveness and cleansing.

God's holiness and his love are not in conflict. The love of God is God willing us to know him and then making it possible to remain in his presence. It is in the context of holiness that we realize the depth of God's love. His very essence naturally recoils at our sin, but he chooses for us to enter into a relationship with him in which we are granted the greatest privilege in the universe. Because of Jesus Christ and in Jesus Christ we dare to approach the Holy Creator of the universe and address him as "Abba, Father."

The vitality and depth of our worship are directly related to our view of God. If we truly know him as he is, three things will characterize our worship: awe before the Wholly Other, shame before the Absolutely Pure, and joyful gratitude before the Merciful One. When we know that he alone is God, we fall before him in awe. When we know that he alone is perfect, we fall before him in shame. But when we know that he, the Holy One, so desires our fellowship that he gave his only Son to make it possible, we fall before him in gratitude and praise and sing the wonder of his holiness and the glory of his amazing grace.

[1]Spencer Marsh, *God, Man and Archie Bunker* (New York: Harper & Row, 1975).
[2]A.W. Tozer, *Knowledge of the Holy* (San Francisco: HarperSanFrancisco, 1961), p. 20.
[3]Emil Brunner, *The Christian Doctrine of God* (Philadelphia: Westminster Press, n.d.), p.58.
[4]Otto Procksch, "αγιος," in *Theological Dictionary of the New Testament,* ed. Gerhard Kittel and Gerhard Friedrich, 10 vols. (Grand Rapids: Eerdmans, 1964-1976), 1:93.

Reading Study Guide

1. Why is the way we think about God crucial to our worship of God?

2. What are the two "laws of the soul" that militate against knowing God as he truly is?

3. Why do we tend to suppress God's revelation of himself?

4. What are the two meanings of *holy?*

   How are they a threat to us in our sinfulness?

5. How does God go about overcoming the gap that stands between his holiness and us?

6. How does your own view of God need to change in order for you to worship more fully?

7. What questions do you have about the reading?

8. Does the reading convict, challenge or comfort you? Why?

Going Deeper

Foster, Richard. "Worship." Chap. 11 in *Celebration of Discipline*. 20th anniversary ed. San Francisco: HarperSanFrancisco, 1998.

Part Two

UNDERSTANDING THE MESSAGE OF CHRIST

This section attempts to capture the content of what we believe. It contains the most heavy theology or doctrine that we will examine. We should not shy away from doctrine, for as Dorothy Sayers says, "The dogma is the drama."[1] The greatest drama ever played out in history awaits our discovery.

We begin our discovery of God and his intent in chapter seven by examining the mystery of the Trinity. We will see what it means that *the three-person God* is a being in community with himself through all eternity.

Chapter eight discusses how we are made in God's image. The clue to understanding the image of God in humans is the trinitarian nature of God. As God is a being in fellowship, so we were made for relationships—with God and with each other.

In chapter nine we discover that something intruded to break our relationship with God and each other. The Bible calls this *sin.* Sin is separation from God in the present and in eternity.

The wonder of wonders is that in spite of our rebellion against God's authority and our distrust of his goodness, God kept coming after us. The demonstration of the extent and extravagance of *God's love* (chapter ten) is the death of Jesus on the cross. And chapter eleven shows how we find *redemption through Christ.*

We can know the story of the gospel, acknowledge that Jesus Christ is God in human form and even affirm his resurrection without it ever making a difference in our life. The way we take these historical events and apply them to ourselves is through faith in Christ. How can a righteous God forgive sinners without compromising his holiness? This is one of the questions about *justification by faith* we will explore in chapter twelve.

This section concludes on the highest of notes—*adoption.* The setting for justification is the courtroom, with God as the presiding judge. But adoption moves us from the courtroom to the family room, from God as judge to God as father. In adoption we are drawn up into the life of God and included in the circle of his love as his sons and daughters.

---

[1]Dorothy L. Sayers, *The Whimsical Christian* (New York: Macmillan, 1978), p. 23.

7 / The Three-Person God

LOOKING AHEAD

MEMORY VERSES: Deuteronomy 6:4; 2 Corinthians 13:14
BIBLE STUDY: Exodus 20:1-7; 3:13-14; John 8:58-59; Acts 5:1-4
READING: Contact

 ## Core Truth

Who is the God a disciple worships and serves?

Though we cannot fully comprehend the nature of God, there is only one eternal God, who though one is at the same time three persons—God the Father, God the Son and God the Holy Spirit.

1. Identify key words or phrases in the question and answer above, and state their meaning in your own words.

2. Restate the core truth in your own words.

3. What questions or issues does the core truth raise for you?

Memory Verse Study Guide

Two memory verses help to capture the biblical emphasis on the oneness of God as well as the threeness of God: Deuteronomy 6:4, which is known as *the Shema* and can be found over the entrance of most synagogues, and 2 Corinthians 13:14.

1. *Putting it in context:* List all the commands mentioned in Deuteronomy 6:1-9.

2. The memory verse is *Deuteronomy 6:4.* Copy the verse verbatim.

3. Why do you think it was necessary to be so adamant that there is one God? What is the relevance of such an insistence today?

4. The next memory verse is 2 Corinthians 13:14. Copy the verse verbatim.

5. What characteristic is associated with each member of the Trinity?

   What does this tell us about their individual roles?

6. What does Paul want the Corinthians to recognize?

   How does this apply to you?

7. How have these verses spoken to you this week?

Inductive Bible Study Guide

Trinity is not a biblical word, nor are there many passages which mention the three persons of the trinity together (Matthew 28:19 and 2 Corinthians 13:14 are a couple of exceptions). How did we come to believe that God is one being who is three persons? It is because the Bible describes all three as divine, with distinct personalities.

God the Father—read Exodus 20:1-7.

1. Put into your own words the prohibitions of the first three commandments in vv. 3-7.

2. Why is there a prohibition against having other gods (v. 3)?

3. What is a graven image?

4. Why is there a prohibition against graven images or any likeness of anything (v. 4)?

5. What does it mean for God to be jealous? (Isn't this a bad thing? Why or why not?)

6. What does it mean to take the Lord's name in vain?

God the Son—read Exodus 3:13-14; John 8:58-59.

7. What claim was Jesus making for himself?

8. How did the religious leaders interpret Jesus' reference to being the "I AM"?

God the Holy Spirit—read Acts 5:1-4.

9. How do these verses demonstrate that the Holy Spirit is a personal, divine force?

10. What questions do you have about these passages?

11. What verse or verses have particularly impacted you? Rewrite key verses in your own words.

Reading: Contact

The hit movie *Contact* (1997) featured a character who was obsessed with making contact with extraterrestrial life. When she was a child, her father instilled in her the fascination that there must be life somewhere in the vast expanse of the universe. Jodie Foster played the role of an astrophysicist whose consuming passion was to receive the signals of intelligent life that must exist somewhere. She spent long, dreary hours listening to sensitive computers and high-intensity speakers that were connected to satellite relays. Suddenly one day the speakers began to pulsate with a rhythmic sound that was out of this world. Contact!

The small lab of offbeat scientists became a beehive of activity. Every scientist and media outlet was focused on the phenomenon of alien life. All effort was put into unscrambling the signal and deciphering the code of this civilization that evidently had progressed far beyond life on Earth. Questions abounded: Who are these beings? What are they like? What are their intentions?

In the first few verses of his Gospel, John declares that contact has been made. His subject is not a life form of higher intelligence that inhabits another planet but the One who brought this universe into being in the first place. This passage sets out to answer certain questions: Who is this being who has made contact with us? Who is Jesus? What is he like? What is his intention for us?

THE WORD

The motif that John selects to convey God's contact with us is *the Word:* "In the beginning was the Word, and the Word was with God, and the Word was God. . . . The Word became flesh and made his dwelling among us" (John 1:1,

14). Why did John select this image to convey the identity of Jesus? The Word has to do with communication—contact. Words are a means of self-revelation, taking hidden thoughts and expressing them in such a way that connection can be made. We cannot be known unless we share our innermost thoughts and feelings, and we do that through words, as does God. Scripture says, "Who has understood the mind of the LORD?" (Isaiah 40:13). We are beholden to God to make himself known.

By using the image of the Word, John is telling us that God is speaking. When God spoke and said all that he had to say to us, his speech materialized in the person of Jesus Christ. "In the past God spoke to our forefathers through the prophets at many times and in various ways, but in these last days he has spoken to us by his Son" (Hebrews 1:1-2).

THE ETERNAL SON OF THE FATHER

John reminds us of another beginning. The book of Genesis starts with "In the beginning God created the heavens and the earth." Genesis 1:1 describes the old creation, whereas John 1:1 introduces the new creation.

Did Jesus have a self-conscious awareness that he existed prior to creation? Quite clearly. On the eve of his crucifixion, during his final meeting with his disciples in the upper room, he expresses a longing to be with the Father in the way he had been before coming to earth. He prays, "And now, Father, glorify me in your presence with the glory I had with you before the world began" (John 17:5). The phrase "The Word was with God" (John 1:1) describes the relationship between the Word and God. In Greek the literal meaning is that the Word was in face-to-face relationship with God. There has always been a close and intimate connection between the Word and God.

This is where things get a little confusing. We have two beings that claim to be eternal yet are different from each other. Do we have two gods? It was verses like John 1:1 and Jesus' speaking of himself as the eternal "I AM" that led to the formulation of our understanding of the plurality within one God. As we shall observe later, the Holy Spirit was also ascribed with divine and personal qualities, yet with a distinct role as separate from the Father and the Son. This then led to the formulation of the Trinity—one God, yet three persons. The singular God is Father, Son and Holy Spirit.

How did this idea come about? There is no chapter in the Bible that begins: "Now concerning the Trinity . . . " *Trinity* is not a biblical word, but it is a description of a biblical reality. The idea of the Trinity came about because of biblical teaching that equated the Son and the Holy Spirit with God and because of our experience of God. I am drawn to C. S. Lewis's description of how our understanding of God as Trinity came into being.

People already knew about God in a vague way. Then came a man who claimed to be God; and yet he was not the sort of man you could dismiss as a lunatic. He made them believe Him. They met Him again after they had seen Him killed. And then, after they had been formed into a little society or community, they found God somehow inside them as well; directing them, making them able to do things they could not do before. And when they have worked it out they found they had arrived at the Christian definition of the three-personal God.[1]

WHY DIDN'T JESUS SAY SO?

If Jesus is God, why don't we have some statement in the Bible that is that straightforward? Why didn't Jesus make the bold claim "I am God"? The reason is that Jesus did not want to be understood as saying that he was identical with the Father. The Father is God and the Son is God, but the Father is not the Son, and the Son is not the Father.

But clearly John is affirming that all that can be said about God can be said about Jesus too. Jesus defended his actions in healing the lame man on the Sabbath, saying, "My Father is always at his work to this very day, and I, too, am working" (John 5:17). Jesus says the Father doesn't take any time off from doing good, and neither does he. How did the Jews understand this comment? "For this reason the Jews tried all the harder to kill him; not only was he breaking the Sabbath, but he was even calling God his own Father, making himself equal with God" (John 5:18). Jesus says later, "I and the Father are one" (John 10:30). Jesus didn't mean one and the same or even one in purpose, but one in essence. This statement is followed by "again the Jews picked up stones to stone him" (v. 31). They explained in verse 33, "We are not stoning you for any of these [miracles], . . . but for blasphemy, because you, a mere man, claim to be God."

John makes other assertions about Jesus' divinity that are indirect claims to deity— Jesus doing things that only God could do. John lists two: Jesus is the agent of creation, and the giver of life.

Jesus, agent of creation. "Through him all things were made; without him nothing was made that has been made" (John 1:3). John makes the all-encompassing pronouncement that everything in the created order came into existence through the agency of Jesus. He states it first positively, "all things were made through him," then negatively, "without him nothing was made that has been made." Note the very careful distinction of roles. Jesus is not the author or the designer of all things but the means by which all things came to be. The Father is the originator of the design, but the Son is the one who carries it out. The Father is the architect and Jesus is the builder.

Jesus, our life source. John affirms a second indirect claim, "In him was life, and that life was the light of men" (v. 4). Throughout John's Gospel, Jesus is said to have life within himself and to give life to whom he wills (5:21). Jesus is self-existent and underived, so he can say what no sinful human being can say about his or her life: "No one takes it [life] from me, but I lay it down of my own accord. I have authority to lay it down and authority to take it up again" (John 10:18).

MAKING CONTACT

So what is God's intent in the contact he has made with us? C. S. Lewis puts it succinctly: "The whole purpose for which we exist is to be taken into the life of God." [2] The Holy Spirit is the life of God in us. Think of the Holy Spirit as the personality that is born from the love between the Father and Son. "The union between the Father and Son is such a live, concrete thing that this union itself is also a Person." [3] The Holy Spirit in us is the one who brings us into the family of God. We are adopted into the life that is shared between the Father and the Son. Paul says that being a Christian means receiving the spirit of adoption. It is the life of the Holy Spirit within us that causes us to cry,

*"Abba,*Father" (Romans 8:15-16).

What does it mean to be adopted into the family of God the Father, Son and Holy Spirit? Imagine that a church picnic is being held at a nearby park. You have many errands to run after the service and don't get around to packing your picnic lunch. You rush home a few minutes before the picnic begins to throw a lunch together. All you find in your refrigerator is a shriveled piece of baloney, two slices of stale bread and some crusty mustard remains. You slap it together and rush off to the park.

When you arrive, you happen to sit at a table already occupied by a large family. You lay your spread out on the table—a puny baloney sandwich. The family proceeds to take from their enormous picnic basket golden-brown fried chicken, mouth-watering potato salad, baked beans that have been simmering for days and two beautiful chocolate cream pies. They look at your baloney sandwich and make an invitation: "Why don't we put it all together?" You protest, but the cook says, "Oh, come on, there's plenty of everything—and we just love baloney sandwiches. Let's just put it all together." You came to the picnic a pauper and are eating like a king.

We came into this world as orphans and Jesus adopted us into his eternal family. "Let's put it all together," the Lord says to us. "Let me draw you into my life, for that is the purpose for which you exist." The Father and Son say to us through the living presence of the Holy Spirit, "Everything that we are and have is available to you."

[1]C. S. Lewis, *Mere Christianity* (New York: Macmillan, 1960), p. 143.
[2]Ibid., p. 141.
[3]Ibid., p. 152.

Reading Study Guide

1. Why does John select the image of the Word for Jesus?

2. What difference does it make whether Jesus is eternal or a created being?

3. What is the relationship between the Father and the Son?

4. How would you explain how we came to believe in the Trinity?

5. Why didn't Jesus simply say, "I am God"?

6. What role does the Holy Spirit have in the life of a believer?

7. What questions do you have about the reading?

8. Does this reading convict, challenge or comfort you? Why?

Going Deeper

Lewis, C. S. "The Three-Personal God." In *Mere Christianity*. New York: Macmillan, 1943.
Packer, J. I. "The Only True God." Chap. 4 in *Knowing God*. Downers Grove, Ill.: InterVarsity Press, 1973.

8 / Made in God's Image

 ## Core Truth

What is humanity?

God, the self-existent Creator, called the world into being through his infinite creativity and power. The peak of God's creative work was humankind, male and female, made exclusively in his image.

1. Identify key words or phrases in the question and answer above, and state their meaning in your own words.

2. Restate the core truth in your own words.

3. What questions or issues does the core truth raise for you?

Memory Verse Study Guide

The place to begin our understanding of the nature of human beings is the beginning. What does Scripture tell us was God's original intent in creating us? These verses contain the clues to what it means to be created in God's image.

1. *Putting it in context:* Starting with Genesis 1:1, the creation formula for each of the six days follows a consistent pattern. How does the formula abruptly change when it comes to the creation of the man?

2. The memory verses are *Genesis 1:26-27.* Copy the verses verbatim.

3. God refers to himself in the plural ("us" and "our"). What could be the reason for this?

What does this reveal about what it means to be created in God's image?

4. Verse 27 says that humankind created as "male and female" is an expression of being created in God's image. How is this another clue for how we are created in God's image?

5. What authority are humans given?

What responsibility does this imply?

6. How have these verses spoken to you this week?

Inductive Bible Study Guide

Some have viewed Genesis 1 and 2 as contradictory accounts of creation. Instead, try to see Genesis 2 as an expansion and further explanation of Genesis 1:26-27. Genesis 1 is an overview, whereas Genesis 2 details the process of creation.

1. *Read Genesis 1—2.* The Bible begins, "In the beginning God . . . " What does this teach us about God?

2. What is the benediction that God pronounces over the created order prior to humankind's coming into being (1:10, 12, 18, 21, 25)?

3. How does the benediction change with the creation of humanity (1:31)?

   What does this tell us about how God views humanity?

4. In Genesis 2 man is created prior to woman, and he is alone. What is not good about being alone (2:18)?

5. How does God go about filling what is missing in the man (2:18-25)?

6. When God presents the woman to the man, how does the man's exclamation (v. 23) express his fulfillment?

7. Genesis 2:24 is the classic biblical definition of marriage, quoted by both Jesus and Paul in the New Testament (see Mark 10:6-9; Ephesians 5:31). According to this verse what are the essentials for a marriage relationship?

8. What questions do you have about these passages?

9. What verse or verses have particularly impacted you? Rewrite key verses in your own words.

Reading: The Jewel in the Crown of God's Creation

German philosopher Immanuel Kant loved to take long walks on summer evenings to meditate and think. On one occasion he was sitting in a park when a policeman noticed that he had been there for several hours. The policeman came up to him and said, "What are you doing?" Kant answered, "I'm thinking." The policemen said, "Well, who are you?" Kant replied, "That's precisely the problem I've been thinking about."

Genesis 1—2 addresses the policeman's question: Who are we? The entire first chapter flows toward the creation of human beings. If the musical score of Genesis 1 were the 1812 Overture, the fireworks would fill the evening sky and the cannons would thunder their salute upon reaching Genesis 1:26-27.

THE PEAK OF GOD'S CREATIVE WORK

In Genesis 1 the structure of the first six days of creation reaches its apex in the creation of humans.

Only God creates. The first evidence of humanity's uniqueness centers around the word *create:* "In the beginning God created the heavens and the earth." The Hebrew word is never used to refer to human creative ability, because God can do something humans can never do—create out of nothing. The Hebrews believed that no material world existed until God called it into being.

The word *create* is also used at a crucial juncture in the creation process—when conscious life comes into being: "So God *created* the great creatures of the sea . . . and every winged bird" (v. 21). And it is used three times of the creation of humans: "So God *created* man in his own image, in the image of God he *created* him; male and female he *created*

them" (v. 27; emphasis added).

The benediction pattern. On the third day God begins pronouncing a benediction at the end of each day of his completed work. Notice that verses 10, 12, 18, 21 and 25 conclude with the same "And God saw that it was good." What does this mean? It means first of all that God is having a great time with his creative work. He is also saying, "I did a great job. This is coming out just the way I intended."

But the jewel of God's creation has not yet been set in the crown. Note that after the humans are created the benediction changes slightly, but very importantly. After God had completed all his work he "saw all that he had made, and it was *very* good" (v. 31).

The creation formula. Throughout the first six days of creation leading up to the creation of humans, God uses an impersonal formula. Starting at verse 3 we read, "And God said, 'Let there be light.'" This same formula, with slight variation, is consistent throughout the passage: "Let there be an expanse," "Let the water . . . ," "Let the land produce vegetation." God speaks and it is so.

But with the creation of the humans the formula abruptly changes. At verse 26 we read, "Then God said, 'Let us make man in our image, in our likeness.'" Human beings are the expression of the personal nature of the Creator and are therefore qualitatively different from the animal world and the rest of creation. Human beings bear the stamp of God.

There is a qualitative difference between beings and things. As an author I have a sense of accomplishment in having a book in print, an expression of my creative work. But that pales in comparison to 5:16 a.m. on August 31, 1975, when our daughter Aimee came into the world. Creating a baby, which expresses personhood, and making a book cannot be compared. God had made things and creatures, but now he creates a being who bears his personal mark.

In what sense are humans created in God's image? The words *image* and *likeness* in verses 26 and 27 indicate that there is something about God that we replicate, copy or resemble something that corresponds to the original. God leaves the distinct imprint of his nature on us. What is it?

CLUES TO THE IMAGE OF GOD IN HUMANS
There are two significant clues in Genesis 1:26-27 that point us toward an exciting discovery.

The plurality of God. The first clue we find in verse 26: "Then God said, 'Let us make man in our image, in our likeness.'" God is using plural pronouns for himself. This is particularly surprising since the verb *make* is singular. The one God speaks of himself as plural.

Who is God talking to? Some say the heavenly host or angelic beings who were present at creation. Yet this couldn't be, because they were just observers, not participants in creating. A better explanation is that the Lord is talking to himself. This is a veiled reference to our New Testament understanding that the one God is three persons. From all eternity God was a being in fellowship. God is his own community, self-existent and self-sufficient. Prior to God's creating the world the only reality was this three-person God.

The New Testament shows us that the Father and the Son have an eternal relationship of love. When Jesus is waiting to be taken to the cross he prays to his Father, "And now, Father, glorify me in your presence with the glory I had with you before the world began" (John 17:5). The Father confirms his eternal love for his Son at the inauguration of Jesus' public ministry. As Jesus came out of the water of baptism, the Holy Spirit descended on him in the form of a dove and a voice spoke from heaven, "This is my Son, whom I love; with him I am well pleased" (Matthew 3:16-17). The Son lived under the pleasure of the Father.

God did not create in order to complete something lacking in himself; he created out of the fullness and overflow of his love. Paul tells us in Acts 17:25, "[God] is not served by human hands, as if he needed anything, because he himself gives all men life and breath and everything else." Out of the exuberance of his love God wanted human beings to be drawn into the circle of his love. Meister Eckhart, the German mystic, said that the creation came into being out of the laughter of the Trinity. God enlarged the circle and drew us in.

The love within the Godhead that produces an object of that love can be seen in a smaller way in the union between husband and wife. My wife and I went spent the first five years of our marriage convinced that we didn't want to have children. We had all the arguments of those raised in the sixties: we wanted to be free and not tied down; it would be cruel to bring a child into the world that lived under the specter of nuclear holocaust. But the arguments seemed silly when we suspected that my wife was pregnant. We admitted to one another that the prospect of having a baby was something we welcomed. Then my wife got word from the doctor that her pregnancy test was negative. We were both surprised by the depth of our disappointment. It had been only a matter of a few suspicious weeks, but during that time our love had already formed for the child of promise. Our union sought completion in one we could love together. Fortunately the pregnancy test was wrong and our joy was fulfilled. Aimee has been the delight of our life ever since.

Much as a child born of the love between a man and a woman reflects the parents' image, we humans reflect the image God planted in us. The first clue to what it means to be created in God's image is that just as God is a being in fellowship, so are we made for relationships. This leads us to the second clue.

Humanity as male and female. The second clue is found Genesis 1:27, "So God created man in his own image, in the image of God he created him; male and female he created them." We could easily pass over this closing phrase and miss its import. Yet humankind as "male and female" is a further indication that we are made for relationships. We mirror God as a being in fellowship, meaning that God made us different so that we could have person-to-person relationships with each other.

In Genesis 2:23 man shouts his joy at the creation of woman. Up to this point the Hebrew word used for man is *adam,* which means humankind. But when the woman is created, the word for man changes.

The man *[adam]* said,
"This now is bone of my bones
    and flesh of my flesh;
she shall be called 'woman' *[ishah],*
    for she was taken out of man *[ish].*"

Man did not become male until there was female. The man is incomplete without his counterpart, and vice versa. Humankind as male and female is another way of saying that what we mirror God in his plurality as humans in plurality. We were created for love relationships, for the vertical love of God and the horizontal love with humans.

IMPLICATIONS OF THE IMAGE OF GOD

The first priority of these love relationships is that we were made to be loved by God. In Genesis 2:2 we read, "By the seventh day God had finished the work he had been doing; so on the seventh day he rested from all his work." God paused to enjoy his creativity.

In the New Testament salvation is spoken of in terms of entering God's *rest.* The *rest* of God is to be included in the pleasure of God and in joining the circle of his love. The oft-quoted statement of Augustine is true: "Our hearts are restless until we find our rest in thee." The first order of priority then is vertical—our relationship with the one who made us for himself.

Second, to be made in God's image means that success in this life is measured by our investment in horizontal relationships.

A counseling session brought this truth into focus for me. The man I had been talking with for over an hour was close to a decision. He was trying to come up with sufficient reason to restoke the fire of his dying marriage. The hostility in the marriage had become so intense that he and his wife needed a rest from each other. The respite had been welcomed by both, and he said that he was enjoying being alone. His business was stimulating and financially rewarding, and he was getting excited about an old hobby that had some promise of being lucrative. The only trouble was that if he pursued the hobby, it would most surely take him further away from his wife. Then he made a matter-of-fact statement—a kind of summary assessment of where he saw his life at that moment. He said it in such a way that the significance of it didn't seem to dawn on him. "Everything in my life seems to be going well . . . except my relationships."

If our primary relationships are in disarray,

what does the rest matter? To be made in the image of God is to be made for love relationships. To be made in God's image is to be made from the motive of love and for love. To be like God is to put our priority time and energy into loving God and others.

Reading Study Guide

1. In examining Genesis 1, what are the indicators that humans are the special creation of God?

2. What does it mean to be created in the image of God?

   How would you support this biblically?

3. What other explanations have you learned for what it means to be created in God's image?

4. What are the implications of the biblical view of humans for how we understand the worth of the individual?

   How might this differ from an evolutionary view of humans as higher-order animals?

5. If being created in God's image means we are made for relationship, what impact should this have on our priorities or how we measure success in life?

What needs to change in your priorities?

6. What questions do you have about the reading?

7. Does the reading convict, challenge or comfort you? Why?

Going Deeper

Lewis, C. S. "Making and Begetting"; "The Good Infection." In *Mere Christianity*. New York: Macmillan, 1960.

Action Page

Reviewing Your Covenant

Once you have established a covenant, it is important to periodically review its expectations and renew your commitment. As with any relationship we can become lax in our attentiveness to what makes it work. These questions will lead you to refine the covenant and recommit your energies to its accomplishment.

1. Review the covenant you made at the beginning of this relationship. On a scale of 1 to 5, 5 being highest, rate yourself on your accomplishment of each of the five elements in the covenant. Share your rating and explain its meaning to each other.

2. As you reflect on the discipling process, what have been the benefits for your growth in Christ up to this point?

3. What have been the disappointments or the unfulfilled expectations?

   How might these be overcome?

4. What changes would you like to make in the disciple's covenant of commitment?

5. To what do you need to recommit yourself in order to be faithful to the covenant?

9 / Sin

LOOKING AHEAD

MEMORY VERSES: Romans 3:23; 6:23
BIBLE STUDY: Genesis 3
READING: Bewitched and Beguiled

 ## Core Truth

What severed the relationship between God and humanity, and what were the consequences?

Though we were created in the image of God and therefore in perfect harmony with him, we willfully disobeyed God's authority and distrusted his goodness. As a consequence our relationship with God was broken, resulting in spiritual death, which in turn tarnished our relationship with ourselves, others and creation.

1. Identify key words or phrases in the question and answer above, and state their meaning in your own words.

2. Restate the core truth in your own words.

3. What questions or issues does the core truth raise for you?

Memory Verse Study Guide

The two memory verses are classics in describing the universal nature of sin and its dire consequences for our relationship with God.

1. *Putting it in context:* Put in your own words Paul's indictment of humanity in Romans 3:9-23.

2. The memory verse is *Romans 3:23.* Copy the verse verbatim.

3. What is the extent of our sin? Does it make any difference in our standing before God that we might not all sin to the same extent?

4. How is sin defined? Is the glory of God a fair standard to be measured by?

5. The second memory verse is Romans 6:23. Copy the verse verbatim.

6. *Putting it in context:* Note Paul's argument from Romans 6:15-23, contrasting being slaves to sin with being slaves to righteousness. How does 6:23 summarize Paul's line of reasoning?

7. What do we earn by our sin?

8. What is meant by "death"?

9. How have these verses spoken to you this week?

Inductive Bible Study Guide

Genesis 3 tells the story of the fall of humanity, which ushered sin into the world. The very nature of sin—its ability to deceive and confuse us and distort our knowledge of right and wrong—is exemplified in the serpent's beguiling persuasion of Eve to taste the forbidden fruit and then in Adam and Eve's hiding in shame from God.

1. *Read Genesis 3.* What was the serpent's ploy in verse 1?

   How does he distort God's generous words from Genesis 2:16-17?

2. In 3:2-3 how does the woman demonstrate that she is already distrusting God?

3. What temptation is placed before the woman in verses 4 and 5?

4. From observing the serpent's strategy, how would you define sin?

5. How do the consequences of sin affect humankind's relationships with self (v. 7)?

   with God (vv. 8-10)?

   with fellow humans (vv. 11-16)?

   with creation (vv. 17-19)?

6. What questions do you have about this passage?

7. What verse or verses have particularly impacted you? Rewrite key verses in your own words.

Reading: Bewitched and Beguiled

Bill Hybels, the pastor of Willow Creek Church near Chicago, preached a sermon one Sunday on the theme that we are all sinners in need of a Savior. After the service a salesman came forward to tell Hybels that he didn't see himself as a sinner. Hybels asked him if he had been absolutely faithful to his wife. The man hedged a bit. "Well, I travel a lot, you know . . . " Then Hybels asked about his expense account. "Oh, everybody stretches the truth a bit," the man said defensively. Finally Hybels asked him if he ever overstated or exaggerated a claim. "That's standard practice in the industry," the man told him. Hybels responded, "Well, let's see. You've just told me you're an adulterer, a cheater and a liar." This man was appalled by Hybels's brash insensitivity. "How dare you call me those awful things!" he exclaimed. He, like all of us, wanted to see himself in the best possible light.[1]

It has been said that the Christian faith makes no sense unless you start with the assumption that there is something drastically wrong. Can anyone deny that there is something insidious at work in this world? The Bible places the problem for the ills of humanity not on a societal flaw but in a character defect in the heart of every individual.

Alexander Solzhenitsyn spent eight years in a Soviet gulag following World War II. He entered prison a die-hard communist, believing that a new social order could create new people. But it was in prison that he discovered that the core issue was not the economic or government system. Solzhenitsyn writes,

It was only when I lay there on rotting prison straw that I sensed within myself the first stirrings of good. Gradually, it was disclosed to me that the line separating good and evil passes, not through states, nor between classes, nor between political parties, but right through every human heart, and through all human hearts.[2]

THE SOURCE OF THE PROBLEM

The first five verses of Genesis 3 reveal the core of the human problem—us. In this account humans turn away from their Creator, giving up their idyllic state of innocence, their perfect fellowship with God in a lavish garden where all their needs and wants were abundantly supplied.

God had given these humans a risky gift—freedom of choice. Without the ability to choose, humans would be robots. Without choice there is no love. Without freedom, love is a preprogrammed response. For example, how do you think my wife would have reacted to me if instead of asking, "Will you marry me?" my proposal for marriage was a command, "You will marry me"? Her response would have been "Oh, no I won't!" Love cannot be forced; it must be chosen. God honored us by giving us the risky gift of freedom as a necessary condition for love.

In Genesis 3 we are immediately confronted by the one who would lure away this innocent couple from their trusting and obedient relationship with God: "Now the serpent was more crafty than any of the wild animals the LORD God had made" (3:1). This talking snake, Satan, is the evil opposition to the good God. He is "more crafty" than any other creature; he is the master of the half-truth and the innuendo, and he begins to do his work on the woman.

DISTRUST THE GOODNESS OF GOD

The serpent's first strategy is to cause the

woman to question whether God is for her. "He said to her, 'Did God really say . . . ' " When we hear something that doesn't seem to square with the integrity of the source, we say, "Did they really say that?" Satan's tactic is to begin to sow doubt, to cause the woman to question whether God is too restrictive.

In her defense of God the woman is showing signs that the seeds of doubting God's goodness are taking root. "The woman said to the serpent, 'We may eat from the fruit of the trees in the garden'" (v. 2), but she slightly alters God's original command. God had said to Adam, "You are free to eat from any tree in the garden; but you must not eat from the tree of the knowledge of good and evil, for when you eat of it you will surely die" (2:16-17). Eve shows that she is becoming fixated on God's restrictions. "We may eat fruit from the trees in the garden, but God did say, 'You must not eat fruit from the tree that is in the middle of the garden, *and you must not touch it,* or you will die'" (3:3). God had restricted eating, but he never said anything about touching. This was Eve's added restriction.

Restrictions are often interpreted as harsh confinements, yet unrestricted freedom leads only to destruction. Laws such as the Ten Commandments are given so that we honor the Creator and keep from bringing harm to ourselves. God forbade Adam and Eve from eating of the tree of the knowledge of good and evil so they would avoid the consequence of dying.

What if we had the attitude of unrestricted freedom when it came to driving a car? *No one is going to make me drive within the confines of these road lines,* we think. *If I feel like zigzagging across lanes, then I will. If I decide to take a shortcut across someone's front lawn, that's up to me. No one can hem me in.* Laws for driving are obviously meant to protect us as well as others who share the road. Our best interest is always freedom within limits, within defined boundaries.

Rebel Against God's Authority

The serpent now becomes more brazen. He knows the woman is staggering. The wedge of doubt is working its way into her spirit. She is questioning what she had come to believe about God's abundant care. Satan closes in for the kill, openly challenging the authority of God. "You will not surely die," the serpent says to the woman. "For God knows that when you eat of it your eyes will be opened, and you will be like God, knowing good and evil" (3:4-5). Satan implies that God is jealously guarding his position of authority, which he doesn't want to share with anyone else. But if Eve eats of the tree, he lets her think, she can attain the same level as God.

What exactly is the tree of the knowledge of good and evil? What did it signify to the original hearers? The phrase *good and evil* is synonymous with all knowledge. It means to aspire to knowledge on the level that only God has—omniscience. Biblical scholar Daniel Fuller says that to aspire to the knowledge of good and evil is to seek "that maturity which frees one from being dependent on someone else for guidance on how to act wisely." [3] The first humans were forbidden from aspiring to a knowledge possessed only by God himself, whereby they might consider themselves free from dependence on him. By this restriction God is saying to them, "I have made you dependent on me for life, for wisdom. You work correctly only when you keep your connection with me. As soon as you aspire to be equal with the Creator, you lose all the good that I intended for you."

We even have an acceptable name for this god of independence—individualism. The protection of individual rights and the freedom from tyranny are deeply rooted in our society, but we crave much more, individualism without limits. Robert Bellah's masterful study on the American character, *Habits of the Heart,* found that freedom was the most resonant, deeply held American value. But the freedom he discovered was lopsided. We want to be left alone, to be free from other people's values and beliefs, free from arbitrary authority in work, family and political life. Freedom is defined solely in terms of being free from something. We want rights without responsibility.

We might expect that God would wash his hands of us disobedient creatures, but the good news is that our Lord came looking for us in the person of Jesus Christ in order to provide new hearts for us. In response to our distrust he demonstrated beyond a doubt that he can be trusted.

Paul said, "If God is for us, who can be against us? He who did not spare his own Son, but gave him up for us all—how will he not also, along with him, graciously give us all things?" (Romans 8:31-32). The effects of the Fall can be reversed in only one way—by putting our trust in Christ, who is for us. Christ died the death we deserve. We are given new hearts when we submit ourselves to God's authority and trust his goodness, even while confessing that we have committed high treason against our Maker. John Stott summarizes this powerfully.

> The concept of substitution may be said to lie at the heart of both sin and salvation. For the essence of sin is man substituting himself for God, while the essence of salvation is God substituting himself for man. Man asserts himself against God and puts himself where only God deserves to be; God sacrifices himself for man and puts himself where only man deserves to be. Man claims prerogatives which belong to God alone; God accepts penalties which belong to man alone.[4]

The only appropriate response is to cast ourselves on the mercy of God.

---

[1]Bill Hybels, *Honest to God?* (Grand Rapids: Zondervan, 1990), p. 22
[2]Alexandr Solzhenitsyn, *The Gulag Archipelago, 1918-1956* (New York: Harper & Row, 1975), p. 612.
[3]Daniel Fuller, "The Fall" (unpublished class lectures, 1972), p. 11.
[4]John R. W. Stott, *The Cross of Christ* (Downers Grove, Ill.: InterVarsity Press, 1986), p. 160.

Reading Study Guide

1. What are some of the ways people attempt to deflect personal responsibility for sin?

2. What is the biblical diagnosis as to why "something is drastically wrong"?

3. How does the serpent sow seeds of doubt in the woman?

4. What seeds of doubt do we allow to take root in our own minds?

5. Why would a good God establish boundaries or restrictions?

6. What is the meaning of the tree of the knowledge of good and evil?

7. In what ways do you see people acting as if they were God?

   Where do you see that tendency in yourself?

8. What is God's solution to the stain of sin on the human heart?

9. What questions do you have about the reading?

10. Does the reading convict, challenge or comfort you? Why?

Going Deeper

Lewis, C. S. "The Great Sin." In *Mere Christianity*. New York: Macmillan, 1960.
Stott, John R. W. "The Consequences of Sin." Chap. 6 in *Basic Christianity*. Downers Grove, Ill.: InterVarsity Press, 1958.

10 / Grace

 **Core Truth**

What is God's response to our distrust and disobedience?

The Bible is the love story of God's revelation of himself in pursuit of wayward humanity. This pursuit reaches its climax in the cross with the gift of God's Son, Jesus Christ.

1. Identify key words or phrases in the question and answer above, and state their meaning in your own words.

2. Restate the core truth in your own words.

3. What questions or issues does the core truth raise for you?

Memory Verse Study Guide

1. *Putting it in context:* In Romans 5:6-11, what amazes Paul about God's action at the cross?

2. The memory verse is *Romans 5:8.* Copy the verse verbatim.

3. What condition were we in when Christ demonstrated his love for us?

4. How did he demonstrate his love for us?

   What makes this demonstration so astounding?

5. This verse teaches us that God took into account everything there was to know about us and still decided to lay down his life for us. How is this liberating?

6. How has this verse spoken to you this week?

Inductive Bible Study Guide

The story of Jesus that takes us to the heart of the gospel and the heart of God is the parable of the prodigal son. But on further study we see that the story is not so much about the rebellious son as it is about the waiting father.

1. *Read Luke 15:11-24.* What was the younger son saying to his father by asking for his share of the property (v. 12)?

2. How far down did the son go (vv. 14-16)?

3. What do you think the phrase "he came to his senses" means (v. 17)?

4. Why did it take so long for the son to turn back to his father?

5. What was the son willing to say and do on his return to his father (vv. 18-19)? What did the son leave out of his practiced speech (v. 21)? What does this indicate?

6. What was the father's response to the return of his son (vv. 20, 22-24)?

7. How would you feel if you were the prodigal son?

8. Summarize the gospel message contained in this story.

9. What questions do you have about this passage?

10. What verse or verses have particularly impacted you? Rewrite key verses in your own words.

Reading: The Waiting Father

Have you ever seen a two- or three-year-old child look in the mirror for the first time? The child does not initially recognize the smiling face staring back at her. Then in a moment of insight she exclaims delightedly, "That's me."

As Jesus tells the story of the prodigal son in Luke 15:11-24, he holds a mirror up to us. Initially we read this story and think, *Yeah, I know people like that.* Then all of a sudden it dawns on us, *That's me.* Jesus tells a story that becomes our story.

AN UNGRATEFUL SON AND A LOVING FATHER

Through the character of the younger son, Jesus puts his finger on the essence of the human problem from which almost every human misery derives. Our problems all begin in the conspiracy for autonomy from the One who made us. Freedom for the younger son meant doing what he wanted to do, beholden to no one.

But even more disturbing than the son's desire for freedom is the pain he inflicts on the heart of his father. There is no precedent in the customs of the Jewish and Arab world for a father to divide his property with his children before his death. When the son demands, "Father, give me my share of the estate," he is in essence saying, "Father, I want you dead so that I can get what is coming to me." In the face of such a horrible insult, the cultural expectation would have been for the father to assert his authority and uphold the family honor by beating the son into submission, then disinheriting him.

But the father does the unprecedented. He acts in a way contrary to everything that a father in the ancient Near East was supposed to

stand for: "He divided his property between them" (15:12). The father chooses to remain the young man's father even though the son no longer wants to be the son. In order to keep the door open for the son's possible return, the father chooses to bear the pain of rejection. The father could have deadened his wound by cutting himself off from his son, but he chose to live with the open sore as the price for his son's eventual return.

And of course the son's plans for greatness and glory are over in the blink of an eye. He loses it all, and to survive he attaches himself to a citizen who raises pigs. Knee deep in the mud of a pig sty, tending to animals that a Jewish boy is forbidden to touch, "he came to his senses" (v. 17). The phrase "He came to his senses" is a Hebrew way of saying that he repented. In other words, this is his turning point, his fork in the road indicating it is time to start walking back home.

THE ROAD HOME

But even though the son is ready to start back home, it is evident that he does not yet appreciate that waiting for him is a brokenhearted father. He returns home out of self-interest, not because he feels bad for what he has done. Pain prods him home. We catch his true motivation at the end of verse 17: "I am starving to death." Though he would face certain shame when he encounters the villagers, his family and especially his father, his pain and hunger overwhelmed the shame.

We humans are a curious lot. It seems that only when the pain increases to an intolerable level are we finally motivated to change. We can endure and tolerate our self-destructive habits until something bad happens that finally makes us ask, "What am I doing to my-self?" Many of us begin our walk toward the Father because the way we are currently living is not working. We are pragmatists at heart. The words of Jesus are an invitation to come home: "Come to me, all you who are weary and burdened, and I will give you rest" (Matthew 11:28).

Further evidence that the son didn't fully appreciate how he had hurt his father is that he thought he still had some bargaining power left. Though he acknowledged his sin to some extent by saying, "Father, I have sinned against heaven and against you. I am no longer worthy to be called your son" (15:18-19), he had the audacity to make the request "make me like one of your hired men."

He did acknowledge his unworthiness by realizing that he had forfeited his right to ever be called a son. He sought the lowliest possible role as a hired servant. In Middle Eastern culture there were two kinds of servants, household slaves that would have been permanent residents in the father's house, and hired servants. Household slaves had living quarters built for them, and their daily needs were provided for by the master. But hired servants were day laborers with no security or longevity. Unscrupulous landowners would hire day laborers and not pay their wages, but the father was so just that even the lowliest and most exploitable workers had "food to spare" (v. 17).

Even though the son was willing to be the lowest of the low, it still appears to have been a calculated move. Perhaps it was his goal to pay back over time the wealth that he had taken from the family. Did repentance for the son mean earning his way back into the good graces of his father? If he could just repay his debt, then he could earn back his freedom and

sonship. But he still had not come to terms with his father's pain, only his own.

A WELCOME OR A REJECTION?

What might the father's reaction be at the return of the son? As the patriarch of the clan the father would be expected to uphold family honor by humiliating the son and making him bear his shame. When the son arrived at the house and the servants announced his arrival, the father could have said to them, "What son? I don't have a son. He is dead."

Instead the unexpected occurs. "But while he was still a long way off, his father saw him and was filled with compassion for him; he ran to his son, threw his arms around him and kissed him" (v. 20). I am convinced that the whole gospel is contained in one word, *but*. The son braces for a public humiliation, flogging, recounting before the family how he had wasted the family income—but! That little conjunction expresses a reversal, an antithesis, something contrary to all that should be.

Critics of the Christian faith, especially Muslims, have questioned the necessity of the incarnation and the cross for forgiveness. They say that if God is God, he simply forgives. Why is it necessary for God to become human and die on the cross? They point to this parable as evidence. There is no incarnation or cross here, and yet Christians say that this story is the gospel. Where are the incarnation and cross in this story?

THE INCARNATION

Jesus' identification with us in the incarnation is captured in the sentence "but while [the son] was still a long way off, his father saw him and was filled with compassion for him." Where was the father when the son returned? Was he at home waiting for the son to return so that he could lower the boom? No. He was out on the road leading to the village, daily waiting for the return of his son. Likewise, instead of being safely cloistered in heaven, God came to seek and to save the lost. The father wanted to be the first to greet the son. He had closed the gap, shortened the distance.

When the father saw his boy, his heart went out to him. The word *compassion* comes from a word associated with guts or innards. Compassion denotes a gut reaction, an intense visceral response, a deep feeling that clutches at the stomach. In the Middle East when a particularly moving story is told that draws forth pity from the listeners, a person can be heard to respond, "You are cutting up my intestines." Compassion means "to suffer with." The father's reaction was to come alongside his pained son.

THE CROSS

Where is the cross in the story of the waiting father? The cross is here, but we are culturally blind to its presence. It is contained in the phrase "[the Father] ran to his son, threw his arms around him and kissed him." In the Middle East a man of mature years always walks in a slow, dignified manner. Walking with a measured pace is a way of commanding respect and projecting deserved honor. It is very undignified for a man to run in public. The word Jesus uses here for *run* is one that Paul uses to describe the Christian life as a race. For the father to run in this fashion he would have to lift up his robes, expose his undergarments and sprint down the road. This itself would have been a shameful, humiliating act. Instead of the son bearing the shame, the father in his running to the son bears it for him. The father reaches his son before the village children, his servants or the village elders do, and he places

himself between his son and the shame that would be heaped on him. The father bears the shame that would have been directed toward the son.

Up to this point there are no words from the father. He substitutes kisses for words. Only now does the son know what repentance is. Notice what the son does not say when it comes time to deliver his prepared speech. He says, "Father, I have sinned against heaven and against you. I am no longer worthy to be called your son" (v. 21), but leaves out "make me like one of your hired men." Was this a calculated move? Perhaps he saw the response of his father and said to himself, *Hey, this is going much better than I had imagined. Maybe I can get a better deal.*

But I believe that when the son saw his father sprinting toward him, his heart collapsed within him. How could he strike a bargain? How could he pay back that kind of love? When someone has given their life for you, what can you give back in return? The son could only throw himself on his father's mercy.

The father then set about to systematically restore the son's broken relationships. He turns to the servants who had run with him and gives several quick commands.

- *"Quick! Bring the best robe."* The best robe was reserved for an honored dignitary. This was the signal to the village elders to treat his son with respect.

- *"Put a ring on his finger."* This is not any ring but the family signet ring that says that the son has been restored to a position of authority within the family.

- *"[Put] sandals on his feet."* Slaves were barefoot, but a son wears sandals.

- *"Bring the fattened calf and kill it."* Meat was a rare delicacy. The fattened calf was a grain-fed animal raised for the specific purpose of celebrating the presence of an honored guest. It was also a signal that the whole community was invited because it could feed over one hundred people.

While the son focused on his unworthiness, the father is absorbed with his joy over the son's return. God wants us to take our eyes off our disqualification and look into his face and see his affection for and delight in us. The good news is that the way is open to come home. He is calling us home.

Reading Study Guide

1. Why is this story our story?

2. What finally made the son come to his senses?

3. What bargain was the son hoping to strike with the father?

   What does this tell us about the state of his heart?

4. What evidence do we see in this story of the presence of the incarnation and the cross?

5. When did the son finally understand the cost of his father's love?

6. Describe the state of the father's heart in your own words.

7. How does God's story of loving pursuit become our story? Talk with your partner(s) about your experience of God's love in these areas:

the nature of your life before Christ

how you came to Christ

how life is different for you in Christ

8. What questions do you have about the reading?

9. Does the reading convict, challenge or comfort you? Why?

Going Deeper

Packer, J. I. "The Love of God." Chap. 12 in *Knowing God.* Downers Grove, Ill.: InterVarsity Press, 1973.

11 / Redemption

LOOKING AHEAD

MEMORY VERSES: Isaiah 53:4-6
BIBLE STUDY: 1 Corinthians 15
READING: The Hope Jesus Offers

 **Core Truth**

How did Christ reconcile the severed relationship between God and humanity?

Jesus Christ was sent by the Father to be the one mediator between God and humanity (1 Timothy 2:5). Through Christ's substitutionary death on the cross the penalty of sin has been paid, and by his bodily resurrection from the tomb, death has been defeated.

1. Identify key words or phrases in the question and answer above, and state their meaning in your own words.

2. Restate the core truth in your own words.

3. What questions or issues does the core truth raise for you?

Memory Verse Study Guide

There are numerous biblical passages that attest to the substitutionary nature of Christ's sacrificial death. But when the New Testament writers wanted us to understand the significance of Christ's death, they found in Isaiah's prophecy the truth that the Messiah would be a sacrificial servant before he became the reigning king (see Matthew 8:17; Acts 8:32-33; 1 Peter 2:22-25).

1. *Putting it in context:* What characteristics of the Messiah do you notice in Isaiah 52:13—53:12?

2. The memory verses are *Isaiah 53:4-6*. Copy the verses verbatim.

3. What did Isaiah prophesy that Jesus would take upon himself?

4. What did he accomplish for us?

5. What was our condition while Jesus was doing what he did for us?

6. What is our hope for wholeness through the cross?

7. In what ways have these verses spoken to you this week?

Inductive Bible Study Guide

In 1 Corinthians 15 Paul reminds the Corinthian church of the teachings about Jesus' resurrection—and ours, in the last days. He counters the claim some were making that Christ was not raised from the dead and goes on to discuss the necessity for a body to die in order for it to be raised again in glory.

1. *Read 1 Corinthians 15.* What is Paul's summary of the core of the gospel in verses 1-4?

2. In verses 5-11 Paul catalogs the resurrection appearances of Jesus. Why is it important to establish these?

   Why does Paul find it necessary to establish his own encounter with the resurrected Christ?

3. Look at verses 12-19. What are the consequences if Jesus had not been raised from the dead?

4. In verses 20-23 Paul identifies Jesus as the "firstfruits" of the resurrection. What does he intend to convey through this image?

5. How would you describe our resurrection bodies in light of verses 35-50?

6. Verses 51-57 state the ultimate victory won by Jesus' resurrection. How does Jesus' resurrection remove death as the last barrier?

7. What questions do you have about this passage?

8. What verse or verses have particularly impacted you? Rewrite key verses in your own words.

Reading: The Hope Jesus Offers

Paul viewed the gospel as a treasure that had been deposited in his account to be preserved intact as an inheritance for the next generation. Paul exhorted Timothy, "Guard the good deposit that was entrusted to you" (2 Timothy 1:14). When the owner demanded an accounting, Paul, like a good steward, wanted to make sure that the gospel message was delivered in exactly the same way that he had received it. "For what I received I passed on to you as of first importance: that Christ died for our sins according to the Scriptures, that he was buried, that he was raised on the third day according to the Scriptures" (1 Corinthians 15:3-4).

The good news is the death, burial and resurrection of Jesus. It is through the work of Christ on the cross and his resurrection from the dead that we are redeemed from the guilt of our sin and are born again to new life.

WHY WAS JESUS ABLE TO FORGIVE US FOR OUR SIN?

"Christ died for our sins," wrote Paul. The objection that immediately comes to mind is: What does Jesus' death on the cross have to do with me? Jesus seems to take my sin personally, as if it were directed toward him.

When King David confessed his sin of adultery with Bathsheba and the murder of her husband to cover up Bathsheba's pregnancy, he said to the Lord, "Against you, you only, have I sinned and done what is evil in your sight" (Psalm 51:4). Though David had sinned against people and certainly needed to ask for their forgiveness, ultimately all sin is disobedience against God's authority.

Jesus was offered by God as the substitute to pay the guilt of our sin. He is qualified to be the sacrifice for our sin because he was unlike any person who had ever walked on the earth: he was without sin. What good would a substitute be if he had to be concerned with his own sin? In the book of Hebrews Jesus is described as the ultimate high priest, who represents us before God. "Unlike the other high priests, he does not need to offer sacrifices day after day, first for his own sins, and then for the sins of the people. He sacrificed for their sins once for all when he offered himself" (Hebrews 7:27-28).

Jesus was sent by God to be the perfect mediator for our sin. "For there is one God and one mediator between God and men, the man Christ Jesus, who gave himself as a ransom for all" (1 Timothy 2:5). Jesus was the only qualified mediator between God and humankind because he was the God-man. What set Jesus apart and gave him the credentials to act on our behalf was that he was divine, God in the flesh (John 1:14).

What evidence do we have for the deity of Christ? John Stott in his book *Basic Christianity* has a very helpful summary of the self-consciousness of Jesus.[1] Stott approaches the deity of Christ through the claims of Christ. How did Jesus view himself?

HIS SELF-CENTERED TEACHING

Jesus' self-centered teaching is striking when compared to the self-effacing teaching of other religious leaders. Jesus said, "I am the truth, follow me," whereas others said, "There is a truth, path or way. Follow that." The words *I* and *me* were often on his tongue.

- "I am the bread of life" (John 6:35).
- "I am the light of the world" (John 8:12).
- "I am the resurrection and the life" (John 11:25).

- "I am the way and the truth and the life" (John 14:6).
- "Come to me ... and I will give you rest" (Matthew 11:28).

The most astonishing of Jesus' words came in a hostile dialogue with the religious leaders. These men rested secure because they could trace their religious lineage back to Abraham, to which Jesus retorted, "Your father Abraham rejoiced at the thought of seeing my day; he saw it and was glad" (John 8:56). Astonished, the Jewish leaders responded, "You are not yet fifty years old, . . . and you have seen Abraham!" Jesus answered, "I tell you the truth, . . . before Abraham was born, I am" (John 8:57-58). In referring to himself as "I am" Jesus was identifying himself as God. When Moses was called by God to deliver the Israelites from captivity in Egypt, Moses wanted to be able to tell the elders who had sent him. When Moses asked God who he was, God answered, "I AM WHO I AM. This is what you are to say to the Israelites: 'I AM has sent me to you'" (Exodus 3:14). Jesus is clearly stating that he is none other that the great I AM who was present as the companion and power of Moses.

The title Jesus most often used for himself was "Son of Man." It is common to contrast this title with "Son of God," as if "Son of Man" refers to Jesus' humanity and "Son of God" expresses his divinity. In fact "Son of Man" was the title for the Messiah taken from the book of Daniel. Daniel had a vision of a figure coming down from heaven to establish his rule on earth. "In my vision at night I looked, and there before me was one like a son of man, coming with the clouds of heaven. . . . He was given authority, glory and sovereign power; all peoples, nations and men of every language worshiped him" (Daniel 7:13-14). So when Jesus referred to himself as the Son of Man he

was associating himself with one who would come from outside this world and who is worthy of worship.

As we saw in our reading on the Trinity in chapter seven, Jesus had a consciousness of an intimate and transparent relationship with his heavenly Father.

WHAT WAS ACCOMPLISHED IN CHRIST'S DEATH ON THE CROSS?

Christ's death on the cross was God himself paying the penalty for our sin. Paul writes, "God made him who had no sin to be sin for us, so that in him we might become the righteousness of God" (2 Corinthians 5:21).

The image that most powerfully captures the substitutionary work of Christ on the cross is that of the lamb of God. When John the Baptist saw Jesus walking by, he said, "Look, the Lamb of God, who takes away the sin of the world" (John 1:29). The image of the lamb of God is a combination of the Passover lamb and the offering associated with the annual Day of Atonement.

The Passover lamb. Paul writes, "Christ, our Passover Lamb, has been sacrificed" (1 Corinthians 5:7). When the Israelites were in captivity in Egypt, the last of the plagues sent upon the Egyptians was the death of the firstborn. God told Pharaoh that he would send the angel of death throughout the land. The Israelites were instructed to sacrifice a one-year-old lamb without blemish and smear the blood on the doorframes of their houses. That night, when the Lord came to strike down the firstborn, he passed over the homes that were under the protection of the blood (Exodus 12). The blood was a symbol of sacrificial death and substitution.

The Day of Atonement. When the image of the Passover lamb is combined with the substitutionary sacrifice of the Day of Atonement, this powerful convergence of symbols captures the work of Jesus. Once a year on the Day of Atonement (Yom Kippur) the high priest entered into the holy of holies in the temple where the glory of the holy God was said to reside. No sinful human being dared enter this space, so the high priest took with him the blood of a goat that had been sacrificed on behalf of the people's sins. The blood was sprinkled on top of the mercy seat as an act of atonement. God's anger against the sins of the people was assuaged by this substitute. Equally powerful is the image of the high priest placing his hand on the head of a second goat, the scapegoat, confessing the sins of the nation and then sending the goat into the wilderness. "The goat will carry on itself all their sins" (see Leviticus 16).

Christ's death on the cross satisfied God's justice and purchased mercy. Justice demands that sin be paid for. Dying on our behalf, Jesus died the death we deserve so that we could have mercy that we don't deserve. He bore the brunt of God's fury toward sin and faced abandonment, isolation and separation from his Father while on the cross. At the moment when Jesus cried out from the cross, "My God, my God, why have you forsaken me?" (Mark 15:34), the Father turned away from the Son, who bore our sin. Payment had been made. When we acknowledge our need for forgiveness through repentance and believe in Christ's sufficient sacrifice, we are given the gift of mercy.

WHY WAS THE BODILY RESURRECTION OF JESUS NECESSARY?

The central symbol of our faith is the empty cross. The unoccupied cross is a sign that we do not seek the living among the dead. Christ is alive. But what difference would it have made if Christ had not been raised? Why is the resurrection necessary to complete our redemption?[2]

Without the resurrection we would have sympathy without victory. The cross is the demonstration of God's love for us (Romans 5:8), but we need more from God than just understanding. Empathy with our brokenness is welcome, but we need someone who has overcome it and shown us the way out. Hope comes not just with sharing the darkness but with leading us out into the light.

Satan would have won. Paul implies that the cross was a trap into which Satan blindly walked. Being limited in knowledge, Satan did not see God's plan to use the cross for redemption or to follow it by a resurrection. "None of the rulers of this age understood it [the cross]," Paul writes, "for if they had, they would not have crucified the Lord of glory" (1 Corinthians 2:8). Satan used the human rulers of this age to bring about the death of Jesus, and in so doing brought his own downfall. "Having disarmed the powers and authorities, [Jesus] made a public spectacle of them, triumphing over them by the cross" (Colossians 2:15).

Death would remain the final enemy. The final obstacle we all face is death. Jesus took on our humanity "so that by his death he might destroy him who holds the power of death—that is, the devil—and free those who all their lives were held in slavery by their fear of death" (Hebrews 2:14-15). By his triumph over death in the resurrection, Jesus has taken the fear and sting out of death. Through Christ's rising from the dead, "death has been swallowed up in victory. Where, O death, is your victory? Where, O death, is your sting?" (1 Corinthians 15:54-55).

There would be no newness of life. The cross brings forgiveness of sin, but the resurrection offers us new life. Paul sees in the act of baptism by immersion the two movements of death and resurrection. When we are lowered under the water, a watery grave rolls over us. In this act we are identifying with Christ's death on the cross. All of our sin is nailed to the tree. The debt has been forgiven. As we rise from the water we leave that old life in the grave and come forth to newness of life. "The old has gone, the new has come" (2 Corinthians 5:17). "We were therefore buried with him through baptism into death in order that, just as Christ was raised from the dead through the glory of the Father, we too many live a new life" (Romans 6:4).

MAKING THE WAY

A missionary to Brazil served a native tribe in a remote part of the jungle. A contagious disease was ravaging the population. The missionary determined that the only hope was to take the tribe to a hospital in another part of the jungle for treatment. In order to reach the hospital it was necessary to cross a large river. Yet the tribe refused to cross, believing that the waters were inhabited by evil spirits.

The missionary explained how he had crossed the water and no harm had come to him, but the people didn't care. He next led them to the river bank and placed his hand in the water. The people still were too afraid. He walked out knee-deep into the water and splashed around, and they wouldn't budge. Finally he turned around and dove into the water and swam beneath the surface until he emerged on the other side. As he came out of the water he punched his hand in the air as an act of triumph. The people broke into cheers and followed him across.

Jesus emerged from a grave that represented the fear of death and guilt of sin, thrust his fist in the air with the triumph of resurrection and someday will call us all to follow him across. The way has been made safe.

---

[1]John R. W. Stott, "The Claims of Christ," chapter 2 in *Basic Christianity* (Downers Grove, Ill.: InterVarsity Press, 1958).
[2]In "The Resurrection of Christ," chapter 4 of *Basic Christianity*, Stott has an excellent discussion on the evidence for the resurrection. The bodily resurrection of Jesus is a well-attested historical event. Reasonable people can believe in the resurrection.

Reading Study Guide

1. What does the image of the gospel as a deposit say to you?

2. Why is the deity of Jesus a necessary prerequisite for what Christ accomplished on the cross?

3. Of the claims to Christ's deity, which do you find most compelling?

4. What was accomplished through Christ's death on the cross?

5. How does Christ's death satisfy God's justice and purchase our mercy?

6. Which benefit of the resurrection provides you the most hope?

7. What questions do you have about the reading?

8. Does this reading convict, challenge or comfort you? Why?

Going Deeper

Stott, John R. W. "The Claims of Christ," chap. 2; "The Resurrection of Christ," chap. 4; "The Death of Christ," chap. 7 in *Basic Christianity*. Downers Grove, Ill.: InterVarsity Press, 1958.

12 / Justification

LOOKING AHEAD

MEMORY VERSES: Ephesians 2:8-10
BIBLE STUDY: Romans 3:21-31
READING: Surprised by Joy

 ## Core Truth

How are the benefits of the cross transferred into our lives?

It is by faith in Jesus Christ alone that we are declared right (justified) before God. God's gift of faith is the recognition of our utter moral bankruptcy and our inability to earn God's favor and that we must receive and rest on Jesus Christ, who has done it all.

1. Identify key words or phrases in the question and answer above, and state their meaning in your own words.

2. Restate the core truth in your own words.

3. What questions or issues does the core truth raise for you?

Memory Verse Study Guide

We struggle with the place of good works in the Christian life. These memory verses clarify the proper balance. Good works or our human efforts to please God can never be the basis for our salvation but are clearly the evidence of it, according to Ephesians 2:10.

1. *Putting it in context:* Read Ephesians 2:1-7. In what terms does Paul describe the hopelessness of humanity (vv. 1-3), and what is the surprising reversal starting at verse 4?

2. The memory verses are *Ephesians 2:8-10*. Copy the verses verbatim.

3. What is the relationship between grace, faith and being saved (v. 8)?

4. How has God taken away our grounds for boasting about our salvation?

5. According to verse 10, what is the place of good works in the life of the believer?

6. How have these verses spoken to you this week?

Inductive Bible Study Guide

Paul has laid out the argument against humanity in devastating terms in the early chapters of Romans. We are all under a death sentence, deserving the wrath of God, but God sent Jesus Christ to do for us what we could never do for ourselves. Our response to Christ's saving act of grace is faith.

1. *Read Romans 3:21-31.* How would you define the righteousness of God?

2. What does it mean that the righteousness of God "has been made known" apart from the law (v. 21)?

3. How do we get the righteousness of God (vv. 22, 24, 26, 28, 30)?

4. What does it mean to have faith in Jesus?

5. Why must the righteousness of God be a gift apart from the law?

6. What has Jesus Christ accomplished for us?

7. Why does the principle of faith remove the grounds for boasting (vv. 27-28)?

8. What questions do you have about this passage?

9. What verse or verses have particularly impacted you? Rewrite key verses in your own words.

👓 Reading: Surprised by Joy

Performance-reward is the value system that drives the world today. Our worth is measured by our ability to live up to certain standards. Expectations are conveyed to children very early. A parent rewards desirable behavior and punishes undesirable behavior. Love and worth are often seen as conditional.

Since the performance-reward system is part of the air we breathe, we assume that this is the way God operates as well. We think God runs the universe using the scale of justice. When our life ends we expect that there will be an accounting of our deeds. All of our good deeds will be piled on one side of the scale and all of our bad deeds on the other side, and our only hope is for the scale to tip the right way.

Yet the gospel is revolutionary because its message is contrary to all that we have been programmed to believe. Paul writes, "But now a righteousness from God, apart from law, has been made known" (Romans 3:21). In other words, being made right before God has come to us apart from our ability to live up to God's expectations. Paul contrasts the righteousness that comes from God with the righteousness we attempt to attain by being good people.

THE RIGHTEOUSNESS OF GOD

In the early sixteenth century, Martin Luther struggled to comprehend "the righteousness of God," and his struggle led to the Protestant Reformation and the rediscovery of the truth of justification by faith alone. When Luther heard the phrase "the righteousness of God," he cowered in fear before a threatening deity. An Augustinian monk, Luther felt he was in bondage to an exacting God, who could never be pleased. To Luther God was a terror. His religious devotion was prompted by his need to assuage God's anger. It was out of fear that he gave up a potentially lucrative career in law to enter the monastery. The turning point came on a sultry July afternoon in 1505. As he approached the Saxon village of Stotterheim, the skies grew more and more menacing. Suddenly there was a crashing storm, punctuated by a bolt of lightning that knocked him to the ground. Fearing for his life and convinced this was a message from God, Luther cried out in terror, "St. Anne, help me, and I will become a monk!"

For Luther God was to be feared and placated. This terror culminated when he had to serve his first Communion. The thought of taking in his hands the very body and blood of Christ was too much for him. When he came to the prayer of consecration, he froze at the altar, his eyes glazing over and beads of sweat forming on his forehead. A nervous hush filled the congregation. Luther could not speak. He had to stop and take a seat in disgrace.

When Luther came to the prayer of consecration for the Communion elements, he was supposed to say, "We offer unto Thee, the living, the true, the eternal God." Luther wrote about this moment in reflection, "At these words I was utterly stupefied and terror-stricken. I thought to myself, 'Who am I, that I should lift up mine eyes or raise my hands to the divine Majesty?' Shall I, a little pygmy, say 'I want this, I ask for that?' For I am dust and ashes and full of sin and I am speaking to the living, eternal, and the true God."[1]

Yet Paul's positive use of the phrase "the righteousness of God" intrigued Luther. Paul was saying that this was a good thing rather than something harmful. Luther came to realize that his view of God was only half correct.

The New American Standard Version is the best translation of Paul's point: "That he might be just and the One who justifies the person who has faith in Jesus" (v. 26). The righteousness of God is twofold: God is just, but he is also the justifier.

Luther was right to say that God is just. The justice of God is an expression of his holiness, which is in total opposition to our sin. There is a genuine hostility that God feels when we flagrantly violate his will. To violate God's holy standard is to incur a penalty that must be paid. Justice must be satisfied with judgment. This Luther understood all too well.

But that is not the whole story, as Luther came to realize. God is just, but he also justifies. He not only exacts demands, but shows mercy as well. *Justification* is a legal term, but it does not mean we are not guilty or declared innocent before God. Justification is full recognition that the crime has been committed and there must be a payment for it. So on the one hand God's verdict is "Guilty as charged," and on the other hand it says "You're free. Payment for the crime has been made." Justification means that all the demands of the law have been met. Equally balanced in the phrase "righteousness of God" are justice and mercy. But how can we be guilty yet also be free to go? How can God remain just and also release us from payment of sin?

GOD'S MERCY: REDEMPTION AND PROPITIATION

Paul addresses this seeming paradox with two key words: *redemption* and *propitiation*. "They are justified freely by his grace through the redemption that came by Christ Jesus" (v. 24). *Justification* is a word associated with law courts, whereas *redemption* is a word connected to the marketplace. Slaves sold in the

marketplace and then set free were said to be redeemed. Redemption is the price paid to set one free. A ransom is the price paid to free one from captivity to a kidnapper. Jesus said that he "did not come to be served, but to serve, and to give his life as a ransom for many" (Mark 10:45). "You were bought at a price," Paul says. "You are not your own" (1 Corinthians 6:20, 19).

There was a young boy who lived in a New England seaport and loved to watch the boats come in from their daily catch. One day he decided to build a little sailboat all his own. He worked for weeks, making sure every detail was right. The big day finally arrived when he would launch his boat. As he watched triumphantly, the wind changed suddenly and his little boat was swept out of sight. He was brokenhearted. Every day he went to the beach to see if his boat had washed up on shore, but it was never there. Then one day he saw his boat in a store window. He ran inside and excitedly told the shopkeeper that it was his boat. The woman informed him that the boat would cost him five dollars. After pleading to no avail, the boy pulled out the money and gave it to the woman. As he left the store, he was heard to say, "Little boat, you are twice mine. You are mine because I made you, and you are mine because I bought you." The death of Jesus was the purchase price of our life. We have been bought back.

Propitiation is the second word used to describe God's gift of righteousness. The NIV translation avoids this technical word with the phrase "sacrifice of atonement." A more literal translation of the text would read, "They are justified by his grace as a gift, through the redemption which is in Christ Jesus, whom God put forward as a propitiation by his blood" (Romans 3:24-25).[2]

To propitiate is to satisfy anger, a concept prevalent in pagan mythology. In a story of the Trojan War, Paris carried off Helen to Troy. The Greek force sent to rescue Helen was held up by ferocious winds, prompting Agamemnon, the Greek general, to send for his daughter, who was ceremonially sacrificed to mollify the anger of the gods. The gods, now satisfied, caused the winds to blow in the right direction so that the rescue could be performed.

But instead of humans making offerings to satisfy God's anger, God himself takes the initiative and puts forth his own Son as the offering for our sin. Jesus paid the penalty for our sin by bearing it on the cross and satisfying God's justice, and at the same time offering us mercy as the One who took our place. God is just and the justifier of all who have faith in Jesus.

FAITH IN JESUS CHRIST

"Faith in Jesus Christ" is the second key phrase in Romans 3:21-31. How do we make God's righteousness our own? "This righteousness from God comes through faith in Jesus Christ to all who believe. . . . [We are] justified freely by his grace through the redemption that came by Christ Jesus . . . through faith in his blood" (vv. 22, 24-25). Faith is the instrument by which we attach ourselves to Christ. It is the conduit that carries grace to the heart of the believer. But to understand true, biblical faith we must first realize what it is not.

Faith is not temporal. Temporal faith is synonymous with foxhole faith, faith on reserve for trying circumstances. People sometimes treat faith like a spare tire: they hope never to have to use it. As long as we can handle things, our faith is in ourselves. But when we are in over our heads, we suddenly plead for God to straighten things out. People become instantaneous believers when their world comes crashing down around them. Temporal faith is using God as a temporary means to retrieve us from a bad situation. When the circumstance eases, then the faith disappears.

Faith is not mere intellectual assent. Biblical faith is not just acknowledging a certain set of facts to be true. We might be able to agree with certain propositions—Jesus is God's Son, he died for our sins on the cross, the Bible is God's Word. But holding these rational convictions doesn't mean we have saving faith.

Take the life of Elvis Presley as an example. He grew up in a Christian home in Mississippi. During his childhood he attended summer church camp for five consecutive years, and each summer he went for free because he memorized 350 Scripture verses. Yet this intellectual knowledge of Scripture didn't seem to have an effect on his life. Head knowledge is not the same as saving faith. So what is real, saving faith?

Faith is putting your trust or confidence in the right object. Faith is only as good as the object you have faith in. This is conveyed in the Chinese symbol for faith, *hsin*. The character pictures a man and a square with several short lines depicting his speech. The meaning of the symbol is that faith is the confidence that one has in a person and his or her words. And even more reliable than words is Jesus Christ, the ultimate object of our faith.

Faith is an admission of our bankruptcy. The principle of faith is very different from what our works-oriented society teaches us. Works-oriented success tells us to hold on to our pride and show God that we are pretty good people. Faith says that we realize that our bank account is overdrawn and we will never have the resources in ourselves to make ourselves right before God. Faith is declaring bankruptcy and throwing ourselves on the mercy of the court.

Faith is an act of commitment. Faith means putting our entire trust in Jesus Christ. Paul uses the phrase "the obedience that comes from faith" (Romans 1:5). This means that our entire life is placed at the disposal of Jesus.

Faith is a decision. We must decide where to place our confidence. Ultimately there are only two options. One option is to trust that we can make ourselves right before God and can control our destiny. But as Luther discovered, this leads only to the burden of condemnation and never knowing when we have done enough. The second option is to relinquish control and place our faith in Christ, who alone is the one who gives us the free gift of righteousness. He then credits our account with his righteousness and stamps "paid in full" on our life. "There is now no condemnation for those who are in Christ Jesus" (Romans 8:1).

May we discover what Luther found: "If you have a true faith that Christ is your savior, then at once you have a gracious God, for faith leads you in and opens up God's heart and will, that you should see pure grace and overflowing love. This is to behold God in faith, that you should look upon his fatherly, friendly heart, in which there is no anger nor ungraciousness."[3]

---

[1]Roland Bainton, *Here I Stand: A Life of Martin Luther* (Nashville: Abingdon, 1950), p. 30.
[2]For a discussion of the meaning of *propitiation,* see J. I. Packer, *Knowing God* (Downers Grove, Ill.: InterVarsity Press, 1975), pp. 162-65.
[3]Bainton, *Here I Stand,* p. 50.

Reading Study Guide

1. How is being made right with God contrary to performance-reward?

2. How did Martin Luther misunderstand God's righteousness?

3. What two elements are included in the righteousness of God?

4. How does God satisfy his justice and mercy?

5. What is so startling about the biblical concept of propitiation?

6. What is saving faith?

7. Do you feel that you have exercised saving faith? Why or why not?

8. What questions do you have about the reading?

9. Does the reading convict, challenge or comfort you? Why?

Going Deeper

Bainton, Roland. "The Gospel." Chap. 3 in *Here I Stand: A Life of Martin Luther.* Nashville: Abingdon, 1950.

13 / Adoption

LOOKING AHEAD

MEMORY VERSES: Romans 8:15-16
BIBLE STUDY: Galatians 4:1-7; 1 John 3:1-2
READING: Abba's Child

 ## Core Truth

What is the greatest benefit we receive from our new standing with God?

The highest privilege of the Christian life is our adoption as children into God's eternal family through God's natural Son, Jesus Christ.

1. Identify key words or phrases in the question and answer above, and state their meaning in your own words.

2. Restate the core truth in your own words.

3. What questions or issues does the core truth raise for you?

Memory Verse Study Guide

In this section of Romans Paul discusses what it means to be sons and daughters of God. The Holy Spirit testifies to our adoption, and through becoming part of God's family we are also entitled to an eternal inheritance.

1. *Putting it in context:* Trace the concept of adoption through Romans 8:12-17.

2. The memory verses are *Romans 8:15-16.* Copy the verses verbatim.

3. How does being a child of God negate our former slavery to fear?

4. What does it mean to cry, *"Abba,* Father"?

    Why is this something that only a person indwelt by the Holy Spirit can say?

5. What does Paul mean when he writes that "the Spirit himself testifies with our spirit that we are God's children"?

6. When have you experienced a little of what it feels like to be God's child?

7. How have these verses spoken to you this week?

Inductive Bible Study Guide

These passages describe the process and privilege of becoming God's adopted children.

1. *Read Galatians 3:26—4:7.* On what basis are we all equal in Christ (3:26-29)?

2. In 4:1-3 Paul describes the status of those who are still under the law. How does Paul use the analogy of a child who is an heir to convey his relationship to the law?

3. Why was Jesus sent (4:4-5)?

4. What is the evidence that we are adopted children of God (4:6)?

5. What does it mean to be an heir? How does this make you feel?

6. *Read 1 John 3:1-2.* What privilege does being children of God bestow on us?

7. What can we look forward to becoming as children of God?

8. What questions do these passages raise?

9. What verse or verses have particularly impacted you? Rewrite key verses in your own words.

👓 Reading: Abba's Child

Do you know who you are? Do you know who you were designed to be? Do you know the Father's intent for your life? You are meant to hear in your spirit the same thing Jesus heard when he came out of the waters of baptism at the beginning of his ministry: "You are my Son, whom I love; with you I am well pleased" (Mark 1:11).

Romans 8:15-16 attests to the highest privilege of the Christian life and the deepest longing of our hearts: knowing God as our perfect Father. "For you did not receive a spirit that makes you a slave again to fear, but you received the spirit of sonship [adoption]. And by him we cry, '*Abba*, Father.' The Spirit himself testifies with our spirit that we are God's children."

J. I. Packer puts it simply. "What is a Christian? The question can be answered in many ways, but the richest answer I know is that a Christian is one who has God for his Father."[1] In other words, we are designed to live in a family. Our highest privilege and deepest need is to experience the holy God as our loving Father, to approach him without fear and to be assured of his fatherly care and concern.

GOD AND OUR EARTHLY FATHERS

It has been observed that our first impressions of God are derived from the model of our parents. Our ability to trust God, to become intimate and self-revealing with him comes from the model for good or for ill that we have in our parents.

Corrie ten Boom, the great Dutch Christian, tells how she learned to trust God when she was in a German concentration camp because of the model of her father. As a child she would call out in the evening, "Papa, I'm ready for bed." Her father would come to her room

and pray for her before she went to sleep. He would then place his hand gently on her face and say, "Sleep well, Corrie. I love you." She would remain very still because she wanted to feel the touch of his hand as she fell asleep. Years later in the concentration camp she remembered the feel of her father's hand on her face. When lying on a wretched, dirty mattress she would say, "O Lord, let me feel Your hand upon me."[2]

Some argue that if we had an inadequate human father who lacked wisdom or the ability to show affection, or who abandoned or abused us, we can't see God as a loving Father. But the good news is that our relationship with God as Father is not limited to our experience with our parents. God is a Father who is faithful in love and care, generous and thoughtful, interested in all we do, skillful in training, wise in guidance, always available, helpful in teaching us maturity and integrity—no matter what our earthly fathers were like.

OUR DAD

Scripture teaches that our Father can be the same one Jesus had. Paul tells us that the indwelling Holy Spirit causes us to cry out, "*Abba*, Father," words spoken by Jesus. In the garden of Gethsemane just hours before his crucifixion, Jesus poured out his soul to his Father. Mark tells us that Jesus threw himself to the ground not far from his dozing disciples. In evident pain he cried out, "*Abba*, Father. . . . Take this cup from me [the cup of his sacrificial death]. Yet not what I will, but what you will" (Mark 14:36). What is unusual here is the way Jesus addresses God. *Abba* is an Aramaic word that expresses an intimate family relationship, a word used by a completely trusting and dependent child wholly secure in the loving arms of a father. "Dearest Father" is an equivalent expression in English. Old Testament scholar Joachim Jeremias thoroughly searched literature leading up to New Testament times to see if anyone had dared address God in such familiar terms, and he found no previous usage. It would have been scandalous to address the Holy One this way, the One whose name was so sacred that it was not even spoken, yet Jesus was on a first-name basis with the God of the universe.[3]

How did the Father feel about his Son? At the beginning of his public ministry Jesus presented himself for baptism to John the Baptist. As Jesus came out of the water, a dove representing the Holy Spirit descended on him, and a voice spoke from the heavens. Matthew records this as an announcement of God's pleasure with his Son: "This is my son, whom I love; with him I am well pleased" (Matthew 3:17). Mark records the message as a more personal statement from Father to Son: "You are my Son, whom I love; with you I am well pleased" (Mark 1:11).

Every parent knows on a human level what the great God of the universe felt toward his eternal Son. When our daughter went to college, my wife and I certainly had heightened feelings of pride and protection. As we walked back to the car to leave her in her new environment, I wanted to turn to the campus and say, "Do you know who I have delivered here? The most precious person in my life." The Father knew the danger into which he was sending his Son. He knew that his life would end in torture on the cross and that when faced with the separation that the cross would bring, Jesus needed to know that his Father took pleasure, delight and pride in him.

ADOPTED CHILDREN OF GOD

When the Holy Spirit takes up residence in our lives, we too can cry, "Abba, Father." The same Spirit that proceeds from the relationship between the Father and the Son is implanted in us. The difference between us and Jesus is that he is the natural Son of the Father, whereas we are adopted into the family through his sacrifice.

We are all spiritual orphans. Our rebellious and sinful nature cut us off from God the Father. The Bible says quite clearly that we are not born children of God and therefore must go through an adoption process. The price of our adoption was the death of God's Son. C. S. Lewis wrote, "The Son of God became a man to enable men to become the sons of God."[4]

The good news is that when we recognize that we are spiritual orphans in need of the Father, we can go through the Son. When we acknowledge that our sin has severed the relationship with the Father, that Jesus is the gracious payment for our sin and then accept the gift of forgiveness offered by inviting the Spirit of Jesus into our life, then we can cry, "Abba, Father." We are at home at last, welcomed into God's family.

As adopted children we can enjoy the same favor that Jesus has with the Father. We too are the apple of God's eye, the pleasure of his love, the delight of his focus. And if we didn't get all that we wanted or needed in our human fathers, we are invited even more deeply into the pleasure that the Father of heaven and earth takes in his Son, and us. We have been included in the family and hear the Father say, "You are my child, whom I love; with you I am well pleased." We now have the Father we always needed and wanted.

OUR RICH INHERITANCE

But that's not where the text ends. If we are full-fledged members of the family, there is an inheritance waiting for us. "If we are children, then we are heirs—heirs of God and co-heirs with Christ" (Romans 8:17). We have been included in the will and stand to inherit such things as resurrection bodies that do not decay, and a new heaven and new earth, for starters. The will also mentions that we'll have a family to spend eternity with, in a life free of pain, crying, disease and death. But that's still not the best part. The best part is that we are heirs of God. The will reads: "I, God, bequeath myself to you for all eternity."

We are heirs of God and coheirs with Christ, and therefore we get in on all that Jesus inherits. When Jesus was in the upper room before going to the cross, he longed to return to the presence of his Father. He prayed in John 17:5, "Father, glorify me in your presence with the glory I had with you before the world began."

Jesus was looking forward to the joy on the other side of the cross. The writer of Hebrews says that "for the joy set before him [Jesus] endured the cross" (Hebrews 12:2). As coheirs with Jesus we get to share in the glory that the Father bestows on the Son. As Jesus prayed moments before his arrest, he made our inheritance with him plain: "Father, I want those you have given me to be with me where I am, and to see my glory, the glory you have given me because you loved me before the creation of the world" (John 17:24). Jesus wraps up his prayer by asking the Father to bestow on us the same love that he has for Jesus: "I have made you known to them . . . in order that the love you have for me may be in them and that I myself may be in them" (v. 26).

We are drawn into the family circle and get to enjoy the spillover of the Father's love for the Son. As we bring this section on the message of Christ to a close, we end where we started. We began examining the meaning of being created in the image of God and discovered that this meant we were created for relationship. To be adopted into God's family is to be restored to paradise lost. God sent Jesus as the image of the invisible God (Colossians 1:15) to restore the image of God in us. We find our way home only when the Holy Spirit comes to take residence in us and we cry out, "*Abba*, Father." Welcome home!

---

[1]J. I. Packer, *Knowing God* (Downers Grove, Ill.: InterVarsity Press, 1973), p. 181.

[2]David Seamands, *Healing Grace* (Wheaton, Ill.: Victor, 1998), p. 50.

[3]Joachim Jeremias, *The Central Message of the New Testament* (Philadelphia: Fortress, 1981), quoted in Michael Green, *I Believe in the New Testament* (Grand Rapids: Eerdmans, 1975), p. 54.

[4]C. S. Lewis, quoted in *Hymns for the Family of God* (Nashville: Paragon, 1976), p. 167.

Reading Study Guide

1. What is the fundamental definition of what a Christian is?

2. What points stood out to you in the discussion of our concept of God coming from our parents?

3. What does being able to call God *Abba* and Father convey about the nature of our relationship with him?

4. The Father has the same view of us as he has of his Son since we are his adopted children. Is it difficult for you to believe that God takes pleasure in, is proud of and delights in you? Why or why not?

5. What does Paul mean when he calls us "heirs of God and co-heirs with Christ"?

6. How does this study on adoption bring us full circle to what it means to be created in the image of God?

7. What questions do you have about this reading?

8. Does the reading convict, challenge or comfort you? Why?

Going Deeper

Packer, J. I. "Sons of God." Chap. 19 in *Knowing God.* Downers Grove, Ill.: InterVarsity Press, 1973.

Part Three

BECOMING LIKE CHRIST

The words of C. S. Lewis serve as an excellent transition from the previous section: "The Son of God became a man to enable men to become sons of God."[1] God acted in Christ to restore our relationship with the Father, which in turn restores God's image in us. What God is after is new people who reflect his life in them.

The new life in us is the Holy Spirit (chapters fourteen and fifteen), sent to indwell us. The first two chapters of this section complete the trinitarian structure that began in chapter seven, "The Three-Person God." Chapters seven and eight focused on the sovereign God whose likeness we share. As God is a being in fellowship, so we were made for relationships. Chapters eleven through thirteen focused on the person and work of Jesus Christ. We begin this third section, "Becoming Like Christ," by focusing on the third person of the Trinity, the Holy Spirit. The indwelling presence of the Holy Spirit is what makes us Christians. Chaper fourteen introduces what it means to be *filled with the Holy Spirit,* whose primary role is to point to Jesus Christ, and chapter fifteen describes the *fruit of the Holy Spirit*. The amazing truth Christians celebrate is that the life of Christ lives within us: "Christ in you, the hope of glory" (Colossians 1:27).

Chapter sixteen reminds us that the place where we entered our relationship with Christ is the place from which we continue. Paul exhorted the Galatians not to start in faith and end in self-effort (Galatians 3:3). Another word for faith is *trust*. Trust is inseparable from obedience. In trust we follow the God of adventure wherever he leads us. Trust means having confidence in our promise-keeping God.

The quintessential quality that defines a disciple of Jesus is *love* (chapter seventeen). What Francis Schaeffer called "the mark of a Christian" is a powerful call to the church to exhibit "observable love." Jesus has given the world the right to judge whether we are Christians based on the love the world sees among Jesus' followers.

Love with a social conscience turns our hearts to the poor and needy (chapter eighteen). Biblical *justice* is combination of addressing the spiritual, emotional and physical needs of society's vulnerable ones, as well as exposing the injustice and exploitation in oppressive societal structures.

Finally, *witness* must also be in words, as well as deeds, for it is proclaiming the gospel that is the "power of God for . . . salvation" (Romans 1:16). God has entrusted us with his message to break down the strongholds of sin in people's hearts and reconcile them to himself (chapter nineteen).

---

[1]C. S. Lewis, quoted in *Hymns for the Family of God* (Nashville: Paragon, 1977), p. 167.

14 / Filled with the Holy Spirit

LOOKING AHEAD

MEMORY VERSES: Ephesians 5:18-20
BIBLE STUDY: John 14:15-18; 16:5-15
READING: The Intimate Presence

 Core Truth

How are we empowered by God to want to follow Jesus?

Jesus promised that he would not leave us alone but would send the Counselor, who would come alongside to help. This Counselor, known as the Holy Spirit, is free to work in us as we empty ourselves of known sin and seek to be continuously filled with his indwelling power.

1. Identify key words or phrases in the question and answer above, and state their meaning in your own words.

2. Restate the core truth in your own words.

3. What questions or issues does the core truth raise for you?

Memory Verse Study Guide

Paul urges the Ephesians to imitate God by being filled with the Holy Spirit, always giving thanks and praising the One who sent his Spirit to be with us.

1. *Putting it in context:* Read Ephesians 5:1-20. Make a list of Paul's exhortations in Ephesians 5:1-17. What general impression do you get from these exhortations?

2. The memory verses are *Ephesians 5:18-20.* Copy the verses verbatim.

3. What is Paul's point in contrasting being filled with the Spirit with getting drunk with wine (see Acts 2:13-17)?

4. What does it mean to be "filled with the Spirit"?

5. In verses 19 and 20 Paul lists three characteristics of those who are filled with the Spirit. What are they?

   Why are they evidence of the Spirit's filling?

6. How have these verses spoken to you this week?

Inductive Bible Study Guide

Though Jesus had spoken of the Holy Spirit at other times in his ministry, the Holy Spirit takes center stage on the eve of Jesus' departure. On the night before his crucifixion Jesus gathers with his disciples in the upper room (John 13—17). He says to them, "My children, I will be with you only a little longer" (John 13:33). He then assures them that it was to their advantage that he go away, for he would send the Holy Spirit to be with them and live in them.

1. *Read John 14:15-18; 16:5-15.* Jesus calls the Holy Spirit "another Counselor" (John 14:16). What does this tell us about the role of the Holy Spirit? (Read this verse in different translations. What different words for "Counselor" do you find?)

2. What does Jesus teach us about the Holy Spirit in John 14:15-18?

3. How could it possibly be to the disciples' advantage that Jesus go away (16:7)?

4. What is the ministry of the Holy Spirit (16:8-13)?

5. What is the Spirit's relationship to Jesus (16:14-15)?

6. What questions do these passages raise for you?

7. What verse or verses have particularly impacted you? Rewrite key verses in your own words.

Reading: The Intimate Presence
Darrell Johnson

John 14—16 is a record of the last words our Lord spoke to his disciples the night before he was crucified. Picture yourself in that context, in the place called *the Upper Room*. You are reclining on the floor around a large table. The food and drink of the Passover meal are spread over the table. Although there is much joy, there is also a feeling of heaviness in the room.

As the evening progresses, Jesus does a number of surprising things. He begins by changing the prescribed order of the Passover meal at two places. He takes a loaf of bread, and after saying the traditional blessing he breaks it and hands it to you, saying, "This is my body." He then takes a cup of wine, and after saying another traditional blessing he offers it to you, saying, "This cup is the new covenant in my blood."

Then he gets up from the table, takes off his outer garments, wraps a towel around his waist, gets down on his knees and begins washing your feet. After doing this for everyone in the room he returns to his place around the table. And then comes the biggest surprise of all: devastating news. "Children," he says, "I will be with you only a little longer" (John 13:33). And for the rest of the evening Jesus prepares you and the others to go on living in the absence of his physical presence. "I am going to him who sent me" (John 16:5).

A TROUBLING REVELATION
No wonder Jesus begins by saying, "Do not let your hearts be troubled" (John 14:1). The word for *troubled* used here is a strong, emotional feeling-word. It means to shudder, to be thrown into confusion. Jesus' announcement made the disciples shudder and threw them into profound confusion. For three wonderful years they had enjoyed his company. They had come to depend on his intimate companionship. When they were with Jesus they felt secure, they had hope, they were not as afraid, and they knew themselves to be loved unconditionally. "I am going away": they shuddered at those words, and their hearts were filled with fear, the fear of being left alone, of having to face the rest of life without this trusted companion.

What startles the disciples then, and us now, is what Jesus says in John 16:7: "But I tell you the truth: It is for your good that I am going away."

How could that be? How could it possibly be to the disciples' advantage to live in the absence of Jesus' physical presence?

Jesus continues: "Unless I go away, the Counselor will not come to you; but if I go, I will send him to you" (16:7).

The word translated "Counselor" is notoriously difficult to render with one English word, which is why different translations of the Bible use different terms. The King James Version translates it "Comforter." The NIV and RSV have "Counselor." The New English Bible, New Jerusalem Bible and NRSV have "Advocate." The NASB has "Helper." J. B. Phillips uses the phrase "Someone to stand by you." Although that is a mouthful, the latter is probably the best. The verb form of the word for the Spirit has a wide variety of meanings: to call in, send for, exhort, encourage, comfort, strengthen, console, connect, convince. In classical Greek the word is a legal term. It refers to someone called in as a representative and advocate to plead another's case.

John uses the term in the "advocate" sense in 1 John 2:1 where he writes: "My dear children, I write this to you so that you will not sin. But if anybody does sin, we have one who speaks to the Father in our defense—Jesus Christ, the Righteous One." Jesus, sent from the Father to the world, returns to the Father to be our advocate, representing us and pleading our case.

In the upper room Jesus claims that it is for the good of all of his disciples that he go away physically. Unless he goes, the Spirit will not come. But if he goes he will send "One called in alongside." The disciples and we will not be alone in Jesus' physical absence.

Why is this better than Jesus' physical presence? Jesus says:

> And I will ask the Father, and he will give you another Counselor to be with you forever—the Spirit of truth. The world cannot accept him, because it neither sees him nor knows him. But you know him, for he lives with you and will be in you. I will not leave you as orphans; I will come to you. (John 14:16-18)

CHARACTERISTICS OF THE SPIRIT

What is the Spirit like? Following are four key characteristics.

■ A Person

The word for "spirit" is a neuter noun, neither male nor female. John breaks all the rules of Greek grammar when he refers to the Spirit with masculine personal pronouns! The point is that the Holy Spirit is not an "it." The Spirit is not an impersonal force or influence. This is important because as long as the Spirit is thought of as "it," we can distance ourselves

from it. But when the Spirit is thought of as "he," we have to decide how we are going to respond to him.

We find the personhood of the Spirit celebrated in the book of Acts. Luke tells us that the Spirit

- speaks (1:16; 8:29; 10:19)
- is lied to (5:3)
- is tempted (5:9)
- bears witness (5:32)
- is resisted (7:51)
- snatches (8:39)
- gives orders (13:2)
- sends (13:4)
- thinks (15:28)
- forbids (16:6)
- prevents (16:7)
- appoints (20:28)

The personhood of the Spirit is also affirmed in the New Testament letters. The Spirit *helps* us pray (Romans 8:16), *searches* our hearts (1 Corinthians 2:10), *teaches* (1 Corinthians 2:13), *leads* (Romans 8:14; Galatians 5:18), *speaks* (1 Timothy 4:1; Hebrews 3:7; 10:15), *predicts* (1 Peter 1:11), is *grieved* (Ephesians 4:30).

■ Another Like Jesus

The passage says that the Holy Spirit is "a second of the same kind and not of a different kind." Who is the first Counselor of whom the Spirit is the same kind? Jesus of Nazareth. He is the first one called in alongside as comforter, counselor, helper, advocate. He promises that when he goes away physically, he will send in another of the same kind. In Jesus' physical absence "another", just like Jesus, comes in alongside, which is why Jesus says to the disciples, "You know him." The "another" has been abiding in Jesus all along. The "another" is stamped with the very personality of Jesus. When the Spirit comes, we disciples do not meet a stranger.

Thus the rest of the New Testament speaks of the presence of the Spirit and the presence of Christ in the same breath. They cannot be separated. To be "in Christ" is to be "in the Spirit"; to be "indwelt by Christ" is to be "indwelt by the Spirit"; to have Christ "make intercession for us" is to have the Spirit "make intercession for us" (see Romans 8:9-10; 8:26, 34).

■ With Us Always

At Jesus' first coming his presence was restricted by geography and time. If Jesus was in Capernaum and the disciples were in Jerusalem, he could not be with them. In the coming of "another Counselor" the presence of Jesus is no longer restricted. Michael Green writes, "In the days of His flesh Jesus was limited by space and time. His physical departure made possible the coming of the Spirit, . . . and there would be no barriers of space and time to prevent disciples being in intimate contact with Him."[1]

In the coming of the Holy Spirit Jesus fulfills his promise: "And surely I am with you always" (Matthew 28:20). In the presence of the Spirit the reality of Jesus as Immanuel, God with us, is realized. That is why it is to our advantage that Jesus went away physically!

■ Dwells in Us

"I will ask the Father, and he will give you another Counselor. . . . He lives with you and will be in you" (John 14:16-17). The disciples would now "find the relationship even closer than companionship with Jesus in the days of His flesh. . . . He has dwelt with them, but the one whom He promises as another Paraclete

[Counselor] will dwell in them."[2] Because of the coming of the Spirit, our bodies, mortal and sinful though they are, have become the Holy of Holies, the sacred dwelling place of the living One!

THE WORK OF THE SPIRIT

Jesus refers to the "Holy Spirit" and the "Spirit of truth." We say the word *holy* so often we forget that it means "wholly other," "distinct," "pure." The Spirit dwelling alongside and within us is pure and is working to purify us, to cleanse us, to free us from all that displeases God.

The indwelling Spirit is fulfilling God's Word: "Be holy, because I, the LORD your God, am holy" (Leviticus 19:2; 1 Peter 1:15-16). That is why, even though the presence of the Spirit comforts, it also disturbs. The Spirit creates a holy discontent with the way things are in ourselves and in the world. The Spirit will not rest, nor let us rest, until we become like the One who sent him.

"Spirit of truth" will teach and guide into all truth (John 14:26; 16:13). The indwelling presence teaches us the truth about ourselves, about the world and about God. We should not be surprised, therefore, that the rest of the New Testament puts such an emphasis on knowing, doing and speaking the truth. Indeed, not speaking the truth grieves the Spirit of God (Ephesians 4:25-30). When we find ourselves having to hide, deny or stretch the truth, we can be sure that we are not being guided by the Spirit. The uneasiness we feel when we exaggerate or lie or otherwise play with the truth is not simply the result of compromising our own conscience; the uneasiness is due to the Spirit's disappointment.

The good news is that the Spirit is at work wooing, pulling, pushing, leading us into truth. He is constantly leading us to Jesus Christ, who is the truth incarnate (John 14:6). As the apostle Paul says, in Christ "all the treasures of wisdom and knowledge" are hidden (Colossians 2:3). The great passion of the Spirit is that human beings know Christ in all his fullness and then evaluate everything in light of him. The Spirit is radically Christ-centered.

"HE WILL GLORIFY ME"

"He will bring glory to me," says Jesus of the Spirit of truth (John 16:14). The Holy Spirit is the "shy member of the Trinity," as Dale Bruner says. He constantly turns the spotlight off himself and shines it on the God-man. Any moving of the Spirit, therefore, that does not lead people to Christ is not the moving of the Spirit of God. The passion of the Spirit of God is to make the living Christ the center of our lives.

It *is* to our advantage that Jesus goes away physically. When Jesus goes he sends another, a Person of the same kind as himself who continues Jesus' presence with us, who comes to live in us, slowly, but surely, making us more like the Holy One and helping us see all of life in light of the One who is the Truth.

---

[1]Michael Green, *I Believe in the Holy Spirit* (Grand Rapids: Eerdmans, 1975), pp. 42-43.
[2]Ibid., p. 43.

Reading Study Guide

1. Describe in your own words the setting in which Jesus speaks of the Holy Spirit.

2. Why is it to our advantage that Jesus sent his Holy Spirit?

3. What new insights about the person and work of the Holy Spirit did you receive as a result of this study?

4. What misconceptions about the Holy Spirit were clarified as a result of this study?

5. How do you view the purpose of the Holy Spirit in your life?

6. What questions do you have about the reading?

7. Does the reading convict, challenge or comfort you? Why?

Going Deeper

Watson, David. "Life in the Spirit." Chap. 5 in *Called and Committed: World-Changing Discipleship*. Wheaton, Ill.: Harold Shaw, 2000.

15 / Fruit of the Holy Spirit

LOOKING AHEAD

MEMORY VERSES: Galatians 5:22-23
BIBLE STUDY: Galatians 5:16-26
READING: The Fruit of Christ's Character

 ## Core Truth

What is the role of the Holy Spirit in transforming us into the image of Christ?

The Spirit is holy, for he produces the character of Christ in those in whom he dwells. These character qualities are known as the fruit of the Spirit.

1. Identify key words or phrases in the question and answer above, and state their meaning in your own words.

2. Restate the core truth in your own words.

3. What questions or issues does the core truth raise for you?

Memory Verse Study Guide

We are called to exhibit the fruit of the Spirit in our lives, which is listed in Galatians 5:22-23.

1. *Putting it in context:* We will examine the larger context in our study on Galatians 5:16-26. Simply note at this point the principal force in opposition to the fruit of the Spirit.

2. The memory verses are *Galatians 5:22-23.* Copy these verses verbatim.

3. Why is *fruit* in the singular instead of the plural?

4. Does *fruit* in the singular mean that all of these characteristics are equally present in our lives? Why or why not?

5. What does Paul mean by the phrase "against such *things* there is no law"?

6. Where do you sense Jesus is stretching your character to be more like him?

Inductive Bible Study Guide

The teaching on the fruit of the Spirit is set within the context of the battle raging inside of us between our old and new natures.

1. *Read Galatians 5:16-26.* Put in your own words the nature of the battle between the Spirit and the flesh.

2. What does Paul mean by "the desires of the sinful nature"?

3. Paul indicates that we have the ability to exercise our will. What is the nature of our choice?

4. As you read the list of the acts of the sinful nature, what still needs to be put to death in you and replaced by the fruit of the Spirit?

5. Why is one who is led by the Spirit not under the law?

6. What does it mean to have crucified the sinful nature (v. 24)? How then does God produce his life in us?

7. What questions does this passage raise for you?

8. What verse or verses have particularly impacted you? Rewrite key verses in your own words.

👓 Reading: The Fruit of Christ's Character

A little girl and her mother were talking as they walked out of church. The mother asked her daughter how she liked church that day. The girl replied that she thought it was good, but she was a little confused. She said, "The pastor said that God was bigger than we are. Is that true?" Her mother responded that it was true. "He also said that God lives inside us. Is that true, Mommy?" "Yes." "Well then," said the girl, "if God is bigger than we are, and if he lives inside us, then shouldn't some of him show through?"

This cute story points to the heart of what it means to be a Christian. A Christian is one in whom Christ dwells. One of Paul's favorite shorthand phrases that captures this is "Christ in you." Earlier in his letter to the Galatians Paul portrayed himself as a midwife vicariously experiencing labor pains on behalf of the Galatians, who are going through the birth process. "My dear children, for whom I am again in the pains of childbirth until Christ is formed in you" (Galatians 4:19).

As the living Christ takes over more and more of our will, we will give off the scent of Christ. This is how Paul describes himself and his companions: "But thanks be to God, who . . . through us spreads everywhere the fragrance of the knowledge of him. For we are to God the aroma of Christ" (2 Corinthians 2:14-15).

So whether we use the image of spreading the scent of Christ or of producing the succulent fruit of Christ, Christ is to be manifest through our personality. Galatians 5:16-23 reminds us of Jesus' description of our relationship to him as branches connected to a vine (John 15:1-11).

What is the fruit we are to bear? The clue to the nature of the fruit we are to bear is the cu-

rious use of the singular *fruit*. Paul writes, "But the fruit of the Spirit is . . . , " when we might expect the plural, "The fruits of the Spirit are . . . " (Galatians 5:22). This is because the fruit is the multifaceted character of one person, Jesus Christ. The Holy Spirit is the Spirit of Christ. The image of the vine and branches describes the fruit of the Spirit as being like a cluster of grapes. There is a single stem attached to a vine, from which a cluster grows. Each grape in the cluster is a characteristic of Jesus.

Let's take a look at the grapes in this cluster, one at a time. Then we will examine how they are grown in us.

LOVE: UNCONQUERABLE BENEVOLENCE

Heading the list is the definitive quality that shines through Jesus and is to mark his followers. Jesus said, "By this all men will know that you are my disciples, if you love one another" (John 13:35). To love your enemies and forgive those who intend your destruction is a love that comes from above.

The story of a Korean couple illustrate this kind of love. Their son, Ho Ho, had graduated with honors from Eastern College and was completing his medical degree at the University of Pennsylvania. While mailing a letter to his family, Ho Ho was surrounded by a gang of teenage hoods, robbed of his pocket change and beaten to death. Ho's parents sat through the entire trial saying nothing. Only after the guilty verdict was announced were they given the opportunity to speak. They stepped forward and knelt in front of the judge's bench. The crowd sat in stunned silence as the parents begged for mercy for their son's murderers. And not only that, but they asked the judge to release the teenagers so that they could give these boys the home they never had. They told the judge that they were Christians and therefore wanted to show the same grace they had received from God to those who had done this grievous evil.

Love is God's unconquerable benevolence.

JOY: BASKING IN THE FATHER'S DELIGHT

When we see ourselves as street urchins deserving punishment and yet are forgiven by the same one who should condemn us, joy is the result. The prodigal son came home to a father's embrace and became the honored guest at a party. Joy is living under the pleasure of the Father's delight in you. It is knowing that we are the apple of his eye. Can you believe that the Lord considers us his inheritance? What the Lord deems as his treasure for all eternity is us.

Joy transcends circumstances. We often confuse happiness and joy. Happiness has to do with "everything going my way," whereas joy can coexist with suffering and grief. Joy is stable, because it is rooted in hope. Jesus said, "Take heart! I have overcome the world" (John 16:33). Hope grounded in Christ's death and resurrection is knowing how the story ends. Joy is that we know there is a happy ending.

PEACE: SERENITY FROM SECURITY

"Therefore, since we have been justified through faith, we have peace with God through our Lord Jesus Christ" (Romans 5:1). Our peace is a result of God's making his peace with us. The Holy God, whose very being is at war with our sinful character, reconciled us to himself by putting forward Jesus Christ as the peace offering for our sin. R. C. Sproul says, "When God signs a peace treaty, it is signed for perpetuity. . . . When we sin, God is displeased, and He will move to correct us and convict us of our sin. But He does not go to war against us."[1]

The Hebrew word for peace is *shalom*. Shalom is not so much the absence of war but the presence of a benevolent, just and honorable king. Shalom reigned in the land of Israel when the people knew that their sovereign was a man of character. We live in peace knowing that our Sovereign, who has made peace with us, sits on the throne of the universe, moving "all things . . . for the good of those who love him, who have been called according to his purpose" (Romans 8:28). It is serenity from security.

PATIENCE: LONGSUFFERING

The word translated "patience" is a compound word meaning longsuffering. When the father of the prodigal son waited for his son to return, he did so with an open heart. He was living with the open wound of rejection. The father could have cauterized the open wound by disowning his son with a furious dismissal, yet instead he displayed one of the ingredients of patience: being slow to anger.

We often do not extend the same patience to others that we want God to have with us. I try to remember the following story when my patience has run out for those who are not living up to my expectations. A medieval peasant woman happened upon a Benedictine monk. She fell down before him and blurted out, "Please tell me, holy father, what do you men of God do up there in the monastery on the hill?" The monk answered wisely, "I will tell you, my child: We fall down and we get up! We fall down and we get up! We fall down and we get up!" If God suffers when I stumble, can't I wait in suffering for others?

KINDNESS: FIRM BUT GENTLE

Simple kindness is often missing in our world. We live in an "in your face" culture marked by belligerence, intimidation and incivility. We get what we want through bullying and boisterousness. The level of public hostility has reached frightening proportions.

Jesus was no pushover and displayed firmness and righteous anger toward the religious establishment, but to the vulnerable and hurting he was tender. A woman was caught in the act of adultery by the self-righteous elite who wanted to bury her under a mound of stones. Jesus said, "He who is without sin, cast the first stone" (see John 8:7). When they all walked away in self-condemnation, Jesus said to the ashamed woman, "Neither do I condemn you. . . . Go now and leave your life of sin" (John 8:11). The Spirit speaks a gentle word through us to other bruised people, a healing salve in a hostile world.

GOODNESS: LOVE FOR THE HOLY, MAGNANIMITY OF SPIRIT

Jonathan Edwards, the eighteenth-century Puritan preacher, wrote, "Holiness is the most amiable and sweet thing that is to be found in heaven or earth." The psalmist says, "Taste and see that the LORD is good" (Psalm 34:8).

One of the definitions of goodness is a love for the holy. Goodness can also mean a generosity or magnanimity of spirit. We live in a world full of hurts, bumps and bruises. To get through this life we need a big heart. We need a generosity of spirit to survive with grace.

FAITHFULNESS: KEEP OUR PROMISES

God is a covenant maker and a covenant keeper. The first covenant the Lord made with Abraham was sealed in such a dramatic way that it shows us that keeping promises is at the

heart of his character. Two altars were erected. On each sat half the carcasses of a bull, a goat, a ram and two birds. Passing between these two altars were the symbols of God in the form of a blazing torch and a smoking pot. It was as if the Lord were saying to Abraham, "May I be cut in two like these animals if I fail to keep my covenant to make of you a great nation" (see Genesis 15).

Lewis Smedes said, "We are most like God when we keep our covenants." We keep the covenants we make. Integrity must be our middle name. Jesus said, "Let your yes be yes, and your no, no" (Matthew 5:37). May it be said of us, "If she said she would do it, you can count on it."

GENTLENESS: POWER UNDER CONTROL

Jesus said of himself, "I am gentle and humble in heart" (Matthew 11:29). *Gentle* is also translated as "meek," yet "meek" does not carry positive connotations. But Jesus said, "Blessed are the meek, for they will inherit the earth" (Matthew 5:5). It was said of Moses that he was the meekest man in all the earth. This is the same one who took on the potentate of the age, the pharaoh, and led his people from captivity. Meek has nothing to do with being weak. It is the same word used to describe a snorting stallion whose power has been harnessed and brought under the control of the bit. Submission to the power of God is what gentleness conveys.

SELF-CONTROL: DISCIPLINE AND DIRECT OUR ENERGIES WISELY

Self-control means not allowing our passions to run wild but harnessing them in the direction God would have them go. It's as if we were orchestra conductors with powerful players down in the pit of our lives—passions, desires, anger, sex drives, terrifying memories. Any one of these could take off and ruin the symphony. But the Holy Spirit gives us the power to stop these from destroying us. Take lust, for example. Lust is born when we allow a simple awareness of another person's attractiveness to become a sexual fantasy. We lose control when we dwell on sexual thoughts so that they are fanned into a flame of passion. Luther said, "We cannot help it if birds fly over our heads. It is another thing if we invite them to build nests in our hair." Self-control is keeping the birds out of our hair.

How Are These Qualities Produced in Us?

We have described our Lord when we group together the qualities of love, joy, peace, patience, kindness, goodness, faithfulness, gentleness and self-control. Since the Spirit indwells believers, these are the qualities that emerge as we abide in the vine.

In this age of self-improvement programs, self-help books and makeovers, we may think we can grow the fruit of the Spirit through sheer willpower and personal discipline: grit your teeth and out pops patience. We can try to act out the qualities that we think make up love, joy or peace, but this will be artificial fruit.

To think we can produce fruit through self-effort is failing to see that the Christian life is a battle. Our old nature, though defeated, is not dead, and it holds on and fights against the new nature of the Spirit. A university student who became a Christian soon discovered that there was now a battle waging in him for supremacy that he had not faced before. The student described to a Christian counselor what he was experiencing: "It's like there is a mutt and a pedigreed dog inside my life, and they are fighting all the time." The counselor asked him which dog was winning. The student thought for a moment and replied, "I guess the one I feed the most."

We cannot pit our will against our sinful nature, but we must submit our will to the Spirit. Feeding the purebred dog means to submit to the rule of God in our lives. Life will flow through us when we know that apart from Christ we can do nothing. When we come to terms with the inability to change ourselves, then we allow the Lord to be our source.

Trying to see the fruit that God has produced in us is like trying to look at our eyes. You can't see that which you see through. The Holy Spirit is like our eyes. But others can see the evidence of the Spirit in our lives in a way we can't. As an exercise to close my small group, the members affirmed the fruit of the Spirit by declaring what we saw in each other. We delighted in telling each other of the evident ways that Christ's character was finding expression through our lives. I found myself saying, "Really? You see that in me? Thanks, Lord, for being at work in transforming me into your image and likeness even though I can't see it myself." We dragged our weary bodies into the meeting and walked out flying high. What a joy to know that God isn't finished with us yet!

---

[1]R. C. Sproul, *The Holiness of God* (Wheaton, Ill.: Tyndale House, 1985), p. 197.

Reading Study Guide

1. What is at the heart of what it means to be a Christian?

2. What does the singular use of the word *fruit* in Galatians 5:22-23 indicate?

3. Write a one-sentence definition of your understanding of each one of the fruit of the Spirit.

   love

   joy

   peace

   patience

   kindness

   goodness

   faithfulness

   gentleness

   self-control

4. From this list, pick one quality where you have seen growth in your own life and another quality where you need God's grace for growth.

5. As an exercise in affirmation, focus on each person in your group and identify the fruit of the Spirit that you see showing through. What Christlike qualities mark your lives?

6. What questions do you have about this reading?

7. Does this reading convict, challenge or comfort you? Why?

Going Deeper

Take the list of the fruit of the Spirit and find examples in the Gospels of each of these qualities displayed in Christ's life.

16 / Trust

LOOKING AHEAD

MEMORY VERSES: Proverbs 3:5-6
BIBLE STUDY: Hebrews 11
READING: God Works Everything Together for Good

 **Core Truth**

How are we to grow in the knowledge of Christ?

Paul exhorts the Colossians, "So then, just as you received Christ Jesus as Lord, continue to live in him" (Colossians 2:6). By faith in God, who is absolutely good, we plug in to the power of the Holy Spirit and set off on a risky adventure to follow wherever Jesus Christ leads.

1. Identify key words or phrases in the question and answer above, and state their meaning in your own words.

2. Restate the core truth in your own words.

3. What questions or issues does the core truth raise for you?

Memory Verse Study Guide

These memory verses focus our attention on the source of wisdom and insight for our life. Because these verses are life directional, they are some of the most memorized.

1. *Putting it in context:* Examine the setting of the command and promise of Proverbs 3:5-6 by reading Proverbs 3:1-10. What themes do you discover?

2. The memory verses are *Proverbs 3:5-6.* Copy the verses verbatim.

3. In order to trust in God with all our heart, what must be true about the Lord?

4. We are told to "lean not on your own understanding" (v. 5). What does that mean? Does this imply that Christians are not to use reason? Explain.

5. What is the importance of the qualifier "in all your ways acknowledge him" (v. 6)?

6. What is the promised outcome? What does this mean?

7. How have these verses spoken to you this week?

Inductive Bible Study Guide

Hebrews 11 is often called the Hall of Fame of Faith because it catalogs the faithfulness of the great ones who have gone before us. Allow their sense of adventure in following wherever God would lead to enhance your sense of anticipation and risk.

1. *Read Hebrews 11.* Rewrite in your own words the definition of faith (v. 1).

2. "Without faith it is impossible to please God" (v. 6). Why is faith necessary to please God?

3. What are the common elements in the faith of the heroes listed?

4. With which of these heroes of faith can you most identify? Why?

5. How are you challenged by the faith of these heroes?

6. What questions do you have about this passage?

7. What verse or verses have particularly impacted you? Rewrite key verses in your own words.

Reading: God Works Everything Together for Good

The test of faith is the ability to trust God when life is at its worst. But on what is that trust based? The promise on which all the promises of God rest is: "And we know that in all things God works for the good of those who love him, who have been called according to his purpose" (Romans 8:28).

We might miss the depth of this verse because of its familiarity, and we might also miss its hope because of the flippant manner in which it is tossed around as a superficial cliché within the Christian community. We throw this verse at people's trauma like a doctor who doesn't want to be bothered by an after-hours call: "Take this verse and call me in the morning."

Paul does not write this to make light of the depth of sorrow that we face. He is saying that everything that happens to us in this world can be viewed from the standpoint of our good God, who rules this world with sovereign power and therefore moves everything after the benevolence of his will.

Let's explore the depth of this verse by first stating what Paul is *not* saying.

THIS PROMISE IS FOR EVERYONE

There are two conditions that must be met for this promise to apply to someone's life. The first condition is emphatic in the Greek structure of this verse. Our English translations tend to tack on "to those who love God" to the phrase "in all things God works for the good." The phrase "to those who love God" in the Greek text precedes the promise "in all things God works for the good." It is clear that to be able to stand under the protection of God we must evidence a love for God. To love God is to obey him.

Some translations say, "We know that in everything God cooperates for good." In other words, our willing and free submission to God's plan is the way that God moves all things after his will. One person put the intent of the condition of our love like this: "If a person loves God and trusts God and accepts God, if a person feels and knows and is convinced that God is an all-wise and all-loving Father, then he can humbly accept all that God sends to him. Without trusting the grace of God to bring good out of any situation, we will fight God's plan and purpose and then end in bitterness." Our love for God is our statement to God that we will cooperate with his larger will.

The second condition we must meet so that in all things God will work for our good is to be "called according to his purpose." To be called is to be summoned, to hear and respond to Jesus' "follow me." It is to submit ourselves to the training of Jesus Christ, whose purpose is to conform us to his image. We can't claim God's promise of working all things together for good unless we have responded and entrusted our lives to a God who *is* good.

PAUL IS NOT MAKING LIGHT OF EVIL

In the summer of 1993, while speaking at Whitworth College in Spokane, Washington, it was my privilege to meet a remarkable man, Jerry Sittser. Jerry told my wife and me of an unspeakable tragedy that occurred in the fall of 1991. Jerry, along with his mother, wife and four children, were returning home in their minivan from an outing. It was dusk as they headed down the winding mountain road. Coming from the other direction was a car whose erratic headlights signaled trouble. Jerry noticed the random, zigzag reflection off the mountain on his side of the road. Before he could maneuver out of the way the drunk driver collided head-on with his minivan. In the space of a few moments Jerry lost three generations of women in his family: his mother, wife and four-year-old daughter lay dead on the side of the road.

What took place was evil, the result of the sinful nature of humanity. A person chose to drink and turned his car into a lethal weapon. Before Jerry could get to the point of truly believing that "in all things God works for good," he had to go through the rage he felt toward the driver and toward God, the sense of meaninglessness, as well as summoning the strength to go on while assuming the duties and responsibilities of a single father for three very traumatized children. Did the knowledge of God's goodness keep Jerry from sorrow? No. Believing that God is good is not being protected from life's tragedies.

So what did Paul intend to affirm about this wondrous promise, that in everything God works for the good?

NOT EVERYTHING IS GOOD, BUT GOD WORKS FOR THE GOOD IN EVERYTHING

The promise is that even out of that which is evil, God in his sovereign way brings good. Let's look at a number of implications of this truth.

God incorporates our detours into his road map. Our cul-de-sacs become his open highways. Nothing is wasted in God's kingdom. John Piper puts it like this, "Specifically, the glorious might of God that we need to see and trust is the power of God to turn all of our detours and obstacles into glorious outcomes."[1] One of the characteristics of Persian rugs is that they are full of mistakes, but when the rug maker notices a mistake he has a creative way

of incorporating the mistake into the pattern so that it blends in.

Time gives us perspective. Time transforms the meaning of events in our life. Much of what happens in this world will not be clear or even completed until Christ comes in his kingdom and makes all the wrongs right and settles the score of justice. Jerry Sittser will go to the grave without knowing the full meaning of the loss of his family, but even in the short five-and-a-half-years since this tragedy, time is bringing perspective to Jerry, and the good from the tragedy is starting to emerge. He has written a wonderful book, *A Grace Disguised.*[2] It takes the perspective of time to begin to see the events of our life in the broader plan of God's purpose.

Life is not arbitrary and capricious. Yet when you look at some of life's events, you wonder if there is a plan. Larry Crabb has written, "No one will conclude that God is good by studying life."[3] Jerry Sittser writes, "One of the worst aspects of my experience of loss has been this sense of sheer randomness. The event was completely outside my control—an 'accident,' as we say. The threat of anomie was and still is almost unbearable to me. I began to look with cynicism on the absurdity of life. Maybe, I thought, there really is no God and no meaning to life. I was tormented by an inability to discover any explanation that made sense of this tragedy."[4]

Tragedy is far more bearable if we can come up with some larger purpose for it. Paul grounds the truth that God works everything for good in the conviction that there is a sovereign God who sees the expanse of time and moves all things in accordance with his purpose. Paul moves from the trenches of time in Romans 8:28 to the foundation of the eternal purpose in verses 29 and 30. Verse 28 is true because it rests on the foundation of verses 29 and 30.

We live looking at the underside of the fabric on the weaver's loom. What we see from the underside are dangling threads and random patterns. Paul moves from the underside of the weaver's loom to the perch where the weaver sits. He pulls back to a heavenly perspective by scanning God's view of eternity. He describes five unbreakable links in a chain moving from God's plan before time to his culmination in the glory of eternity. In everything God works for good because he has a purpose for us before we were created and sets about to accomplish it while incorporating our free will in the process. "For those God *foreknew* he also *predestined* to be conformed to the likeness of his Son, that he might be the firstborn among many brothers. And those he predestined, he also *called;* those he called; he also *justified;* those he justified, he also *glorified*" (vv. 29-30).

Let's look at the links in this unbreakable chain.

For those God foreknew. To foreknow is to know beforehand. Some view foreknowledge as God's seeing ahead those who will exercise faith in him and, based on that decision, picking those who will choose. But knowing in Scripture is a personal knowing, not God scanning time at a distance. To know is to regard, to know with a particular interest, delight and affection. Of all the people on Earth, God foreknew Israel as his special people. To foreknow is to "forelove." For a reason known only to God he bestows his love on some.

Those God forknew he also predestined. Predestined means that God decreed in advance that our purpose is to be conformed to the image of his Son, something that does not happen without considerable trial.

Those he predestined, he also called. The

call of God is his eternal summons on our life. We are invited by name to respond to the claim of Jesus on our life. Some have named this God's effectual calling. In other words, God's call effects the desired result. Can we resist the call of God? Never. But we can respond willingly.

Those he called, he also justified. To be called is to be made right with God. All the demands of the law have been met when we place our faith in Jesus Christ alone for our salvation.

Those he justified, he also glorified. So assured is Paul that God will bring his people home that he makes it a completed past action, "glorified." Many have noticed the absence of the step of sanctification. Paul does not say, *"Those he justified, he also sanctified."* So sure is Paul of God's goodness that once we have been declared right before God, future glorification is finished.

HISTORY TELLS THE TALE

This leads us to the ultimate event of history that showcases 'the goodness of God. If we would not conclude by looking at the events of life that the goodness of God will triumph, where can we look? The historical demonstration that in everything God works for good is the cross.

If we had been present the day of Jesus' death, would we have seen anything other than an act of gratuitous violence? If we had been followers of Jesus, would we have walked away in despair, saying, "What was the purpose of that? Why did he have to die?" At best we might have concluded that the cross served to unmask the evil that lurks in the human heart. But evil triumphed. What else could one conclude?

Yet to quote Joseph in Genesis 50:20, "You

intended to harm me, but God intended it for good." Joseph had been left by his brothers for dead, yet God preserved him to become second in command to Pharaoh to further the purposes of God's chosen people. The cross, that which was intended for evil, was—in the plan and foreknowledge of God—the means to redeem lost humanity. If God can bring good out of the crucifixion of his Son, then he can bring good from any horror that befalls his children.

J. I. Packer brings the implication of the cross home.

> As believers we find in the cross of Christ assurance that we, as individuals, are beloved of God; the Son of God . . . loves me and gave himself for me. Knowing this we are able to apply to ourselves the promise that all things work together for good to them that love God and are called according to His purpose. Not just some things but all things! Every single thing that happens to us expresses God's love for us, and comes to us for the furthering of God's purpose for us. Thus so far as we are concerned, God is love to us—holy, omnipotent love—at every moment and in every event of every day's life. Even when we cannot see the why and the wherefore of God's dealing, we know there is love in and behind them; and so we can rejoice always, even when, humanly speaking, things are going wrong. We know that the true story of our life, when known, will prove to be, as the hymn says, "mercy from first to last, and we are content."[5]

[1]John Piper, *Future Grace* (Sisters, Ore.: Multnomah Press, 1995), p. 173.
[2]Gerald Sittser, *A Grace Disguised* (Grand Rapids: Zondervan, 1996).
[3]Larry Crabb, *Finding God* (Grand Rapids: Zondervan, 1993), p. 104.
[4]Sittser, *Grace Disguised*, p. 97.
[5]J. I. Packer, *Knowing God* (Downers Grove, Ill.: InterVarsity Press, 1973), p. 111.

Reading Study Guide

1. How has the promise that "God works all things for good" been misused?

2. Why would the promise that God works everything together for good be limited to "those who love him" and "have been called according to his purpose"?

3. How does the knowledge of God's goodness address Jerry Sittser's tragedy?

4. Share a story from your life in which you have gained perspective.

   • Detours turning into open highways

   • Time bringing a new vantage point

   • Gaining a sense of purpose over time

5. How does verse 28 rest on the foundation of verses 29 and 30?

6. What comfort do you find for yourself in the closing quote from J. I. Packer?

7. What questions do you have about this reading?

8. Does the reading convict, challenge or comfort you? Why?

Going Deeper

Lewis, C. S. "The Three Parts of Morality," and "The 'Cardinal Virtues.'" In *Mere Christianity*. New York: Macmillan, 1981.

Action Page

REVIEWING YOUR COVENANT

Once you have established a covenant, it is important to periodically review its expectations and renew your commitment. As with any relationship we can become lax in our attentiveness to what makes it work. These questions will lead you to refine the covenant and recommit your energies to its accomplishment.

1. Review your most recent covenant. On a scale of 1 to 5, 5 being highest, rate yourself on your accomplishment of each of the elements in the covenant. Share your rating and explain its meaning to each other.

2. As you reflect on the discipling process, what have been the benefits for your growth in Christ up to this point?

3. What have been the disappointments or the unfulfilled expectations?

   How might these be overcome?

4. What changes would you like to make in the disciple's covenant of commitment?

5. To what do you need to recommit yourself in order to be faithful to the covenant?

17 / Love

LOOKING AHEAD

MEMORY VERSES: John 13:34-35
BIBLE STUDY: John 17:20-26
READING: People of the Basin and Towel

 Core Truth

What is the authenticating mark to the unbelieving world that we are followers of Jesus Christ?

Sacrificial love as exemplified in Jesus' voluntary death on the cross is to be reflected in the way Christians relate to each other. This kind of love is so out of step with the world's way that unbelievers will take notice.

1. Identify key words or phrases in the question and answer above, and state their meaning in your own words.

2. Restate the core truth in your own words.

3. What questions or issues does the core truth raise for you?

Memory Verse Study Guide

This lesson connects two passages from Jesus' final words to his disciples in the upper room. The memory verses focus on love as demonstrated in service. The second passage, which is our Bible study, is Christ's call to unity. Love and unity seem to be inseparable.

1. *Putting it in context:* The overall setting for Jesus' command to love one another is the last meal with his disciples. How does the footwashing and prediction of betrayal provide the context for this command (John 13:1-35)?

2. The memory verses are John *13:34-35.* Copy the verses verbatim.

3. Jesus commands, "As I have loved you, so you must love one another." How does the word *as* affect the meaning of the phrase?

4. Why is love the authenticating sign to the world that we are disciples of Jesus?

5. What would others observe when watching you interact with your Christian friends?

6. How have these verses spoken to you this week?

 Inductive Bible Study Guide

Love is the sign to the world that we are followers of Jesus, whereas unity is the sign that Jesus was sent from God. Love and unity are what Francis Schaeffer calls the "final apologetic." The defense to the world of the authenticity of our faith is not right belief, but right behavior.

1. *Read John 17:20-26.* What does Jesus pray about for us (vv. 20-21)?

2. On what is our oneness based (vv. 21-23)?

3. What will our oneness prove to the world (v. 23)? Why?

4. What attitudes and values do you think characterize oneness?

5. What do we as believers allow to divide us from one another?

6. In what current relationship do you need to experience reconciliation?

7. What questions do you have about this passage?

8. What verse or verses have particularly impacted you? Rewrite key verses in your own words.

Reading: People of the Basin and Towel

What is the mark of a Christian? A fish on the back of a car? A cross worn around the neck? The right theology?

How easy it is to look in the wrong places for the sign of authenticity! Jesus told us plainly about the distinguishing mark of a Christian. He raises one quality above all others: "By this all men will know that you are my disciples, if you love one another" (John 13:35).

But what does this love look like? Jesus was concerned to leave an indelible, visual image in the minds of his disciples of what it means to love one another. He models servant-love by washing the disciples' feet.

THE SECURITY OF A SERVANT

John 13 introduces a climactic moment captured in John 13—17, known as the upper-room discourse. John lets us know that Jesus is fully conscious of the importance of the moment. John gives us three insights into Jesus' self-awareness.

1. Jesus knew that the time had come for him to leave this world and go to the Father. A favorite phrase in John's Gospel is "his hour had not yet come." Jesus operated out of the awareness of a divine timetable. Jesus was a man born to die. At one point Jesus' brothers wanted him to go to Jerusalem to make a name for himself, but he responded, "For me the right time has not yet come" (John 7:8), for it was in Jerusalem that his appointment with death awaited him. On another occasion the religious leaders wanted to arrest him for what they thought was a blasphemous statement, but John writes, "No one laid a hand on him, because his time had not yet come" (John 7:30). But in John 13 "the time had come." The

pall of Jesus' death hangs over this last meal with his disciples.

2. Satan makes his move. If this were a cosmic chess match, Satan is about to declare checkmate. He has one final pawn to move into place. "The evening meal was being served, and the devil had already prompted Judas Iscariot, son of Simon, to betray Jesus" (John 13:2). Jesus is aware that in a few hours one of his trusted followers will betray him with a kiss in a garden, the sign for bloodthirsty men to arrest him.

3. In spite of impending death and betrayal, Jesus is fully cognizant of who he is. He is in absolute control. Events of history may appear to be out of control. The mounting forces of evil are a gathering darkness on the horizon, but Jesus has already declared checkmate. "Jesus knew that the Father had put all things under his power, and that he had come from God and was returning to God" (John 13:3). Jesus knew where he had come from and where he was going.

THE FOOTWASHING

With his worth established in his relationship with the Father, Jesus was able to assume a lowly role: "So he got up from the meal, took off his outer clothing, and wrapped a towel around his waist. After that, he poured water into a basin and began to wash his disciples' feet, drying them with the towel that was wrapped around him" (John 13:4-5).

None of the disciples had the humility or the courage to play the role of a household slave. Luke's Gospel tells us that they entered the meal debating among themselves who was the greatest. In Jewish culture footwashing was such a menial task that it was listed as a duty that a Jewish servant should not perform; footwashing was reserved for Gentile slaves, women and children.

When it's time to have his feet washed, Peter can only sputter and stammer out his objection: "Lord, are you going to wash my feet?" (John 13:6). Jesus says something about Peter's not understanding the meaning of what he is doing now, but that he will understand in the future, but none of this sinks in. Peter is too caught up in his own revulsion. "No, . . . you shall never wash my feet!" (John 13:8).

PETER'S REACTION

What was going on with Peter? Why the intense resistance?

Jesus' action violated the entire way that Peter had learned to understand value and worth. The lesser serves the greater; this is the way it is. Peter has been in a competitive discussion with his fellow disciples as to who would receive the position of greatest honor when Jesus sat on the throne. Who would get the seat nearest to the center of glory and power? Now the greater is acting like the lesser. Peter had no frame of reference to understand this.

Second, being served by his Lord was a blow to Peter's pride and self-sufficiency. To be on the receiving end is to be put in a vulnerable position. We want to be in control. It is much easier to condescendingly give to another in need. We get our strokes from being there for others. We love to hear, "I couldn't have gotten through that illness or grief or loss without you." We become addicted to the need to be needed. But to be on the receiving end of help displays weakness that is a blow to our self-control.

Archbishop William Temple said, "Man's humility does not begin with the giving of ser-vice; it begins with the readiness to receive it." Peter had to learn to receive before he was ready to give.

Perhaps the third reason for Peter's resistance was that Jesus came down from the pedestal and began to meddle in the dirt of real life. We want to keep Jesus polished and on a mantle reserved for religious times. We don't want a Jesus who mucks around in the rough-and-tumble of real life.

George MacLeod put it powerfully: "I am recovering the claim that Jesus was not crucified in a Cathedral between two candles, but on a cross between two thieves; on the town garbage heap . . . at the kind of place where cynics talk smut, and thieves curse, and soldiers gamble. Because that is where He died. And that is what He died about. And that this is where churchmen should be."[1]

LESSONS OF FOOTWASHING

Jesus explains the meaning of the footwashing. He points to the deeper meaning of the symbol and then the importance of his model of humility.

Footwashing foreshadows the cross. Taking up this shameful role points to Jesus' death on the cross. The footwashing foreshadows the self-degradation of this hideous means of death. Jesus speaks in a way that gets Peter's attention: "Unless I wash you, you have no part with me" (John 13:8). He is emphatic that *he* must do the washing. Dirty feet are a symbol of the need for the deeper cleansing of the cross. The image of baptism merges with the image of the cross. In the waters of baptism our sins are washed away, but only because the shed blood of Christ is the way God has provided for the cleansing of the guilt of our sin.

Peter remains true to his character to the end. In typical overreaction Peter displays his lack of understanding in his resistance and in his exuberance. Peter says to Jesus, "Then, Lord, . . . not just my feet but my hands and my head as well" (John 13:9). In response to Peter Jesus essentially says, "Peter, it is not the washing of your body that is the issue here. It is the deeper washing of your guilt that I came to deal with. Only I can do that."

Jesus is the model of servant love. After Jesus had bent down before every disciple, including Judas, he resumed his position at the table and took on the role of teacher. He asked the disciples a question and then answered it himself: "Do you understand what I have done for you? You call me 'Teacher' and 'Lord,' and rightly so, for that is what I am. Now that I, your Lord and Teacher, have washed your feet, you also should wash one another's feet. I have set you an example that you should do as I have done for you" (John 13:12-15).

What does this servant-love look like? Mary Rutan tells of meeting one such servant. Her church in Alaska was hosting missionaries who were to live in the homes of the parishioners and rotate among the churches. Just before their house guest was to arrive, the flu arrived first. Her whole family was ill. Before they had time to make other housing arrangements, there was a knock on the door. Mary's husband was the only one well enough to stagger to the door. He explained the situation and suggested that it would be best for the missionary to stay elsewhere. The man's face became serious with concern, but not for himself. He didn't just step through the door, but he strode in with a firm, "Oh, no! You need me here!" To their amazement he put down his luggage, took off his coat, rolled up his sleeves and began to wash the dishes. Mary said she had heard many sermons on servanthood but none so eloquent as those six words, "Oh, no!

You need me here." His eyes were on the lookout for how he could be helpful. A servant doesn't wait to be asked but restlessly looks for unmet needs.

A servant focuses far more on the needs of others than on his or her own. A story illustrates this: "Two brothers shared a field and a mill. Each night they divided evenly the grain they had ground together during the day. One brother lived alone; the other had a wife and large family. Now the single brother thought to himself, 'It isn't really fair that we divide the grain evenly. I have only myself to care for, but my brother has children to feed.' So each night he secretly took some of his grain to his brother's granary to see that he was never without. But the married brother said to himself one day, 'It really isn't fair that we divide the grain evenly, because I have children to provide for me in my old age, but my brother has no one. What will he do when he is old?' So every night he secretly took some of his grain to his brother's granary. As a result, both of them always found their supply of grain mysteriously replenished each morning."[2]

This story illustrates the brothers' willingness to see the other's need, and also that mutual servanthood leads to having our own needs met. I have observed, especially in marriage, how destructive it is to dwell on one's own needs. How easy it is to get into the self-pitying mindset that says, "My needs are not being met. I am putting out more in this relationship than she is." Such thinking is a dead-end street, because we often distort the truth and make ourselves look more heroic than we actually are.

Service requires self-sacrifice. Servanthood is death to self. Being a servant is contrary to our nature, requiring personal crucifixion. Being a servant is the opposite of being full of self. The disciples did not have the servanthood mindset because they were so busy looking out for themselves. They were too busy jockeying for their position in the kingdom. In our society the highest value is looking and feeling good. In Robert Bellah's study of character recorded in *Habits of the Heart,* he says we are allergic to words like *sacrifice* and *self-denial.* "Since the only measure of good is what is good for the self, something that is really a burden to the self cannot be a part of love." He concludes, "It was hard for people to find a way to say why genuine attachment to others might require the risk of hurt, loss, or sacrifice."[3]

In a biblical sense, anything worthy of the name of servanthood will require some sacrifice on the part of the server. It means doing the thankless job: cleaning up after an event, spending the night at a family shelter, having the comfortable routines of life interrupted for needs that don't fit into the preplanned schedule, making lifestyle changes to release more resources for others and fewer for self, not needing to receive attention for good deeds. In other words, servants are not self-absorbed but others-absorbed.

So with the backdrop of the footwashing, Jesus makes the most important point in his speech: "A new command I give you: Love one another. As I have loved you, so you must love one another" (John 13: 34). And then he says this startling thing, "By this all men will know that you are my disciples, if you love one another" (v. 35). It is as if Jesus turns away from the disciples to an imaginary audience made up of the unbelieving world. Jesus is saying to the not-yet followers of Christ, "I give you the right to judge whether these are disciples of mine based on the observable love you see among them." If the unbelieving world says to us, "Why should I believe in your God based on the way I see you treating each other?" we must realize that Jesus has given that right to the world. German philosopher Friedrich Nietzsche challenged the church by saying, "If you want me to believe in your redeemer, you have to look a little more redeemed."

[1]George MacLeod, *Only One Way Left* (Glasgow: Iona, 1956), p. 33.
[2]*Christian Century,* December 16, 1981.
[3]Robert Bellah et al., *Habits of the Heart* (New York: Harper & Row, 1985), p. 109.

Reading Study Guide

1. Why does John reveal what Jesus "knew" as backdrop for washing the disciples' feet?

2. If you were in a position to have Jesus wash your feet, what do you think your reaction would be?

3. How does the footwashing foreshadow the cross?

4. Servant love implies three things. Explain each.

    a. restless eyes

    b. focus on the needs of others, above self

    c. self-sacrifice

5. Where do you need grace to grow in servant love?

6. What questions do you have about this reading?

7. Does the reading convict, challenge or comfort you? Why?

Going Deeper

Schaeffer, Francis. *The Mark of the Christian*. Downers Grove, Ill.: InterVarsity Press, 1970. This is a prophetic word to the church about the need for visible unity in the body of Christ based on forgiveness.

18 / Justice

LOOKING AHEAD

MEMORY VERSES: Isaiah 58:6-7
BIBLE STUDY: Matthew 25:31-46
READING: God Loves the Poor

 **Core Truth**

How is sacrificial love expressed among those broken by the world?

When love intersects broken lives, Christ's disciples are called to stand for justice. Biblical justice means lifting the bonds of oppression, identifying with the cause of the poor and meeting the needs of the downtrodden.

1. Identify key words or phrases in the question and answer above, and state their meaning in your own words.

2. Restate the core truth in your own words.

3. What questions or issues does the core truth raise for you?

Memory Verse Study Guide

1. *Putting it in context:* Isaiah 58:1-12 is the setting for God's call to repent with a fast. According to verses 1-5, how have the people corrupted the practice of fasting?

What are the promised results of a true fast, according to verses 8-12?

2. The memory verses are *Isaiah 58:6-7.* Copy the verses verbatim.

3. What is the evidence of a true fast?

4. What common threads do you observe in the acts of a true fast? (What are we required to do?)

5. What do these verses tell us about the heart of God?

6. How have these verses spoken to you this week?

Inductive Bible Study Guide

There is a healthy tension in Scripture between deeds done for salvation and deeds done as evidence of salvation. It is clear that we cannot earn a righteous standing before a holy and perfect God, yet it is also clear that if we do not show evidence of a changed heart through our deeds of compassion, the reality of our salvation can be questioned. In the following passage Jesus is not saying that we must earn our salvation but rather that we will be judged on the basis of the evidence for it.

1. *Read Matthew 25:31-46.* Who is the Son of Man, and what is the context of his appearance?

2. On what basis will the sheep be welcomed into the kingdom?

3. Think and pray over the people with whom Jesus identifies: the hungry, the thirsty, the stranger, the naked, the sick, the prisoners. Where do you see each of these in your community?

4. What is Jesus' relationship with the downtrodden?

5. On what basis will the goats be excluded from the kingdom?

   What will be their end?

6. Does the message of this passage disturb you? Explain.

7. What questions do you have about this passage?

8. What verse or verses have particularly impacted you? Rewrite key verses in your own words.

👓 Reading: God Loves the Poor

Economics is one of the most frequent topics discussed in Scripture, second only to idolatry in the sheer number of verses. In the New Testament alone five hundred verses, one out of every sixteen, address material matters. And when it comes to the first three Gospels, the ratio increases to one in ten verses that discuss wealth and poverty. If we were to focus on Luke's Gospel alone, which is most concerned about the physical implications of Jesus' kingdom, the ratio is one in seven verses.

The Bible's view of the poor and the use of material resources is at the heart of our discipleship. After all, Jesus said, "Where your treasure is, there your heart will be also" (Matthew 6:21).

WHO ARE THE POOR?

Who are the poor? And why are they poor? There are four categories into which the poor fall in the Bible.

1. Poverty is chosen for righteousness' sake. Some have a spiritual gift of being able to rid themselves of all but the bare necessities. By their own choice they devote themselves solely to Christ and identify with his poor. The apostle Paul in the love chapter speaks of those who "give all [they] possess to the poor" (1 Corinthians 13:3). Those who enter Roman Catholic orders take a vow of poverty, best illustrated by Mother Teresa, who identified with the destitute, diseased and dying.

2. Poverty is a result of calamity. A natural disaster sometimes wipes out all physical possessions and means of livelihood. The obvious biblical example is Job, a man blessed by God with seven thousand sheep, three thousand camels, and a family of seven sons and three daughters. This man was "the greatest man

among all the people of the East" (Job 1:3). Instantaneously all that he had was taken from him.

3. Poverty is the result of sin or laziness. Sinful behavior, such as drunkenness, can cost a job, family and relationships. Others are poor because they lack industry and drive. Paul in his second letter to the Thessalonians castigates "some among you [who] are idle" (2 Thessalonians 3:11). He goes on to say, "'If a man will not work, he shall not eat.' . . . Such people we command and urge in the Lord Jesus Christ to settle down and earn the bread they eat" (vv. 10-12).

4. Poverty is a consequence of oppression by the powerful. Injustice is by far the predominate reason for poverty. Most poor people in the world are poor because they are exploited by economic and political manipulators. The Bible concerns itself overwhelmingly with this group, using the terms *needy, poor, oppressed, widows, orphans* and *sojourners* (or *strangers*). What these people have in common is that they can easily have their rights taken away from them. They are the exploitable, weak and defenseless. They are open to abuse and are the prey of the powerful.

BIBLICAL JUSTICE

In the Bible the needy are often equated with the "innocent" and "righteous." Note the parallel construction in Amos 5:12 that interchanges *righteous* and *poor:* "You *oppress* the *righteous,* . . . and you *deprive* the *poor* of justice in the courts" (emphasis added).

The righteous in a legal dispute are the innocent who should have justice rendered in their favor. There is an important difference between biblical justice and our societal view of justice. The symbol of justice in our society is a blindfolded woman, indicating that justice is blind. The fair judge is dispassionately objective, free from bias, who rationally decides what is right before an impersonal law. On the other hand, the role of the judge and justice in Israel was to actively and redemptively seek to protect the poor from the wiles of the rich and powerful. So strong was the skepticism toward the powerful that the poor in the courts were often viewed collectively as the innocent and righteous. The law in Exodus 23:6-8 reads, "Do not deny justice to your *poor* people in their lawsuits. Have nothing to do with a false charge, and do not put an *innocent* or *honest* person to death, for I will not acquit the guilty. Do not accept a bribe, for a bribe blinds those who see and twists the words of the *righteous*" (emphasis added).

It is the subversion of the justice system that is on the prophet Amos's heart: "You hate the one who reproves in court and despise him who tells the truth" (Amos 5:10). The court was an enclosure just inside the walled city where the elders gathered to render decisions related to the life and property of the citizens according to the law. The rendering of just decisions was the basis for a righteous order under the rule of God. But the wealthy and powerful had taken over the courts, buying justice for themselves.

The picture in Amos is one of marked disparity between rich and poor. "You trample on the poor and force him to give you grain. Therefore, though you have built stone mansions, you will not live in them; though you have planted lush vineyards, you will not drink their wine" (Amos 5:11). Archaeologists have confirmed Amos's picture of shocking extremes of wealth and poverty. In early Jewish settlements of the Promised Land there was an equal distribution among families and tribes. All Israel enjoyed a similar standard of living. This was still true in the tenth century B.C., but two hundred years later, archaeologists have discovered, there were bigger, better-built homes in one area and poor houses crowded together in another. The poor in Amos's day no longer owned their own land but worked as tenant farmers for the landowners, who took as their payment exactions of wheat far beyond what was reasonable.

In Amos we see that poverty is not the result of laziness but because of the unjust distribution of wealth and power into the hands of a few. John Perkins, an African American and native of Mississippi, tells how he came to understand this system of inequality. In the 1940s, when he was eleven, he was away from home visiting relatives. He decided to make some money in order to buy a gift for his family, so he hired himself out to a white farmer as a day laborer. At the end of the twelve-hour day he was handed his pay: fifteen cents. The farmer owned the plow, the land and all the means of production. All John had was his labor. He also knew that the last black man to talk back had been chained to the back of a car and dragged through the streets of the town on Saturday afternoon. He learned what the Bible teaches: exploitation and oppression are the primary reasons for poverty.[1]

GOD'S ATTITUDE TOWARD THE POOR

What is God's attitude toward the poor? Theologian Karl Barth summarized it provocatively: "God in no wise takes up a neutral position between the poor person and the rich person. The rich may take care of their own future; He is on the side of the poor. . . . Thus the Bible is on the side of the poor and the destitute. He who the

Bible calls God is on the side of the poor."[2]

God's compassion is evidenced in his hearing the cries of the poor and delivering them from oppression. The nation of Israel was formed from a slave people. For four hundred years the Hebrew people labored under the whip of the economic tyranny of the Egyptian overlords. They cried out to God as their backs broke under the burdens they bore. Scripture records God's heart for his people, "The LORD said, 'I have indeed seen the misery of my people in Egypt. I have heard them crying out because of their slave drivers, and I am concerned about their suffering. So I have come down to rescue them" (Exodus 3:7-8). God chooses a people who know the chains of oppression. After the exodus God instructed this new nation never to turn their backs on the destitute, weak and widows, for this was their origin. "Do not mistreat an alien or oppress him, for you were aliens in Egypt" (Exodus 22:21). And if Israel treats the defenseless as Egypt treated the Hebrews, God will hear their cries, for his ear is especially tuned to the downtrodden. "For I am compassionate," says the Lord God (Exodus 22:27).

God shows that he is partial to the poor when he executes justice to redeem the downtrodden and to crush the oppressor. When Scripture applies the justice of God to the poor and needy, we see God showing mercy to the downtrodden and bringing down the powerful.

Endow the king with your justice,
    O God,
    the royal son with your
        righteousness.
He will judge your people in
    righteousness,
    your afflicted ones with justice. . . .
He will defend the afflicted among
    the people

and save the children of the needy;
    he will crush the oppressor.
(Psalm 72:1-2, 4)

God is the defense attorney for the poor. God will be the spokesperson for the poor if there's no one else. He will plead their cause and trumpet justice on their behalf. If nobody hears the cries of the poor, God will stand with them. God raised up prophetic voices like Amos, Isaiah and Micah to make clear that he was not a detached observer.

If justice for the poor means mercy and redemption, then justice for the powerful means judgment and being brought low. During the brief period of Amos's prophesy in 760 B.C. there were three sins the prophet railed against, the poor were being economically exploited; the wealthy hoarded for themselves without concern for the plight of others; and the court system had become a tool of the powerful rather than a protector of the weak. Yet the people of Israel continued their practices of worship and offering sacrifices for sins in the temple. Amos states in the strongest terms that God will not abide with worship that does not issue in justice: "I hate, I despise your religious feasts; I cannot stand your assemblies" (Amos 5:21). Worship that does not lead to righteousness, defined here as concern for the poor, is a stench in the nostrils of God. Enough of this outward show. "But let justice roll on like a river, righteousness like a never-failing stream" (Amos 5:24). Treat the poor with equity, have compassion on the lowly, feed the hungry, clothe the naked, and then I will receive your worship, says the Lord.

How does God respond to the needy? His heart accompanies them in compassion, for he hears their agony. As a defense attorney he takes up their cause and executes justice by redeeming the needy and judging the powerful.

OUR RESPONSE TO THE POOR

After peering into the heart of God and seeing what is important to him, what are we individually and collectively to do in regard to the poor?

Our first act must be to repent of our disdain and disgust toward the poor. We must acknowledge our self-righteousness that views all poor as welfare cheats and lazy indigents. We must confess that our prejudice toward different classes of the poor, such as illegal immigrants, is a selfish disguise for not wanting to have our standard of living disrupted. We must remember that the poor are poor because of systematic racial prejudice, repressive political regimes and economic exploitation. Most of us have what we have by privilege of birth alone.

Secondly, we are called to identify with and stand for the poor, because the One we claim to follow as Lord did so. Jesus was born in a small, insignificant province of the Roman Empire. The first visitors at his birth were poor shepherds, the rogues of society. His parents, too poor to bring the normal offering for purification, offered two pigeons in sacrifice instead of a lamb. Jesus was a refugee from political oppression; his family fled to Egypt and then migrated back to Galilee. As a rabbi he received no fees for his teaching and had no regular means of income. Having no home of his own, he said, "Foxes have holes and birds of the air have nests, but the Son of Man has no place to lay his head" (Matthew 8:20). So complete was his identification with those on the fringes of life that he said to his followers, "Whatever you did for one of the least of these brothers of mine, you did for me" (Matthew 25:40).

Third, our response to God's heart for the poor will cause us to examine how we can lead a compassionate lifestyle. What does a compassionate lifestyle look like? A young woman in her fourth year of medical school completes her work so that she can live among and serve the poor. Others simplify their lifestyle, reduce their overhead and live on less in order to release resources. A very practical step toward implementing a compassionate lifestyle and putting a governor on our greed is to obey God by tithing at least 10 percent of our income to the Lord's work. What resources could be unleashed for world mission and for those who live on the edge of survival!

Our fourth response to God's heart for the poor is to preach the gospel to them. Jesus inaugurated his ministry with a quote from the prophet Isaiah, "The Spirit of the Lord is on me, . . . to preach the good news to the poor" (Luke 4:18). Throughout history it often is among the poor that the gospel has found receptivity. Historians credit the Great Awakening with heading off a growing spirit of rebellion among the poor. John Wesley was a key figure in taking the gospel from the established church to the streets. He was initially resistant to going beyond the "orthodox" ways of getting out the good news. He recorded in his journal, "In the evening I reached Bristol, and met Mr. Whitefield there. I could scarce reconcile myself at first to this strange way of preaching in the fields, of which he set me an example on Sunday; having been all my life (until very lately) so tenacious of every point relating to decency and order, that I should have thought the saving of souls almost a sin if it had not been done in the church."[3]

As we look at the world today, where is the gospel finding receptivity and spreading like wildfire? Traditional Western Christendom is in shambles. In North America faith has been privatized and marginalized. Europe is spiritually dead. The West, comfortable in its affluence, is spiritually powerless. But in Latin America, Africa and Asia the gospel is spreading at twice the rate of the population growth. Soon 60 percent of all Christians will reside in these three areas. "Has not God chosen those who are poor in the eyes of the world to be rich in faith?" (James 2:5).

At the heart of our discipleship is a call to minister to the poor. We are to be where our Lord's heart is. We must repent of our disdain for the poor, identify with and stand for the poor, commit ourselves to a compassionate lifestyle, and use our financial and human resources to aid the spread of the gospel among the poor. A number of years ago Mark Hatfield, a disciple of Jesus Christ and a retired senator from Oregon, spoke these words at a presidential prayer breakfast: "We sit here today as the wealthy and powerful, but let us not forget that those who follow Christ will more often find themselves not with the comfortable majorities but with the miserable minorities."

[1]John Perkins, *Let Justice Roll Down* (Ventura, Calif.: Regal, 1976), pp. 47-48.
[2]Karl Barth, "The Call to Discipleship," in *Church Dogmatics* (Edinburgh: T & T Clark, 1969), 4:543-55.
[3]Garth Lean, *Strangely Warmed: The Amazing Life of John Wesley* (Wheaton, Ill.: Tyndale House, 1964), p. 47.

Reading Study Guide

1. Why do you think so much of the Bible focuses on economic issues?

2. What are the four reasons for poverty?

What is the predominant emphasis in the Bible? Does this surprise you? Explain.

3. What view of justice is behind the equation of the poor with the innocent and righteous?

4. What is God's attitude toward the poor?

How does the Lord show it?

5. Consider the four suggestions given for responding to the poor. How are you moved to respond?

6. What questions do you have about the reading?

7. Does the reading convict, challenge or comfort you? Why?

Going Deeper

Perkins, John. *Let Justice Roll Down.* Ventura, Calif.: Regal, 2006.
Sider, Ronald J. *Rich Christians in an Age of Hunger.* Dallas: Word, 1997.

19 / Witness

LOOKING AHEAD

MEMORY VERSE: Acts 1:8
BIBLE STUDY: Acts 4:1-30
READING: Sharing Our Faith with Our Friends

 ## Core Truth

How does the world come to know the love and justice of Jesus Christ?

Jesus Christ has entrusted to his followers the message of the gospel, which contains the power of God unto salvation. The authority to share the good news comes through the Holy Spirit, who makes us witnesses. A witness is one who declares on the basis of personal experience what he or she knows to be true about Christ.

1. Identify key words or phrases in the question and answer above, and state their meaning in your own words.

2. Restate the core truth in your own words.

3. What questions or issues does the core truth raise for you?

Memory Verse Study Guide

1. *Putting it in context:* Examine Acts 1:1-14. How does Jesus redirect the focus of the disciples to their task ahead?

2. The memory verse is *Acts 1:8.* Copy the verse verbatim.

3. What do you suppose is the nature of the power we receive when the Holy Spirit comes on us?

4. Being a witness appears to be the inevitable consequence of receiving the power of the Holy Spirit. What does this teach us about how we are motivated for this call?

5. Put in your own words what it means to be a witness.

6. What is the extent of Jesus' vision for our witness?

7. How has this verse spoken to you this week?

🖊 Inductive Bible Study

The story of Jesus' encounter with the woman at the well serves as a model for how we are to share our faith. Notice how Jesus piques the woman's interest on the way to the ultimate goal of revealing his identity.

1. *Read John 4:1-30.* What words or phrases are used to describe the person of Christ throughout the passage?

2. What barriers were between Jesus and the woman?

   How did Jesus overcome them?

3. In the conversation with the woman, Jesus mentions living water. What is it (vv. 7-15)?

   What is Jesus revealing about himself?

4. In the discussion on the proper place of worship, Jesus says, "True worshipers will worship the Father in spirit and in truth." Why does Jesus interject this truth in the discussion (vv. 20-24)?

5. Why did Jesus have this conversation with the woman?

6. How did Jesus reveal his identity to the woman?

7. What can we learn about witnessing from observing Jesus in this passage?

8. What questions does this passage raise for you?

9. What verse or verses have particularly impacted you? Rewrite key verses in your own words.

Reading: Sharing Our Faith with Our Friends

Is there anything that produces more anxiety than the pressure we experience in our call to be witnesses? Rebecca Pippert conveys our experience when she describes her anxieties about witnessing in her book *Out of the Saltshaker and into the World*. She was laboring at that time under a view of witnessing that could be summarized as "offending people for Jesus' sake." She had gotten the impression that witnessing was where she trapped an unsuspecting victim who was forced to listen to her speech about Jesus. With this image of witnessing she writes, "The result was that I would put off witnessing as long as possible. Whenever the guilt became too great to bear, I overpowered the nearest non-Christian with a nonstop running monolog and then dashed away thinking, 'Whew! Well, I did it. It's spring . . . and hopefully the guilt won't overcome me again till winter.'" The next potential victim was hoping the same.[1]

To be effective witnesses we need anxiety reduction. How can we lower the anxiety level so that we can allow a natural joy to flow from our lives with the belief that we have the best news to offer? There is nothing like anxiety to block authenticity. In order for our witness to be compelling it must be experienced as congruent with who we are. The last thing people want is to be our project, someone we are working on.

The most effective witness occurs in the context of authentic, caring relationships. Relationships built over time with trust have earned us the right to share the difference that Jesus Christ makes in our lives. We don't want witnessing pressure to build in us to such an extent that we regurgitate the gospel over some hapless victim merely to relieve the pressure for the time being.

Contained in John 1:35-42 are six anxiety-reducing principles that free us to witness in the context of authentic friendship.

REDUCE SELF-CONSCIOUSNESS AND INCREASE GOD-CONSCIOUSNESS

Our anxiety is heightened when we are so self-conscious that we are afraid what we might say will reflect badly on us. If we are too concerned with what people will think of us, then we will be tied up in knots. We need to lose ourselves in the joy of Jesus.

What we want is to become like John the Baptist, who was not concerned about his own reputation but about the reputation of Jesus. What is impressive about John the Baptist is his willingness to let his disciples follow Jesus. "The next day John was there again with two of his disciples. When he saw Jesus passing by, he said, 'Look, the Lamb of God!' When the two disciples heard him say this, they followed Jesus" (John 1:35-37).

One of the hardest things to do is to take second place, especially if you are in first place. John had acquired his group of followers. Now there was one on the scene who eclipsed him, and John willingly pointed his followers to Jesus.

John's lack of pride is remarkable. Pride is competitive at its root. It is an unnatural act of the sinful heart to exalt someone else's glory and diminish our own. So much of our worth is derived from comparing how we are doing to how others are doing. When pastors get together the undercurrent is comparing how their churches are doing, especially whether they are growing. We are naturally inclined to want recognition. I am ashamed to say how much I feed off people's comments about my effect on their lives. And as much as I like to take pleasure in shining the spotlight on others, I still twinge with the desire for recognition, especially when I am feeling overlooked or underappreciated.

How liberating it would be to be free of self-consciousness, as John the Baptist was. Humility is an anxiety reducer. "People with humility don't think less of themselves, they just think of themselves less." Jim Elliot defined witnessing as "a bunch of nobodies trying to exalt Somebody." Thomas Merton caps this decrease in self-absorption when he writes, "When humility delivers a person from attachment to their own works and reputation, they discover true joy is only possible when we have completely forgotten ourselves."[2]

OUR WITNESS IS ONLY ONE OF MANY INFLUENCES

The two disciples who responded to John's designation of Jesus as Lamb of God were fully prepared to follow him. We meet them at the very end of a long process of preparation that got them to this point of openness. What we don't see are the many people and influences that the Spirit used to get them there. I have been privileged to pray with people to receive Jesus in their lives, knowing that I did nothing to get them to that point. I have often visualized myself with a basket in my hand, standing under a tree of ripened fruit, waiting for it to fall into my basket. Later they tell me the story of the friends, family and life situations that brought them to this point over a long period of time.

Think of conversion as a journey from one to one hundred. We may intersect someone's life at the beginning, middle or end of that journey, but we most likely will be only five of the one hundred points along the scale. We may be the one who destroys someone's negative stereotypes of what it means to be a Christian. A member of my congregation told me that his son paid me the highest complement. "What was it?" I asked. He said, "You don't act like a pastor." Given this young man's negative association with pastors, I had given him hope that things could be different. Every life is in process, and we intersect somewhere along the way.

Anxiety comes by putting pressure on ourselves to be the one who takes a person from one to one hundred. We think that we must plant the seed, water it, nurture it to maturity and bring in the harvest. Even Paul didn't put that kind of pressure on himself. Paul wrote to the Corinthians, "I planted the seed, Apollos watered it, but God made it grow. So neither he who plants nor he who waters is anything, but only God, who makes things grow" (1 Corinthians 3:6-7). May our prayer be simply that God would use us to help every person we know to take that next step in their journey toward the decision to follow Jesus.

LISTEN BY ASKING PROBING QUESTIONS

"Turning around, Jesus saw [the two disciples] following and asked, 'What do you want?'" (John 1:38). To our ears that question sounds more rude and abrupt than is meant. The NRSV better captures the tone and intent of Jesus: "What are you looking for?"

Jesus was the master at guiding the discoveries of the heart with great questions. Telling people something they are not ready to hear only raises their defenses. Compassionately asked questions are like the Trojan horse that gets through the gate. Good questions are used by the Holy Spirit to crack open a heart that can lead to a full-fledged quest.

I am convinced that if our witness consisted of becoming caring listeners who attend to the needs of those around us, there would be no end of the opportunities to share Christ. On the surface people may not evidence much spiritual hunger, but I believe that hunger lurks just below the surface. In our secular age we don't usually pepper polite conversation with questions such as "What is the meaning of life? What is your purpose for breathing the air on this planet? What kind of God do you believe in?" But if we listen to people's self-doubts—about their jobs, the challenges of raising kids—we will get below the surface to spiritual matters. Our message of hope will be pertinent to the needs people are expressing.

A poem, "Cold Water, Hot Coffee," expresses the challenge to listen.

> Sometimes that cup of cold water,
> turns out to be a cup of hot coffee,
> and what we're asked to do is
> to pour it . . . and to listen.
> Sometimes we Christians
> in our enthusiasm
> think we were asked
> to save the world,
> when what we were asked to do
> is to go into it
> and tell God's story
> to people in need of
> some good news.
> Anxious activists forget
> that just listening is an act
> of compassion.
> Driven disciples forget
> that just listening is an act
> of faithfulness.
> Guilty givers forget
> that just listening is an act
> of stewardship.
> Since we church people

> have a tendency to be
> driven and anxious and guilt-ridden
> perhaps we should
> read the directions again
> and pour a cup of hot coffee
> and listen
> in His name.
> (Anonymous)

ASK PEOPLE TO INVESTIGATE JESUS

In response to Jesus' question, the two disciples responded with a question that conveyed what they were looking for. "They said, 'Rabbi' (which means Teacher), 'where are you staying?' 'Come,' he replied, 'and you will see.' So they went and saw where he was staying, and spent that day with him. It was about the tenth hour" (John 1:38-39). The disciples didn't want a casual and brief conversation with Jesus in the streets, but they wanted to spend some substantial time with Jesus, checking out his authenticity.

Eventually any genuine spiritual quest must center on an investigation of Jesus. What I love about the Gospel of John is that every passage we study in this book leads us to ask the question, "Who does this Jesus think he is, anyway?"

Jesus is the destination. The journey and search end with Jesus, but in many people's minds Jesus is just another way station in life's journey. There is no destination, no place to arrive. All truth is personal or individual. Feelings tell us the truth that is personally designed to work for us. A campus Christian worker made one of the great spiritual observations of our day when he said, "It is all right today to search for truth, as long as you don't find it." It is the quest that counts. Be on the journey, but don't arrive. Yet as we understand Jesus' truth claim, he is not just another point along the way. He is the One where the quest stops.

At some point we must ask people to examine Jesus. Ask people to read John or Mark and ask, "What are your impressions of this person? What do you say about him?" Ultimately that is the key question.

SHARE OUT OF JOY

Witness at its best is contagious joy. Andrew, the brother of Peter, embodies sharing his faith with his friends. For Andrew being a witness was natural. "Andrew, Simon Peter's brother, was one of the two who heard what John had said and who had followed Jesus. The first thing Andrew did was to find his brother Simon and tell him, 'We have found the Messiah' (that is, the Christ)" (John 1:40-41). Andrew couldn't contain the joy of his discovery. He had to tell his brother what he had found.

I pray that I would be like the Christians who influenced the lives of Sheldon and Davy Vanauken. Sheldon describes one of the early points in his process of coming to faith in Christ. It was the quality of Christians he and his wife, Davy, met at Oxford University that caused them to consider following Christ. A group of five Christians became their closest friends. "These were our first friends, close friends. More to the point, perhaps, all five were keen, deeply committed Christians. But we liked them so much that we forgave them for it. We began, hardly knowing we were doing it, to revise our opinions, not of Christianity but of Christians. Our fundamental assumption had been that all Christians were necessarily stuffy, hide-bound, or stupid—people to keep one's distance from. Then the astonishing fact sank home: our contemporaries could be at once highly intelligent, civilized, witty, fun to be with—and Christian."[3] There is

nothing like contagious joy to share our faith with our friends.

THEIR BEST SELVES AWAIT THEM

To know that Christ turns us into what we were designed by God to fully be is to offer the best gift to someone. Peter discovered his potential in his first encounter with Christ. "And he [Andrew] brought him [Peter] to Jesus. Jesus looked at him and said, 'You are Simon son of John. You will be called Cephas' (which, when translated, is Peter)" (John 1:42). *Cephas* means "rock." Jesus certainly didn't get that name for Peter by looking at who he was at that moment. *Rock* is about the last word you would use to describe Peter's personality and temperament; instead words like *impulsive, volatile* and *unreliable* come to mind. But John says that Jesus "looked at him," meaning he saw beyond the surface into Peter's heart. Jesus saw Peter for what he would become, not for what he was at the moment. Our best self awaits us in Jesus.

Am I a better person on the way to becoming my best because of Jesus? You had better believe it. I've got a long way to go, but you don't know how far I've come. Has Christ made a difference in my life? Without a doubt. He took a guy full of fear and transformed him into one with risk-taking confidence; he freed me as a father to give affection, though I had a father who did not know how to do that; he filled me with a passion to see his people mobilized for ministry. Would my life be different without Christ? I shudder to think of what I would be like. So when I offer Jesus to someone, I am giving them the opportunity to discover their best self, which awaits them in Christ.

Are you stopped in your tracks with anxiety when it comes to being a witness for Jesus? My prayer is that you have discovered in this passage one or more truths that allows you to transform witness from an anxiety-ridden, guilty ineptitude to a joyful privilege. Perhaps then the anxiety will recede and in a relaxed, caring way Jesus will authentically make himself known through you.

---

[1]Rebecca Manley Pippert, *Out of the Saltshaker & into the World* (Downers Grove, Ill.: InterVarsity Press, 1979), p. 16.
[2]Thomas Merton, quoted in Tim Hansel, *Through the Wilderness of Loneliness* (Elgin, Ill.: Cook, 1991), p. 123.
[3]Sheldon Vanauken, *A Severe Mercy* (New York: Harper & Row, 1977), p. 77.

Reading Study Guide

1. Are you anxious when it comes to being a witness for Christ? If yes, describe the nature of that anxiety. If no, why do you think that is not your experience?

2. Put in your own words each of the six anxiety-reducing principles.

3. Which of the anxiety-reducing principles spoke most pointedly to your needs and why?

4. Pray for a burden of love for people in your sphere of influence. Who are the people the Lord would have you touch?

5. What questions do you have about this reading?

6. Does the reading convict, challenge or comfort you? Why?

Going Deeper

Take some time to write the story of your own witness. To develop your testimony, answer the following questions.

- What was your life like prior to coming to Christ?

- How did you come to commit your life to Christ?

- How is your life different now that Christ is in it?

Recommended Reading

Pippert, Rebecca Manley. *Out of the Saltshaker & into the World.* Downers Grove, Ill.: InterVarsity Press, 1999.
Watson, David. "Evangelism." Chap. 9 in *Called & Committed: World-Changing Discipleship.* Wheaton, Ill.: Harold Shaw, 2000.

Part Four

SERVING CHRIST

The previous section, "Becoming like Christ," focused on the qualities and responsibilities of individual disciples. This section, "Serving Christ," stresses that an individual cannot and should not be separated or even attempt to live out discipleship apart from the body of Christ. The Holy Spirit is the Spirit of the individual and the life source of the church. God is not only about re-creating individuals in his image but also about forming a new corporate humanity.

The nature of *the church* and its ministry is the subject of chapters twenty and twenty-one. Paul's image of the church as the body of Christ emphasizes the organic and living reality of the church as a people indwelt by Christ. Just as each part of the human body contributes to the health of the whole, so each member of the church through the exercise of unique *ministry gifts* builds up the body of Christ. This chapter explores the process of understanding what spiritual gifts are and how to discover what gifts you have been assigned by God.

Martin Luther summarized our enemies as being the world, the flesh and the devil. We will examine the last two in reverse order. Chapter twenty-two on *spiritual warfare* looks at the reality of our enemy, the devil, and his various schemes to exploit our weaknesses. Chapter twenty-three pinpoints the habits that have become a part of our ways of acting, thinking and feeling that are not God-honoring and shows us what *walking in obedience* is all about. God requires our obedience because he desires our happiness.

At chapter twenty-four, *sharing the wealth,* the pilgrimage with your discipling partner(s) comes to a conclusion, while a new journey is just beginning. Take some time to reflect on what this time together has meant. Think back to where you were spiritually when you started this covenant. What have been some significant landmarks along the way? Were there big insights, turning points, tender moments, deepened convictions, new life directions that came as a result of this time? Share and celebrate these together. Then pray for each other and for those who will be your relational partners on the next leg.

It is my sincere prayer that through this process you have caught a vision and have the deep and abiding conviction that discipling is a lifestyle issue. Wherever you are may you seek out those you can invite into relationship with yourself for the purpose of growing toward maturity in Christ.

20 / The Church

LOOKING AHEAD

MEMORY VERSES: 1 Corinthians 12:12-13
BIBLE STUDY: 1 Corinthians 12:12-27
READING: A Living Organism

 Core Truth

How does Jesus continue to make himself known?

Jesus continues to live out his life on earth through his corporate body, the church. The "body of Christ" is not just a figure of speech but conveys the reality that Christ lives through his people. Together God's people extend the life of Jesus to the world.

1. Identify key words or phrases in the question and answer above, and state their meaning in your own words.

2. Restate the core truth in your own words.

3. What questions or issues does the core truth raise for you?

Memory Verse Study Guide

1. *Putting it in context:* Examine 1 Corinthians 12:1-11. What is the subject matter that serves as the backdrop to the church as the body of Christ, and why is this an appropriate introduction?

2. The memory verses are *1 Corinthians 12:12-13.* Copy these verses verbatim.

3. Paul surprisingly concludes verse 12 with the phrase "so it is with Christ." What does this tell us about the relationship between Christ and his body, the church?

4. What are the two key points that Paul is making about the nature of a body in verse 12?

5. What is the means of entrance to the body of Christ?

6. What is Paul implying with the phrase "whether Jews or Greeks, slave or free"?

7. How have these verses spoken to you this week?

Inductive Bible Study Guide

Here Paul plays with the image of the church as the body of Christ. He describes body parts having a conversation with each other.

1. *Read 1 Corinthians 12:12-27.* How is the human body an appropriate comparison to the church?

2. In what terms is the body's diversity described?

3. What two harmful attitudes undermine the body's proper functioning (see 1 Corinthians 12:15, 16, 21)?

   How do you see these in yourself?

   in the church?

4. Paul seems to be saying that celebrating our diversity in Christ leads to unity. Why might this be?

5. Whom do you suppose Paul had in mind when referring to the "weaker" and "less honorable" in verses 22-26?

   To what rhythm of relationship is Paul calling us?

6. What is the balance that we need to strike, according to verse 27?

7. What questions do you have about this passage?

8. What verse or verses have particularly impacted you? Rewrite key verses in your own words.

Reading: A Living Organism

The body of Christ is the fundamental biblical image for the church. In all, ninety-six word pictures have been identified in the New Testament that convey various aspects and angles of the place of the church in God's plan, but the one that dominates the New Testament and truly defines who we are is the image of the body of Christ. By this we understand the church to be a living organism.

WHAT IS CHRIST'S RELATIONSHIP TO THE CHURCH?

The apostle Paul ingeniously selected the image of the human body to convey the organic manner in which the church is to function. We can look at the human body from two standpoints. First, we see the body as a functional whole with all its part under the central coordination of the head. But on closer examination we notice that the whole is made up of diverse parts, each with a distinctive, unique function. The hands are for grasping, the eyes for seeing, the feet for walking and so on. The body is the prototype of unity in diversity.

Paul uses the human body analogy to convey Christ's relationship to the church in an arresting and even shocking fashion. Note the startling conclusion to 1 Corinthians 12:12: "The body is a unit, though it is made up of many parts; and though all its parts are many, they form one body. So it is with Christ." Is this the way we expect the verse to conclude? We expect Paul to write: "So it is with the church." In fact we tend to read right over Paul's actual words and supply the previous phrase. Paul must mean that the church is like a human body made up of diverse parts and coordinated under its head. But Paul is saying far more than that. For Paul "the body

of Christ" is not just a metaphor or a helpful word picture, but it also points to the reality that Jesus dwells among his people and gives his life to them.

In other words the church is not a human organization that has contracted by common consent to keep alive the memory of a great historical figure. On the contrary, the church is a divine organism mystically fused to the living and reigning Christ, who continues to reveal himself in his people. Ray Stedman put it this way, "The life of Jesus is still being manifest among people, but now no longer through an individual physical body, limited to one place on earth, but through a complex, corporate body called the church."[1]

Paul understood the church as a organism from the moment of his initial encounter with Christ. Saul, the firebrand and self-righteous protector of the Hebrew law, was on his way to Damascus, having received authority to arrest and bring Christians to Jerusalem, but his plans were dramatically altered. A blinding light filled the sky and engulfed his field of vision. Thrown to the ground, he heard a voice, "Saul, Saul, why do you persecute me?" Saul replied, "Who are you, Lord?" The heavenly voice responded, "I am Jesus, whom you are persecuting" (Acts 9:4-6). But wait! Saul was not persecuting Jesus but those who claimed to be his followers.

What does this incident tell us about the relationship between Jesus and his followers? Jesus indwells them. If you touch a Christian, you have touched Christ. Christians are a sacramental people. A sacrament is a means of grace, a symbol that mysteriously bears the presence of Christ and through which believers encounter Christ.

Thomas Oden summarizes Christ's relationship to the church.

> Christianity is distinctive as a religious faith in that it understands itself to be living as a continuing community through the living Christ. . . . Its uniqueness lies in its particular relationship with its founder. . . . It is the resurrected presence of the living Lord that continues to be the sole basis of the present reality of the church. Jesus is not merely the one who founded the community and left it, but rather the one who is present to the community now and in each historical period as the vital essence of the church.[2]

WHAT IS THE CHURCH'S RELATIONSHIP TO CHRIST?

The church is absolutely dependent on its head, Jesus Christ. Max Thurian captures both Christ's relationship to the church and our relationship to Christ: "Jesus does nothing independently of the church nor can the church do anything independently of Christ."[3] The nature of the church's relationship to Christ is implicit in the phrase that Jesus is "head over everything for the church" (Ephesians 1:22).

The word *head* has two meanings in the Bible: "life source" and "ultimate authority." In our society *head* usually connotes authority, the one in charge, but in the original Greek *head* could equally mean "source" or "origin." The source of a river is called the headwaters. When you think of head as the life source, then Paul's use of head in Ephesians 4:15 and 16 makes sense. "Instead, speaking the truth in love, we will in all things grow up into him who is the Head, that is, Christ. From him the whole body, joined and held together by every supporting ligament, grows and builds itself up in love, as each part does its work."

Whoever heard of a body growing into its head? Paul has exhorted the Ephesians to "become mature," to attain "the whole measure of the fullness of Christ" and to "no longer be infants." Paul reminded the Ephesians that the only way to become spiritual adults is to recognize their absolute reliance on Jesus to supply their life and that his likeness is the goal toward which they are growing. So Jesus is the head into whom and from whom we grow.

Second, for Jesus to be head means that the church is under his direct authority. The church's relationship to Christ means accepting obediently and fulfilling faithfully the particular role that God has assigned to each of us through the Holy Spirit. The most basic confession of the church is "Jesus is Lord" (1 Corinthians 12:3), but this is far more than reciting a creed. Paul intends this truth to be a functional, operational reality.

Jesus as head of the church means that he arranges life in the body. Each member is directly connected to the head and therefore is able to receive signals from the head. Paul Stevens says this well,

> There is a direct and living connection between the Head and every member of the body. . . . No church leader in the New Testament is ever called the head of a local body. That title is reserved for Jesus. The head does not tell the hand to tell the foot what to do. The head is directly connected to the foot. Therefore people find their ministries not by being directed by the leaders but by being motivated and equipped . . . by the Head himself.[4]

The church functions as an organism when those who make up the body of Christ obediently seek to fulfill the role God has assigned to them. We return to the analogy of the human body to understand how the church can function as a living organism. The human body functions beautifully when each part operates according to its design. The central command post, the head, sends forth the signals through the nervous system, which activates the body parts. These body parts have no will of their own. The hands and feet, for example, function only in response to the head. If the hand could act independently of the head, there would be chaos in the body. When people in the body takes responsibility before the Head to know and exercise their assigned functions, the church becomes a living organism.

WHAT IS OUR RELATIONSHIP TO EACH OTHER?

We need each other. According to Paul's body image, all the parts are interdependent and necessary for the health of the whole. Robert Banks says, "God has so designed things that the involvement of every person with his special contribution is necessary for the proper functioning of the community."[5] The underlying message of 1 Corinthians 12 is that everyone is valuable. God in his wisdom designed us not as well-rounded, multitalented, thoroughly complete and independent people. He made it so that we need each other and that each of us brings something of value. We are not self-sufficient. As one person put it, "We don't have it all together, but together we have it all."

When we forget this, the body ceases to function according to its design. Paul identifies two devaluing attitudes that undercut the proper functioning of the body.

First, Paul mentions the attitude of *inferiority,* or low self-esteem, as detrimental to a healthy body. To capture this Paul personifies

the body parts and puts them in conversation with each other. The extremities speak first: "If the foot should say, 'Because I am not a hand, I do not belong to the body,' it would not make it any less a part of the body." Then the senses compete with each other: "If the ear should say, 'Because I am not an eye, I do not belong to the body,' that would not make it any less a part of the body" (1 Cor 12:15-16 NRSV).

The Corinthians suffered from the same malady we do today. They exalted some gifts higher than others. They placed gradations of value on gifts. The church today is sick in part because we have so exalted preaching that no other gift can match that level of importance. Hear this statement from Martin Luther as the legacy of the importance of the preacher in the body of Christ: "A Christian preacher is a minister of God who is set apart, yea, he is an angel of God, a very bishop sent by God, a savior of many people, a king and a prince in the Kingdom of Christ and among the people of God, a teacher, a light of the world. There is nothing more precious or nobler on earth and in this life than a true, faithful parson or preacher."[6]

As soon as a hierarchy of gifts in the body is set up, two things happen:

We compare our gifts to others and declare ourselves deficient. We play the "if only" game: if only I could be like so-and-so, then I would have significance and value. When we secretly envy the gifts of others, we denigrate ourselves and the unique design God has placed in us. Instead the Lord would have us believe what Gordon Cosby writes:

> Christ makes each of us something unlike any other creation fashioned by God—something wonderful, exciting, unique; something specifically needed in the total body of Christ. This uniqueness, this very self that is so hard to de-

scribe, this charismatic person is the gift of the Holy Spirit. It is the primary gift we bring to the body, and without it the body is immeasurably impoverished. [7]

We copy those we admire. Instead of being ourselves we mimic others and cease to be the unique creation we were made to be. This is illustrated through a story from Native American lore. An Indian brave found an egg that had been laid by an eagle. Unable to return the egg to the eagle's nest, he put the egg in the nest of a prairie chicken. In due time the little eaglet was hatched alongside the prairie chickens. This little eagle, thinking it was a prairie chicken, did what prairie chickens do: scratched the dirt for seeds and insects to eat, clucked and cackled, flew only a few feet off of the ground.

One day the eagle saw a magnificent bird flying overhead, floating with graceful majesty on the powerful currents. "What a beautiful bird," he said to his fellow prairie chickens. "What is it?" "That's an eagle," they replied, "the chief of the birds. But don't give it a second thought. You could never be like him." Not knowing he was an eagle, he imitated the prairie chickens and never soared to the heights he could have.

Copying is a sin against ourselves and against God. It was the Lord who designed us just the way we are so that we are needed in the body of Christ. "All these [gifts] are the work of one and the same Spirit, and he gives them to each one, just as he determines" (1 Corinthians 12:11). To copy someone else is to be a pale imitation of yourself and to miss seeing the unique way God has designed you. You are needed as you are.

The second disruptive attitude is *devaluing other members of the body by superiority.* In verse 21 Paul sees the upper parts of the body looking down on the lower: eye over hand, head over feet. "The eye cannot say to the hand, 'I don't need you!' And the head cannot say to the feet, 'I don't need you!'" (1 Corinthians 12:21).

Independence and self-reliance are enemies of community. Without vulnerability and an awareness of need there is no basis for community. Unfortunately it is often in the church that we find the façade of having it all together. Keith Miller writes of the average church, "Our churches are filled with people who outwardly look contented and at peace but inwardly are crying out for someone to love them . . . just as they are—confused, frustrated, often frightened, guilty, and often unable to communicate even within their own families. But the other people in the church look so happy and contented that one seldom has the courage to admit his own deep needs before such a self-sufficient group as the average church meeting appears to be."[8] Vulnerability is a gift to the community that says, "I need you. I welcome you into my life. I want you to be a part of me."

Paul is telling us to value the gifts of one another. The actress Celeste Holm spoke for us all when she said, "We live by encouragement and we die without it; slowly, sadly, angrily." Yet we so often devalue others in the body because they don't think as we do or have the personal tastes we do. Practice this personal exercise: Picture those in the body toward whom your attitude is "I have no need of you." As an act of repentance place these people before God and say, *I need you. I benefit because of you. You have gifts and a perspective that I don't have.*

Instead of inferiority or superiority, we need an attitude of interreliance. Interreliance means you are incomplete without me and I am incomplete without you. You need me and I need you. "We don't have it all together, but together we have it all." Or to use Paul's summary, "Now you are the body of Christ, and each one of you is a part of it" (1 Corinthians 12:27).

---

[1]Ray Stedman, *Body Life* (Glendale, Calif.: Regal, 1972), p. 37.
[2]Thomas Oden, *Agenda for Theology* (San Francisco: Harper & Row, 1979), pp. 117-18.
[3]Max Thurian, quoted in Arnold Bittlinger, *Gifts & Graces: A Commentary on 1 Corinthians 12—14* (Grand Rapids: Eerdmans, 1967).
[4]R. Paul Stevens, *Liberating the Laity* (Downers Grove, Ill.: InterVarsity Press, 1985), p. 36.
[5]Robert Banks, *Paul's Idea of Community* (Peabody, Mass.: Hendrickson, 1994), p. 64.
[6]Martin Luther, quoted in *The Ministry in Historical Perspectives,* ed. H. Richard Niebuhr and Daniel D. Williams (San Francisco: Harper & Row, 1983), p. 115.
[7]Gordon Cosby, *Handbook for Mission Groups* (Waco, Tex.: Word, 1975), p. 72.
[8]Keith Miller, *The Taste of New Wine* (Waco, Tex.: Word, 1965), p. 22.

Reading Study Guide

1. According to 1 Corinthians 12:12, what is the surprising reality conveyed in the phrase "so it is with Christ"?

   What is Christ's relationship with the church?

2. The church's relationship to Christ is captured by the image of "life source" and "authority." Put in your own words what you understand the relationship to be.

   life source

   authority

3. How does the confession "Jesus is Lord" become an operational reality in the church?

4. Do a personal inventory. How have you devalued yourself through comparison or copying?

5. The attitude of superiority expresses itself by not valuing the contributions of others. Do an inventory of those in the body of Christ whom you discount, then thank God for them as people you need in your life to be complete.

6. What questions do you have about this reading?

7. Does the reading convict, challenge or comfort you? Why?

Going Deeper

Ogden, Greg. *The New Reformation: Returning the Ministry to the People of God.* Grand Rapids: Zondervan, 1990.

Action Page

INVITING OTHERS TO JOIN US

What criteria should we use while making the decision to invite others to join us on the next leg of this discipleship journey? We should look for the same qualities in people that Jesus looked for in those he called to be among the original twelve.

Jesus did not seem to be in a hurry to issue his invitation. On the eve of his selection of the twelve, Jesus spent the night in prayer (Luke 6:12-16). Jesus knew that the entire future of his work rested upon the quality of those he chose. As Jesus was praying, what qualities was he seeking in those he chose?

LOYALTY

Jesus made Peter a successful fisherman and then called him to leave his big catch to follow him (Luke 5:1-11). All Jesus had to say to the twelve was, "Follow me, and I will make you fishers of men" (Mark 1:17), and they left their trade, families and familiar surroundings to be a part of the troupe. The apostles were appointed to their position only after they demonstrated their willingness to be sold out to him.

A disciple responds to the gracious call of Jesus Christ to follow him as Lord. John the Baptist said of Jesus, "He must increase but I must decrease"(John 3:30 NRSV). We are seeking those who demonstrate a desire to place Jesus above all else in their lives. This is evidenced by a willingness to change in character and lifestyle, an openness to self-examination and a hunger to place themselves at Jesus' disposal in order to discover how their lives can count for him.

TEACHABILITY

Jesus chose the disciples for what they would become, not for what they were at the moment of summons. From a worldly standpoint the disciples did not have much to commend themselves. They were not influential people in key positions who could get the word to the "right" people. They did not have any authority, so they could not throw their weight around. None belonged to the Levitical priesthood, nor were they in high positions in the synagogue. They did not have any academic degrees nor worldly credentials that would make them credible to the populace. None had recognizable names worth printing on a letterhead. In fact, in the book of Acts they were described by the religious leaders as "unschooled, common men" (Acts 4:13).

We must therefore be careful not to be molded by a worldly agenda when it comes to forming our list of candidates. Neither natural leadership ability nor outgoing personality, neither a respected vocation nor advanced academic degrees, neither influential positions nor public notoriety were the criteria that Jesus used. Instead look for a hunger to know the Lord and a willingness to pay whatever price is necessary to become God's person.

In terms of character, the disciples left much to be desired. James and John were unpredictably impulsive, ready to call down fire from heaven on the first unbelieving town. They were temperamental. They fought among themselves and jealously jockeyed for positions of greatness (Mark 10:35-41). They reflected the prejudice of their day, seeing women as second-class citizens (John 4:27). But Jesus noticed in them what they could become over a long period of investment. And these men placed themselves as clay in the potter's hand.

SELECTING FUTURE DISCIPLING PARTNERS
As you are looking toward the completion of your discipleship journey with your current partners, it is time to begin praying about who will join you on the next leg. The topic of "selecting future partners" is placed here so that you can assist one another. Allow the following questions to guide your process.

1. How are you feeling about making an investment in the next generation? Explain.

2. Put in your own words the qualities that Jesus was looking for in those whom he selected to be his disciples.

3. How can these criteria guide you in your selection?

4. The discipling dynamic is most effective when you sense a personal call or leading to give yourself to those whom the Lord especially places on your heart. Over the next few weeks as you pray, begin to record names of people who come to mind.

21 / Ministry Gifts

Looking Ahead

MEMORY VERSE: 1 Corinthians 12:7
BIBLE STUDY: 1 Corinthians 12:1-11, 27-31; Romans 12:3-8; Ephesians 4:11-12;1 Peter 4:10-11
READING: You Are Gifted!

 Core Truth

How can we know what our part is in the body of Christ?

The Holy Spirit graciously gives ministry abilities, "spiritual gifts," so that every Christian can make a valued contribution to the health of the whole body. The church actually operates as the body of Christ when each person seeks to know and function in accord with their role assigned by God.

1. Identify key words or phrases in the question and answer above, and state their meaning in your own words.

2. Restate the core truth in your own words.

3. What questions or issues does the core truth raise for you?

Memory Verse Study Guide

First Corinthians 12 is the classic New Testament passage on the subject of spiritual gifts and the church as the body of Christ. Paul begins this chapter by introducing his topic in the same pattern that he has throughout the book: "Now about spiritual gifts" (v. 1).

1. *Putting it in context:* What misunderstanding about what it means to be spiritual is Paul addressing in 1 Corinthians 12:1-3?

2. The memory verse is *1 Corinthians 12:7.* Copy the verse verbatim.

3. What is the extent of the distribution of spiritual gifts in the body?

4. What does the word *manifestation* tell us about spiritual gifts?

5. What is the purpose of spiritual gifts?

6. How has this verse spoken to you this week?

Inductive Bible Study Guide

Four New Testament passages discuss spiritual gifts for ministry. Some teachers look to the seven gifts identified in Romans 12:6-8 as the "motivational" gifts. One of these seven motivations is seen as dominant for every believer. The gifts listed in 1 Corinthians 12 are then "manifestations" of these motivations, while the four gifts associated with equipping are "offices." I view the gifts that Paul lists as illustrative of the variety of ways that the Holy Spirit works through us. The four categories for the gifts are for descriptive purposes only, as a way to see the variety.

1   *Read 1 Corinthians 12:1-11, 27-31; Romans 12:3-8; Ephesians 4:11-12; 1 Peter 4:10-11.* Paul lists four synonyms for gifts. Write down your own definitions of these terms.

    gifts (1 Corinthians 12:4)

    service (1 Corinthians 12:5)

    working (1 Corinthians 12:6)

    function (Romans 12:4)

2. After reviewing these synonyms, write your own definition of a spiritual gift.

3. Identify the gifts that are listed in the passages and place them in one of the following categories. Under each gift write your own choice for a synonym.

support (Ephesians 4:11)	speaking (use the tongue)	sign	service

4. Paul intertwines what we might humanly distinguish as supernatural (for example, healing) and natural (for example, administration) gifts. What does this teach us?

5. Do you agree or disagree with the following statement: Paul intended to give us an exhaustive or complete list of all the spiritual gifts. Explain.

6. What questions do these passages raise for you?

7. What verse or verses have particularly impacted you? Rewrite key verses in your own words.

⬰ Reading: You Are Gifted!

My first ministry position with college students ended on a high. The ministry in Pittsburgh had grown to three hundred students on Wednesday nights, a core of forty small-group leaders and weekly reports of students coming to Christ. From that position I blew like a whirlwind into a sleepy, declining church with the attitude "I can get this place up and humming." As I look back on my late twenties, my naive conviction was that the context in which one serves doesn't matter, because God can use a person anywhere. To the contrary, I found that context mattered a great deal. During that seven-year pastorate I felt like an eight-cylinder car running on two cylinders. The setting allowed for only a small range of my gifts to be used. I was constricted and lost motivation.

Sometimes we lose motivation because we don't feel competent to do the job or fulfill the role. The position calls for skills that are not natural to us, or we are asked to give our energy to something we don't care about. When my daughter was little, she had a toy sphere into which were cut various geometric shapes. Her objective was to slide a round cylinder through the circle on the sphere. But invariably I would find the cylinder wedged tightly in the square-shaped opening. Round pegs in square holes: they just don't fit. When this occurs we find our energy and motivation dissipating.

The body of Christ is designed in such a way that each of us has a valued role particularly suited for us, but the problem is that we don't always know what it is. It's no wonder that Paul begins his teaching on spiritual gifts in this manner: "Now about spiritual gifts, brothers, I do not want you to be ignorant" (1 Corinthians 12:1). One of the reasons we get into positions for which we are not suited is that we are ignorant of our abilities.

SPIRITUAL GIFTS EXPLAINED

What is meant by *spiritual gifts?* In 1 Corinthians 12:4-7 Paul establishes a vocabulary for spiritual gifts that gives us an insight into what he means by this term. Before we examine Paul's glossary for spiritual gifts, we need to remove the cultural debris surrounding this phrase. The words *gifted* or *gift* are used in a different way in the Scriptures than they are in everyday speech. A gifted person is one who excels in a particular field. Carl Lewis is a gifted track star because he can run faster and jump farther than any other human being. A gifted student is one with above-average intelligence. We hear people say someone has a gift for fixing cars or making cherry pies, or he or she has the gift of gab. The way we use *gifted* or *gift* generally falls into the category of natural talents that God, out of his bounty, gives to Christians and non-Christians alike; whereas spiritual gifts are possessed by Christians, with the purpose of building and strengthening fellow Christians and extending the influence of the church to an unbelieving world. Spiritual gifts are only for those indwelt by the Holy Spirit.

Let's examine the synonyms used in our passage to build a picture of what we mean by spiritual gifts.

> There are different kinds of *gifts,* but the same Spirit. There are different kinds of *service,* but the same Lord. There are different kinds of *working,* but the same God works all of them in all men. Now to each one the *manifestation* of the Spirit

is given for the common good. (1 Corinthians 12:4-7, emphasis added)

Each of us has one body with many members, and these members do not all have the same *function*. (Romans 12:4)

The first thing we notice is a repeated word, *different*, which serves as the common characteristic of spiritual gifts. Variety is an expression of the one God who is three persons. The source of the gifts in verse 4 is the Spirit, in verse 5 the Lord Jesus, and in verse 6 God the Father. Paul is saying that the variety of motivations in the church is an expression of the diversity within the Godhead. As our God is one being who is three persons, so the church is like the God it worships.

Different means distribution, diversity, allotment, apportionment. The Spirit is in charge of the distribution system. The emphasis is that God is the distributor of the gifts, and we are the receivers.

Now let's look at Paul's words for *gifts*.

1. "There are different kinds of *gifts*" (v. 4, emphasis added). The Greek word here is a compound word meaning "grace-gift." Not only are we saved solely by grace, but given to us with our salvation package is a capacity and motivation to serve others in a way that is particular to us.

Deep within us is a basic need. We all have a desire to make a contribution, to make a difference, to be valued because we have left a positive imprint on others. The gifts are our observable contribution to the health of the body of Christ.

2. "There are different kinds of *service*" (v. 5, emphasis added). The word *service* captures the spirit in which our gifts are offered to the body of Christ. Paul makes it clear that the purpose of the gifts is not to attract attention to ourselves but to build up the community. In verse 7 Paul says that the gifts are "for the common good." As much as the gifts help us know our value, their purpose is to serve others.

In saying this Paul was addressing a problem in Corinth that can be found in any age. When the Corinthians came together as a group, the flashy gifts of speaking in tongues and healing took center stage. People were using the community as a platform for show-and-tell. Yet the nature of gifts is that God distributes them, but it is up to us to use them in the right spirit. Gifts can be and are abused when people turn them into a means of self-aggrandizement.

Service also has to do with the sphere in which your gifts are used. Do you function best in a large group, small group or one-on-one? The gift of teaching can be exercised in an auditorium, classroom, living room or face to face. To whom are you drawn in ministry: children, the elderly, women, men? Your call is where the compassion of Christ in you intersects with a need in the world. It is as that point of intersection that we find why God has made us.

3. "There are different kinds of *working*" (v. 6, emphasis added). The word *working* comes from a Greek word whose root means "energy." Other translations give the idea of different kinds of "effects" or "different kinds of impacts." Each gift leaves its own imprint. If you have the gift of teaching, people should be transformed by the truth of the Word. If you have the gift of evangelism, people should be coming to know Christ. If you have the gift of mercy, then the sick and hurting should be comforted.

Using our gifts is like drinking from the well of refreshing waters of God's Spirit. Somewhere along the way, service got a bum rap.

Many have been taught that true service must be sacrificial drudgery. Service is doing what we don't want to do. Ray Stedman has written, "Somewhere this idea found deep entrenchment in Christian circles that doing what God wants you to do is always unpleasant; that Christians must make choices between doing what they want to do and being happy, and doing what God wants them to do and being miserable."[1] But when we operate within our giftedness, we are being carried along in a current of love that says, "You were made for this."

4. "Just as each of us has one body with many members, . . . these members do not all have the same *function*" (Romans 12:4, emphasis added). From the word *function* we derive the English word "practice." In other places in Scripture the word is translated "good deeds," but here it refers to our way of acting, our particular way of doing things that feels comfortable to us. Members of the body can say, "I am a teacher, a prophet, an administrator, a server," because these roles describe who we are inside.

Putting this all together, spiritual gifts can be defined as follows: spiritual gifts are our ministry capacity or abilities given by the Spirit that express our unique motivation for building up the body of Christ.

What is our responsibility? To discover and use the gifts that God has given to us. The Lord is going to ask us to give an account one day for the stewardship and multiplication of the gifts we have been given. In the parable of the talents the Lord says that the one who was given five talents went out and multiplied them into five more. To this servant the Lord said, "Well done, good and faithful servant!" To the one who buried his talent the Lord said, "You wicked, lazy servant!" (see Matthew 25:14-30). It is not an easy process to unearth

our gifts. It is a lifelong quest.

BURYING OUR GIFTS

The primary reason we bury our gifts is fear. This fear comes in a number of forms.

Fear of failure or taking risk. Paul writes to Timothy, who was shrinking from the exercise of his gift of evangelism: "For this reason I remind you to fan into flame the gift of God, which is in you through the laying on of my hands" (2 Timothy 1:6). Timothy's gift was dormant. When our gifts are not used, they atrophy like unused parts of the body. Why did Timothy not use his gift? He was afraid of taking the risk for fear of what might happen. Paul continues, "For God did not give us a spirit of timidity, but a spirit of power, of love and of self-discipline" (v. 7). The fear that locks you up inside yourself does not come from God. The spirit of God thrusts us out into new possibilities.

Fear of confronting pain. Some of us are frustrated because we seem not to know what our gifts are. When we try to get an accurate mirror image of ourselves, the reflection is distorted. For many people the reason for the distortion is that some painful past experience left a spiritual wound and shut off part of our inner world. There is a desire to embrace God's best, but there is an inner wall we can't seem to break through. Only when we get at the root of the problem will we break through what is holding us back.

Fear of commitment. Sometimes we claim ignorance of our gifts because it is safer. We know intuitively that to name our gifts makes us responsible for using them. Denying that we know what our gifts are gives us a reason not to use them, but as soon as we identify our gifts, we are accountable. Elizabeth O'Connor has written, "I would rather be committed to God in the abstract than be committed to him at the point of my gifts."[2] We prefer life as a smorgasbord, where we can sample here and taste there. As soon as we name our gifts we have narrowed our choices. We have to give up straddling the fence and keeping our options open.

Those who have broken through the fear of failure, the fear of confronting personal pain and the fear of commitment have stepped into liberated joy. The energized and fulfilled people have discerned their ministry capacity and are applying themselves to a need they care about.

There is a story about Michelangelo pushing a huge piece of rock down a street. A curious neighbor sitting lazily on the porch of his house called to him. "Hey, Mike, why are you laboring so over an old piece of stone?" Michelangelo reportedly answered, "Because there is an angel in that rock that wants to come out."

You are invited to break free and join the treasure hunt. What discoveries await you!

SPIRITUAL GIFTS CATEGORIZED

Here is a descriptive way of categorizing the spiritual gifts listed in 1 Corinthians 12:8-10, 28-31; Romans 12:6-8; Ephesians 4:11-12 and 1 Peter 4:9-11. Picture them in four groups, as in the table below.

Paul's list of gifts are descriptive, not definitive. He was not giving an exhaustive list. His lists seem to have little concern for uniformity of terminology. The biblical lists give us a good starting point for identifying the shape that God's grace takes.

SUPPORT GIFTS

Those who have support gifts have the responsibility to prepare the rest of the members of the body in the exercise of their ministry gifts (Ephesians 4:11-13). The one thing that apostles, prophets, evangelists and pastor-teachers have in common is the use of the Word as their tool. Ray Stedman uses a life-support analogy for each of the support gifts to define their role in the health of the body. Apostles are the skeletal structure, for it is revelatory truth that serves as the body's frame; prophets are analogous to the nervous system, for messages are sent from the head through the nerves to activate the body parts; evangelists are like the digestive system that takes in nutrients, breaks them down and sends energy to keep the body alive; and pastor-teachers are like the circulatory system that distributes the food of the Word and cleans out the waste.[3]

Apostle (missionary). One who exerts influ-

Spiritual Gifts Categories

Support	Speaking	Signs	Service
apostle	teaching (Rom 12:7;	healing (1 Cor 12:9)	faith (1 Cor 12:9)
prophet	1 Cor 12:28)	miracles (1 Cor 12:10)	helps (1 Cor 12:28)
evangelist	encouragement (Rom 12:8)	tongues (1 Cor 12:10)	administration (1 Cor 12:28)
pastor-teacher (Eph 4:11)	wisdom (1 Cor 12:8)	interpretation of tongues	service (Rom 12:7)
	knowledge (1 Cor 12:8)	(1 Cor 12:10)	giving (Rom 12:8)
			leadership (Rom 12:8)
			mercy (Rom 12:8)
			hospitality (1 Pet 4:9)
			distinguishing between
			spirits (1 Cor 12:10)

ence or authority over others to establish new local churches or to enhance the spread of Christianity into new areas. This gift is especially needed for foundational stages.

Prophet. One who discerns and expresses truth from God in order to exhort, edify and comfort the church or to convince nonbelievers of the truth.

Evangelist. One with a passion to tell the overwhelming grace of God and the overpowering love of a heavenly Father either individually or publicly so that people take the initial steps in Christian discipleship.

Pastor-teacher. One who has a particular concern for the long-term spiritual welfare of a flock and who teaches the Word of God as the primary means to feed, nurture and shepherd.

SPEAKING GIFTS

The distinguishing characteristics of the speaking gifts is not at all profound. The primary part of the body used for those with speaking gifts is the tongue. The support gifts use the tongue as well, but they are united by their equipping role within the body and therefore are worthy of a separate descriptive category. The book of James reminds us that there must be careful governance on the tongue because of its capacity for abuse (James 3).

Teaching. The ability to acquire, organize and communicate God's truth effectively so that there is life transformation in Christ.

Encouragement. The capacity to motivate individuals or a group through comfort, challenge, exhortation or rebuke.

Wisdom. The capacity to apply insight from the Holy Spirit to specific needs.

Knowledge. Depending on your tradition, there are two very different definitions: *scholarship*—the capacity to research, systematize and accumulate facts to help upbuild the body;

and *revelation*—the capacity to receive knowledge directly from God that was not passed on through human channels.

SIGN GIFTS

For two reasons it may appear unfortunate, at first glance, to separate the sign gifts into their own category. First, it may appear that these gifts are more "supernatural" than other gifts, like administration. Yet what is impressive in Paul's writing is that he commingles what we may consider the miraculous and nonmiraculous. This means that in his mind all the gifts of the Spirit, no matter how ordinary, function under the supernatural empowerment of the Spirit.

Secondly, by simply listing these gifts we are drawing attention to the fact that some schools of thought do not consider these gifts valid for today. This author has included them as normative for today for the following reasons: (1) Paul intersperses the natural and supernatural, thus erasing our categories. (2) Nowhere in the New Testament does it say that these gifts will cease once the apostolic era has ended. (3) The Holy Spirit continues the direct presence of Jesus in and through his people in accord with Jesus' promise of "greater things than these [shall you do], because I am going to the Father" (John 14:12).

Miracles. The ability to perform supernatural acts of God that interrupt the natural laws of the universe in a way that brings glory to God and authenticates the authority of the servant of God.

Healing. The ability to intervene in a supernatural way through faith as an instrument of God for the curing of physical, emotional or spiritual illness.

Tongues and interpretation. The ability to supernaturally speak in a human or angelic language given for the purpose of extolling God or interceding for something for which you do not know how to pray.

SERVICE GIFTS

This final category is somewhat of a catchall and is a reminder to us of the spirit in which these gifts should be offered to the body. With the exception of leadership and administration, these gifts might be the least noticed. Those who exercise these gifts tend to have the lowest need for recognition. Yet their quiet faithfulness is the glue that holds the body together. They are the sinews and ligaments that make for fluid motion in the body.

Service. The ability to perform any task or responsibility with joy, benefiting others and meeting practical or material needs.

Helps. The ability to serve by aiding someone in their ministry, by performing duties that release another to pursue their main call.

Mercy. The ability to work joyfully with those whom the majority ignores.

Giver. The ability to give material goods or resources with joy, delighting in the benefit it will be to the recipient.

Hospitality. The ability to entertain guests in your home, with joy and affection.

Leadership faith. The ability to discern clearly God's dreams for a particular body of believers and to empower them to fulfill these dreams.

Administration. The ability to organize a group of people to accomplish goals.

Discernment (NRSV). The ability to judge or determine whether forces acting on a person are from God, Satan or the human spirit.

STEPS IN SPIRITUAL GIFT DISCOVERY

There is no clear process of how to discover your spiritual gifts. To get a clear picture of yourself, you need to come at the discovery process from a number of angles.

Explore the possibilities. Be aware of the biblical definition of the different gifts so you can compare your behavior and motivation with their characteristics.

Discern your motivation. When you operate in accord with your gifts, you should feel that you are doing what you have been specifically designed by God to do, which will lead to inner satisfaction and fulfillment.

Seek feedback from the body. Those who know you best and have observed you are the best candidates for giving you their evaluation of your giftedness. Spiritual gifts have an effect on others and builds them up. Affirm others by sharing how their gifts have strengthened your walk in Christ.

Test the options. Often spiritual gift discovery means taking risks, trying new things. Face the fear that would bind you and try something that stretches you beyond where you have been before. Evaluate past areas of service and attempt to determine which were fulfilling and which were unsatisfactory.

Explore critical feelings. A clue to your giftedness may be indicated by what you criticize in others. Often there is an inner voice that says, "I can do that better than they can." This could be an indication of giftedness because you have identified something in another that you feel capable of doing yourself. It could also mean that you simply have a critical spirit and are in need of repentance.

---

[1]Ray Stedman, *Body Life* (Ventura, Calif.: Regal, 1972), p. 54.
[2]Elizabeth O'Connor, *Eighth Day of Creation* (Waco, Tex.: Word, 1971), p. 42.
[3]Stedman, *Body Life*, p. 70ff.

Reading Study Guide

For the purpose of discipleship we will focus on steps one, two and three in the discovery process. Complete the following:

1. Fill out the Subjective Inventory of Gifts, and after reviewing your answers prayerfully make an estimation of what you believe your gift mix to be. A part of the group exercise can be sharing the insights received and patterns discovered from the subjective inventory.

2. Follow the directions under the heading "Affirming Our Spiritual Gifts."

SUBJECTIVE INVENTORY OF GIFTS

On a piece of paper, complete the following statements as quickly as possible with your first impression.

1. In my work or church ministry I find myself most fulfilled when . . .
2. Others have told me I am most helpful when . . .
3. I am often asked to . . . (e.g., teach or clarify a difficult concept)
4. As a Christian, I most often picture myself as . . . (e.g., a coach)
5. I believe God has given me the responsibility of _____ in my congregation.
6. My biggest concern for this church is . . .
7. If I could be assured of not failing in ministry I would . . .

After reviewing my answers I think I have the gifts of . . . (list as many as you like)

AFFIRMING OUR SPIRITUAL GIFTS

1. List the names of the people in your group and next to them write down as many spiritual gifts as you have experienced through them.

   a.

   b.

   c.

2. Choose a group member. Focus on that person and bombard him or her with the gifts you have identified on your chart. After everyone is finished, go to the next person. There should be no discussion at this point.

Gifts others have identified

1.

2.

3.

4.

5.

The three gifts identified from the subjective inventory:

1.

2.

3.

3. Go around the group again and have each person react to the relationship between the gifts identified by the group and those discovered through the subjective evaluation.

   a. Do they coincide? What can you accept? What can't you relate to?

   b. What new insights have you received?

   c. Affirm what you see in each other and clarify the way you see the gifts functioning in a person's life.

Going Deeper

Bugbee, Bruce. *What You Do Best in the Body of Christ*. Grand Rapids: Zondervan, 2005. This is a helpful workbook that takes you through exercises to help you discover your gifts; it includes a temperament profile so that the ministry you choose will be consistent with the person God has designed.

22 / Spiritual Warfare

LOOKING AHEAD

MEMORY VERSES: Ephesians 6:14-18
BIBLE STUDY: Ephesians 6:10-20
READING: Our Struggle Is Not Against Flesh and Blood

 ## Core Truth

What opposition can a disciple expect, and what resources are available to combat this opposition?

Disciples have an enemy, Satan, who will oppose every step of growth into the sufficiency of Jesus Christ. Disciples must arm themselves for spiritual battle against the ploys of the evil one by putting on the whole armor of God.

1. Identify key words or phrases in the question and answer above, and state their meaning in your own words.

2. Restate the core truth in your own words.

3. What questions or issues does the core truth raise for you?

Memory Verse Study Guide

Christians are to put on the armor of faith when they go and do battle with the forces of the enemy.

1. *Putting it in context:* Read Ephesians 6:14-18, and list each part of the armor and its value as an offensive or defensive weapon.

2. The memory verses are *Ephesians 6:14-18.* Copy the verses verbatim.

3. How do we put on the whole armor of God?

4. Which part of your equipment is lacking?

5. How have these verses spoken to you this week?

Inductive Bible Study Guide

1. *Read Ephesians 6:10-20.* What are we commanded to do? Why?

2. What are the "schemes" of the devil?

   To which particular "schemes" are you susceptible?

3. Ephesians 6:12 portrays a struggle that is beyond flesh and blood. How would you describe this struggle in your own words?

4. What is your reaction to Paul's description of a battle against "rulers, . . . authorities, . . . powers of this dark world and . . . spiritual forces of evil in the heavenly realms"? (Are you skeptical about the reality of evil personified? Explain.)

5. What is the objective of these evil forces?

6. What is your attitude toward the power of evil?

7. What place does prayer have in the battle?

8. What questions do you have about this passage?

9. What verse or verses have particularly impacted you? Rewrite key verses in your own words.

Reading: Our Struggle Is Not Against Flesh and Blood

How do we account for the heinous evil of ethnic cleansing carried out by the Serbians against the Muslims in Bosnia? How do we explain the number of pastors who have sacrificed their call to the temptation of sexual infidelity? How do we understand the disunity and dissension in many churches who are bringing shame on the name of the Christ they follow? How do we make sense of the rapid disintegration of marriages, where the divorce rate has escalated from 11 percent in the 1950s to over 50 percent today? How do we justify our own self-destructive behavior when we violate our own beliefs about what is right, decent and virtuous?

Scripture says we have an unseen enemy who will defeat us if he's not taken seriously. "For our struggle is not against flesh and blood, but against the rulers, against the authorities, against the powers of this dark world and against the spiritual forces of evil in the heavenly realms" (Ephesians 6:12). If we seek human solutions to problems whose origin is supernatural evil, we will fail because we will not have correctly assessed the strength of the enemy. Education and support groups might help to a limited extent, but they are human solutions to spiritual problems.

In his autobiography, *A General's Life*, General Omar Bradley writes of his first meeting with the young William Westmoreland, who would later become commander of the American forces in Vietnam. At the time, Westmoreland was a cadet first captain in the West Point class of 1936. During the summer war games Westmoreland commanded a battalion defending a hill. He performed so poorly in this mock battle that the hill was overrun. Bradley, a major at the time, observed the exercise. He pulled the young field officer aside with this advice, "Mr. Westmoreland, look back at that hill. Look at it from the standpoint of the enemy. It is fundamental to put yourself in the position of the enemy."

WE HAVE AN ENEMY

Paul asserts without embarrassment that standing behind the human face of sin, brokenness and evil are unseen spiritual forces. Paul says that there are powers in our dark world. *Powers* was a term used commonly in astrology for the alignment of the planets, which was thought to control human fate. Paul takes that familiar word and fills it with his own content. By describing these powers as evil Paul means that they are destructive, unscrupulous, ruthless and in pursuit of malicious designs. Peter wrote, "Your enemy the devil prowls around like a roaring lion looking for someone to devour" (1 Peter 5:8).

Though Paul assumed the reality of a personified evil, we cannot. C. S. Lewis said that we make two opposite yet equally destructive errors regarding the devil. In his preface to *Screwtape Letters* Lewis writes, "One is to disbelieve in their existence. The other is to believe, and to feel an excessive and unhealthy interest in them."[1]

Regarding the first error, we disbelieve in the devil because in our scientific age the idea of a supernatural being who is the enemy of God is viewed as a product of primitive times. Now that we have come of age, we have a cause-effect explanation for everything. These notions seem foolish. Skeptical theologian Rudolf Bultmann expressed this attitude, "It is impossible to use electric lights and the wireless, and to avail ourselves of the modern medical and surgical discoveries, and at the same time believe in the New Testament world of demons and spirits."[2]

Richard Mouw, president of Fuller Theological Seminary, took the opportunity to visit a tenured professor at a major university who had recently become a Christian. The conversation began in a strained, awkward fashion until this new believer admitted his nervousness about the conversation. "This may seem strange to you, but you are the first Christian academic I've ever talked with about my faith." Concerned that his questions were too fundamental, he was afraid to ask them. One of the topics concerned the devil. "Before I became a Christian I thought a belief in Satan was a leftover from the Dark Ages—something you found today only on the lunatic fringe. But now as I look back on my own pre-Christian days, I sense that I was held in the grip of a power that tried to dominate my thoughts. Becoming a Christian meant being released from that stranglehold. In Christ I am now free to see things in a different way."[3]

The second mistake that we make regarding Satan, Lewis says, is "to feel an excessive and unhealthy interest" in him.[4] Some Christians are marked by excesses when they see demons as the cause of all problems. If one has an addiction to tobacco or sex, the reasoning goes, a demon of tobacco or sex has entered one's body and must be removed. Excessive interest can be a reason for not accepting responsibility for one's own sin. Comedian Flip Wilson's old line applies: "The devil made me do it."

In addition to disbelief and excessive interest, there is a third problem that may be more prevalent and damaging than the first two. We can say that we believe in the reality of a personified evil, but it has no practical effect in our lives. For example, when illness or depression occur, our means of handling them may be limited to medical or psychological services. Though we say there is an evil one, we operate out of the scientific worldview that asserts that all problems have a natural cause and therefore a natural solution. The truth is that transformation and change, the dislodging of sin and evil from our lives, is an act of the Holy Spirit displacing and confronting the powers of evil and sin. It is easy to be seduced into thinking that we can produce fruit in *our* efforts when in fact we are being called to enter into a realm of spiritual warfare that is not fought with human weapons.

We have an enemy, and the enemy engages us in battle. Paul writes, "For our struggle is not against flesh and blood." The word *struggle* literally means "wrestle" and is taken from the world of athletic competition or hand-to-hand combat. Paul is indicating that the battle is now "up close and personal." Just as a wrestler needs to know the moves of the opponent in order to pin him, so we must know the moves of the one who wants to destroy us. We are to put on the whole armor of God that we may be able to stand against the devil's schemes.

There are four basic strategies that the evil one uses against individuals, the church and the world. We must not think of the work of the evil one as purely personal. Christians have often failed to see that not only is Satan wanting to neutralize us individually, but his strategies relate to destroying the church of Christ and throwing a blanket of darkness over whole cultures.

What are the common strategies of the devil?

Temptation

When Jesus launched his public ministry, the first act of the Holy Spirit was to lead him into the wilderness to face "the tempter" (Matthew 4:1). A primary strategy of the evil one is to be a beguiling serpent whose method is to sow seeds of distrust and doubt about God, whether he has our best interest at heart. The primary tool in the devil's box is the wedge. When we go back to the Garden of Eden, Satan appears to Eve in the form of a serpent. God had promised the original couple abundance of life, the only restriction being not to eat of the tree of the knowledge of good and evil. So what does the serpent do? He raises a question meant to create doubt about God's goodness: "Did God really say, 'You must not eat from any tree in the garden?'" (Genesis 3:1).

Temptation is to sow disbelief that God's way is the most satisfying way for us to live. Though James tells us that temptation originates from within (James 1:13-15), Satan is there also fanning the flames of those desires, creating pictures in our minds and wooing us to do what is contrary to God's intent. The tempter promises satisfaction, but it is hollow and harmful.

Accusation

In Revelation 12:10 Satan is called the "accuser of our brothers." Satan wants nothing more than to tear apart the church from within. Satan's ultimate goal is to attack the glory of God and strike a blow against God's Son. What better way to do that than to sow dissension within the people of God, who are to reflect the glory of God? If Satan can get God's people fighting among themselves, the battle is over. We must beware of how we talk about our leaders or other members of the body, for we could unwittingly become a wedge, causing disunity.

Another way we experience accusation is the inner voice of self-condemnation and despair. Christians often fail to discern the difference between the conviction of the Holy Spirit and the accusations of the evil one. How can we know the difference? In the results. Satan has the capacity to create in our minds a frighteningly accurate picture of our sins and weaknesses. His intent is to lead us into despair. But the conviction of the Holy Spirit is sweet release. Under it we see with incisive clarity the guilt and horror of our sin, but we are lead to the refreshing waters of God's mercy.

Deception

Satan masks himself as an angel of light. The Ephesian believers were acquainted with Satan's attempts to transform himself into a benevolent power. Ephesus was a center for magic and occult practices. The temple of Artemis contained a cultic zodiac that could supposedly manipulate the cosmic forces. When there was a great turning to Christ in the city, "Many of those who believed now came and openly confessed their evil deeds. A number who had practiced sorcery brought their scrolls together and burned them publicly" (Acts 19:18-19).

Johanna Michaelsen tells the story of how she was sucked into the world of occult power through what appeared to be the good of psychic healing. Her story is titled *The Beautiful Side of Evil*. Satan exercises the power of healing and even attempts to co-opt the name of Jesus, but it is his way of taking hold. People innocently dabble in things such as astrology, graphology and palm reading, thinking that these things are harmless, but they are the evil one's point of entry. The lure of the occult is twofold. There is the desire for supernatural knowledge of the future and the desire for acquiring power to manipulate spiritual forces for our own benefit.

Satan doesn't come primarily through the occult. He is much more effective in throwing a blanket of darkness over an entire culture. Satan deceives whole people groups to buy in to worldviews that become dominant thought patterns and assumptions. The acceptance of relativism, for instance, is an ingenious and insidious maneuver on the part of Satan. A recent poll reveals that 67 percent of Americans believed there is no such thing as absolute truth. People won't even search for a truth outside themselves because they don't think there is such a truth to be found.

DIRECT ATTACKS

When Satan gets bold he attacks directly. Our society is openly hostile toward Christians. Christian belief is characterized by the media as narrow and even lunatic. We are living in the rising tide of anti-Christianity. We must be aware that the one who is driving the passions and energizing the antagonism is none other than the enemy whose target is the Lord Jesus Christ. If he can't get at Jesus directly, he will do it through Jesus' people.

We face a formidable enemy, but don't lose heart. "Finally, be strong in the Lord and in his mighty power" (Ephesians 6:10). As powerful as the evil one appears to be, we have the right Man on our side. The head of our army is the One who hung on the cross, unmasking and pronouncing judgment on the evil one and his minions. When Satan thought he had dealt the death blow to Jesus, God raised him from the dead, triumphing over the power of darkness. The power that raised Jesus is available to us. That is why Paul prayed for the Ephesians, "That the eyes of your heart may be enlightened in order that you may know . . . his incomparably great power for us who believe, . . . which he exerted in Christ when he raised him from the dead" (Ephesians 1:18-20).

SUNDAY'S COMING

Tony Campolo dramatizes the power of the cross and resurrection through a Good Friday sermon. On this particular Good Friday Campolo was the sixth of seven preachers at a Good Friday service.

Campolo was hot. After preaching he sat down next to the seventh preacher of the day, leaned over and said, "Can you top that?" The man, his pastor, said, "Just you sit back and watch." For the next forty-five minutes this preacher worked the congregation into a lather, and it was all built around one line: "It's Friday. Sunday's a coming!"

He started off slowly and built to a crescendo. "It's Friday. Jesus is on the cross. He's dead. Gone. He's no more. But that's Friday. Sunday's a coming." He began to take off. "It's Friday. Mary's crying her eyes out. The disciples are running in every direction. No hope in the world. That's Friday. Sunday's a coming."

"Keep going," someone said.

"It's Friday. Pilate's washing his hands. The Pharisees are calling the shots. The Roman soldiers are strutting around. But that's Friday. Sunday's a coming!"

"Preach on, brother!"

"It's Friday. Satan's doing his little jig. He thinks he rules the world. Institutions are at his command, governments do his bidding, and businesses do his work. But that's because it's Friday. Sunday's a coming!"

He ended by yelling at the top of his lungs,   "Sunday's a coming!"
"Friday!" And all 1500 people yelled back,   Take heart. Sunday has come.[5]

[1]C. S. Lewis, *The Screwtape Letters* (New York: Macmillan, 1961), p. 3.
[2]Rudolf Bultmann, *Kerygma and Myth* (London: SPCK, 1953), pp. 4-5.
[3]Richard Mouw, *Distorted Truth* (San Francisco: Harper & Row, 1989), p. 30.
[4]Lewis, *Screwtape Letters*, p. 3.
[5]Tony Campolo, *It's Friday, but Sunday's Comin'* (Waco, Tex.: Word, 1984).

Reading Study Guide

1. What is your explanation for inordinate and heinous evil?

2. Explain why we don't fully appreciate the reality of the demonic.

3. The author identifies four strategies of the devil. Put each in your own words.

a. temptation

b. accusation

c. deception

d. direct attack

4. How can we best arm ourselves against each of these strategies?

5. Where are you most susceptible to Satan's attacks?

6. Where do you see the church being susceptible to Satan's strategies?

7. What are Satan's strategies regarding the culture in which we live?

8. What questions do you have about the reading?

9. Does the reading convict, challenge or comfort you? Why?

Going Deeper

Watson, David. "Spiritual Warfare." Chap. 8 in *Called and Committed: World-Changing Discipleship*. Wheaton, Ill.: Harold Shaw, 2000.

23 / Walking in Obedience

LOOKING AHEAD

MEMORY VERSES: Ephesians 4:22-24
BIBLE STUDY: Ephesians 4:17-32
READING: The Principle of Replacement

 **Core Truth**

How is a disciple transformed into the likeness of Christ?

Sinful behavior is the product of practiced patterns that become habits which sink their roots deep in us. Growing to Christlikeness involves a process of replacing old habits with God-pleasing ones.

1. Identify key words or phrases in the question and answer above, and state their meaning in your own words.

2. Restate the core truth your own words.

3. What questions or issues does the core truth raise for you?

Memory Verse Study Guide

Paul uses a number of images in his letters to describe the process of transformation. He speaks of being conformed to the image of Christ (Romans 8:29), the fruit of the Spirit versus the deeds of the flesh (Galatians 5:16-26), and not being conformed to this world but being transformed by the renewal of our minds (Romans 12:2). In our memory verses sanctification is pictured as taking off old, tattered garments and being redressed with clothing that is honoring to God.

1. *Putting it in context:* Read Ephesians 4:17-32. How are verses 22-24 a transition point from the description of our former manner of life (vv. 17-21) to the new ways of life that replace it (vv. 25-32)?

2. The memory verses are *Ephesians 4:22-24.* Copy the verses verbatim.

3. Whereas Romans 12:2 speaks of the renewal of our minds, here Paul writes of the "attitude" of our minds (v. 23). To what is Paul referring?

4. What does Paul tell us to put off and put on?

5. How much is God responsible to change us, and how much are we responsible for our transformation?

6. How have these verses spoken to you this week?

Inductive Bible Study Guide

Read Ephesians 4:17-32. Whereas Ephesians 4:17-24 describes the need for and the principle of replacement of the old with the new, Ephesians 4:25-32 illustrates the principle that transformation is never complete until the old way of life is replaced with habits empowered by and pleasing to the Lord.

1. One way of looking at sin is to think of it as addictive habits, not isolated, individual acts. Notice phrases in the passage that describe sin as settled habits.

2. In verses 22 and 24 Paul does not say simply to put off the old nature but to put on a new nature in its place. Why can't we simply stop bad behavior?

3. Notice how Paul illustrates the principle of replacement using the phrases "put off" and "put on" in verses 25-32. Record your observations below.

Put off	Put on

4. What questions does this passage raise for you?

5. What verse or verses have particularly impacted you? Rewrite key verses in your own words.

Reading: The Principle of Replacement

In *The Voyage of the "Dawn Treader,"* the third book in the Chronicles of Narnia, C. S. Lewis tells the story of the transformation of the difficult little boy Eustace. Eustace is a passenger on the *Dawn Treader,* which is sailing under the command of Prince Caspian. Being nasty, a complainer and generally obnoxious, Eustace alienates his fellow travelers. When the ship docks on an island, the passengers get out to explore. Eustace intentionally separates himself from the rest, sensing that he is not welcome. He soon comes face to face with a frightful, fire-breathing dragon. Much to Eustace's relief the dragon expires right in front of him, but after a dream-filled night Eustace awakes to find that he himself has become a green, scaly dragon. This was Lewis's way of saying that Eustace became on the outside what he was on the inside.

Eustace sobs when he realizes the meaning of the symbol. How can he rid himself of the scaly skin and be recognized and accepted by those he has estranged? Another night passes full of dreams, or so he thinks. In his dream he is approached by Aslan—a lion and the Christ figure in the story. Aslan takes Eustace to a bubbling well, shaped like a round bath with marble stairs descending into it. The water is deliciously inviting, but Aslan says that before Eustace can get into it he has to undress first. Eustace knows that this means he must remove his scaly surface like a snake sheds its skin. He strips off his skin as if peeling a banana. He steps out of the skin and walks over to the edge of the pool, only to see that his reflection still shows the same rough and wrinkled skin. Two more times he attempts to remove his outer coat with the same results. No matter how much he strips away, he does not change.

Then Aslan says, "You will have to let me undress you." Even though Eustace is afraid of Aslan's claws, he is desperate by now. Eustace lies on his back and allows Aslan to have his way.

> The very first tear was so deep that I thought he had gone right into my heart. And when he began pulling the skin off, it hurt worse than anything I've ever felt. The only thing that made me able to bear it was just the pleasure of feeling that stuff peel off. After he peeled off all the skin, I was as smooth and soft as a peeled switch. He caught hold of me and threw me into the water. At first it smarted, but then it became perfectly delicious. I'd turned into a boy again. . . . And after a bit the Lion took me out of the water and dressed me. New clothes and all.[1]

God intends to make us into new persons who reflect his image. To do so he must remove the old skin that represents our old way of life and clothe us with new skin made in the likeness of him. The image of undressing and re-dressing serves as the frame for Paul's teaching. "You were taught, with regard to your former way of life, to put off your old self, which is being corrupted by its deceitful desires . . . and to put on the new self, created to be like God in true righteousness and holiness" (Ephesians 4:22, 24). Paul is saying that the Christian life is a lifelong process of taking off the soiled, tattered garments of our sinful nature and being dressed with a fresh set of clothes that will transform us into beings reflecting God's holiness and righteousness.

TRANSFORMATION

Let's put the process of transformation in very practical terms. We are creatures of habit. Habits are practiced ways of thinking, feeling or acting. They become so much a part of us that they are second nature. For example, do you button your blouse or shirt from top to bottom or from bottom to top? So well ingrained are our habits that we can master complex behaviors and perform them without conscious thought. Do you remember when you first sat behind the wheel of a car? There were so many things to think about—put the key in the ignition, fasten the seat belt, move the seat into position, keep your eye on the speedometer and the rearview and side mirrors—just for starters. Everything was a conscious effort. But thousands of hours later we can slip into the car in the darkness, find the slot for the key and buckle the seat belt without thinking.

Life is full of good and bad habits. We have habits of thinking, feeling and acting that both honor God and displease him. To follow Christ is to commit ourselves to putting off the old and putting on the new. The Lord desires to build God-pleasing habits into our character. The word "habits" is derived from the Latin word *habitus*. A priest wears a *habitus,* a piece of clothing that represents a commitment to a holy life. We too are to put on habits that are formed in practice so that godliness is a built-in instinct.

In Ephesians 4:17-24 Paul focuses on four steps in the process of removing God-displeasing habits and putting on those habits that reflect God's character.

KNOW THE OLD LIFE FROM WHICH YOU CAME

According to Paul Christians are to live in stark contrast to the dominant culture out of which we have come. In order for us to see the person we are to be, Paul in broad strokes paints the picture of a pagan culture in rebellion against its Creator. Paul's concern is contrast; he makes no effort to balance his description with noble qualities. He wants the believers to see that they are to live a life that stands out in bold relief. "So I tell you this, and insist on it in the Lord, that you must no longer live as the Gentiles do, in the futility of their thinking. They are darkened in their understanding and separated from the life of God because of the ignorance that is in them due to the hardening of their hearts. Having lost all sensitivity, they have given themselves over to sensuality so as to indulge in every kind of impurity, with a continual lust for more" (Ephesians 4:17-19). Paul notes three stages of descent into darkness.

1. Wrong-headedness. Paul says that darkness begins with faulty thinking. Notice the three words in verses 17 and 18—*thinking, understanding* and *ignorance.* Paul says that our entry into darkness occurs with the decision to reject the proper starting point for all of life.

Paul uses three phrases to capture this wrong-headedness. He speaks of the "futility of their thinking." The word *futility* is related to idolatry. Paul is saying that rejecting the true God doesn't mean ceasing to have a god. If one's god is not the true God, then the Lord is exchanged for a lie. Second, "futility of . . . thinking" leads to being "darkened in . . . understanding." If we start with the wrong premise, it makes no difference how impeccable our logic might be, because we will always come to the wrong conclusion. Finally, Paul describes wrong-headedness as the "ignorance that is in them." This is not innocent igno-

---

rance but a willful ignorance that leaves us accountable to God. We are without excuse. God will hold us accountable for our ignorance because it is chosen blindness.

The result of this wrong-headedness is that we are "separated from the life of God." Not only are we cut off from the life source that made us, but we are also in rebellion against and at odds with our Maker.

What form does this take in our society? A sign of our wrong-headedness is a rejection of absolutes. We worship the god of relativism. The prevailing attitude is that we should be faithful to whatever is true *for us*. This is the cultural air we breathe.

2. Hard-heartedness. The descent into darkness moves from wrong-headedness to hard-heartedness. Paul says that our thinking is wrong because our heart is calcified. Wrong-headedness is "due to the hardening of their hearts" (v. 18). The word for "hardness" is derived from the idea of stone that becomes harder than marble. It is comes from a medical term that refers to deposits of calcium between the joints that become harder than bone. They have lost all *sensitivity* (v. 19), a word meaning "ceasing to care," dulled to the point of making right and wrong indistinguishable.

3. Permissiveness. Paul writes that the Gentiles "have given themselves over to sensuality" (v. 19). The Greek word for "sensuality" means shamelessness. When a society can no longer be shocked or no longer has a healthy shame, it is at the point of Paul's description. The second phrase that captures permissiveness is to "indulge in every kind of impurity," that irresistible desire to have what we have no right to have.

Paul goes into a detailed description of pagan culture, for in order to practice godly habits, we must be able to recognize the soiled garments which must be removed.

DON'T UNDERESTIMATE THE GRIP OF THE OLD LIFE

One of the reasons we fail in our attempts to change bad habits is that we don't respect the power of a habit to hold us. It's like removing a tree stump. We might say at first, "This isn't a big job. I'll have that out in an hour." We show up with our shovel and ax to cut the roots. Three hours later we are ready to give up because we have dug a five-foot trench around the tree and exposed the root system, which was far larger than we ever imagined. We have considerably underestimated the task.

Endurance and discipline are key elements in changing habits. Any new habit takes a minimum of three to six weeks to become part of our routine. Most of us get washed out long before that time. We must know the strength of the battle that is ahead so we can call on the Lord's grace for the change.

PRACTICE THE PRINCIPLE OF REPLACEMENT

Paul gives us an often overlooked but necessary step for changing a habit. Our usual approach to change is to stop a habit of thinking, feeling or acting: we reduce our food intake, we try to stop being critical, we try to stop drinking. We do fine for a while. We may even think, *I have this licked.* But then our will crumbles and the former behavior is back, stronger than ever. Jesus tells the story of the man who had a demon cast out of him. The demon finds no place to lodge, so it returns to the place from which it was cast, bringing seven more demons along (Luke 11:24-26). When you simply stop doing an old behavior without putting a God-pleasing one in its place, you create a vacuum that is filled by an even stronger version of the same problem.

Paul says that we must practice the principle of replacement. When we "put off " we must "put on" as well. The first step is to identify the habit of thinking, feeling or acting that needs to be put to death or nailed to the cross. Then we must make a searching and fearless moral inventory of ourselves and admit to God, ourselves and other people the nature of the wrong. Then we must prepare ourselves to remove all defects of character. The Holy Spirit's transformation will not be complete until we practice the principle of replacement.

KEEP IN MIND GOD'S INTENTION FOR YOU

God's intent is for you to reflect his image: "Put on the new self, created to be like God in true righteousness and holiness" (v. 24). Athletes often attain their goal by visualizing their success. A high jumper sees the bar and her body safely flying over it. It is the completion of the goal that motivates her toward what she is to become. We are to see ourselves with the defects of character removed from our lives as Jesus shines through so that we are what God intends us to be.

We must be patient with the process. Richard Lovelace gives us good insight into the process of sanctification: "God will proceed at a rate and follow a course which is ideally suited to the individual, raising successive issues over the years and making a point of the need for growth in one area after another. He seldom shows us all of our needs at once; we would be overwhelmed at the sight."[2] In other words, there is no such thing as instant godliness. To live in a way that is contrary to society, we need to commit ourselves to a lifetime of change under the guidance of the Holy Spirit.

The Holy Spirit is God's tailor: he is ready to give us a new set of clothes and discard the old, threadbare wardrobe. But the old way of life dies a slow, bitter, bloody death. It does not want to give up its grip. Yet the new set of clothes are so much more becoming.

As in Eustace's story, it is the Lord who must be given the permission to dress us anew. We can't remove the scales ourselves. Our prayer should be, "Lord, do what it takes, reach as deep as you need, go after the wrong thinking, wrong feelings, wrong behaviors. Go straight to the heart with whatever pain it will take, because our desire is to be made over in the likeness of God."

---

[1]C. S. Lewis, *The Voyage of the "Dawn Treader"* (New York: Macmillan, 1952), p. 90.
[2]Richard F. Lovelace, *Dynamics of Spiritual Life* (Downers Grove, Ill.: InterVarsity Press, 1980), p. 111.

Reading Study Guide

1. What point does C. S. Lewis illustrate through Eustace in *The Voyage of the "Dawn Treader"*?

2. Does Paul's description of society in rebellion against God seem overstated to you? Why or why not?

3. What habits have you tried to dislodge? If you failed, what do you suppose was the reason for the failure?

4. How would you put each of these steps to enact the principle of replacement into effect?

   a. habit to be replaced

   b. the biblical "instead of"

   c. visualize what God intends you to be

5. What questions do you have about this reading?

6. Does the reading convict, challenge or comfort you? Why?

Going Deeper

Watson, David. "Cost of Discipleship." Chap. 11 in *Called and Committed: World-Changing Discipleship*. Wheaton, Ill.: Harold Shaw, 2000.

24 / Sharing the Wealth

LOOKING AHEAD

MEMORY VERSE: 2 Timothy 2:2
BIBLE STUDY: 1 Thessalonians 2:1-12
READING: Paul's Strategy of Ministry

 **Core Truth**

What is our role in discipling others?

Discipling is the process of allowing God to use us to be a part of helping another disciple to grow. A sign of our maturity is the desire to pass on the "wealth" to the next generation.

1. Identify key words or phrases in the question and answer above, and state their meaning in your own words.

2. Restate the core truth in your own words.

3. What questions or issues does the core truth raise for you?

Memory Verse Study Guide

Second Timothy is a motivational letter from Paul to his son in the faith, Timothy. Paul is at the end of his earthly ministry and deeply concerned that the gospel be transmitted intact to the next generation. Timothy is urged to be that link.

1. *Putting it in context:* Read 2 Timothy 1:1-18. How does Paul's admonition to Timothy, "be strong in the grace that is in Christ Jesus" (2:1), address the fears that Paul identifies in 1 Timothy 1?

2. The memory verse is *2 Timothy 2:2.* Copy the verse verbatim.

3. What is the ministry strategy contained in this verse?

4. Timothy is to look for those who are "reliable." What qualities should you look for in a future discipling partner?

   Does this mean that some Christians are not suitable for a discipling relationship? Why or why not?

5. William Barclay has said that every Christian stands as a link between two generations. How do you feel about being in that link?

6. In what ways has this verse spoken to you this week?

Inductive Bible Study Guide

In the first chapter of Paul's letter to the Thessalonians he commends them for many good qualities. He then goes on in the second chapter to describe the qualities that he exemplified as well as the methods he used to urge the Thessalonians to maturity.

1. *Read 1 Thessalonians 2:1-12.* Read Acts 16:11-40 to see the treatment of Paul and Silas in Philippi, the community he visited just prior to going to Thessalonica (Acts 17:1-10). What impresses you about Paul and Silas?

2. What character qualities does Paul exhibit that are worthy of imitation?

   Which of these challenge you in your discipleship?

3. What was Paul's method of instilling these qualities in the Thessalonians (notice verses 7 and 11)?

4. How do these images instruct you in how to invest in others?

5. What questions do you have about this passage?

6. What verse or verses have particularly impacted you? Rewrite key verses in your own words.

Reading: Paul's Strategy of Ministry

Paul saw himself as one to be imitated. In so many words Paul said, "If you copy my life, then you are following Christ." To the Corinthians he could be so bold as to say, "I urge you to imitate me" (1 Corinthians 4:16). A key element in teaching is modeling. What was there about Paul's life that was worth copying?

PAUL'S MODEL

From 1 Thessalonians 2:1-12 certain qualities stand out in Paul's life.

Paul exhibited courage in the Lord (v. 2). Paul proclaimed the gospel in spite of the opposition he received in Philippi (Acts 16:11-40). Paul and Silas were cast into jail because Paul had cast an evil spirit from a woman who could divine the future. They demonstrated trust in God's deliverance through prayer and singing hymns during a desperate situation. When their resources were spent, God made his resources available, even though they had "been insulted," probably a reference to the abuse of Paul's Roman citizenship.

Paul's message and motives were true (v. 3). His message was not based on error, even though his hearers thought it to be sheer delusion. To the Greeks his message of incarnation and resurrection was madness, a foolishness that did not accord with reality. The intimation was that Paul was a fraud, a wandering impostor and propagandist. But Paul claims the source of his message to be from God and the foolishness is really God's means of salvation.

The Greek word translated "impure motives" comes from an impurity related to sexual matters. Stories were circulated to discredit Paul—that Christians were involved in secret immoral practices such as drinking the body and blood of Christ and greeting each other with a holy kiss. Paul preached against the backdrop of the Greek mystery religions, where temple prostitution was part of their worship.

Further, Paul's conduct was *above board.* There was no intention to deceive or lead astray, but he was open and honest, convinced of the truth of his message. He was not a crafty person with an intention to deceive.

Paul spoke to please God, not people (v. 4). Paul lived with a sense of obligation because he had been entrusted with a message from God. He therefore had no right to change its content or blunt its thrust. Paul refused to be swayed by the need for human acceptance.

Paul was not out for personal gain (v. 5). Paul never tried to derive financial gain from his preaching. Paul worked as a tentmaker, so the accusation of greed could not be leveled at him.

PAUL'S METHOD

Paul's method was personal investment. The only way to make disciples is to get involved intimately in the lives of the people you are trying to influence. God got involved with us in Jesus Christ, and he uses us to the extent that we give ourselves to others personally. Let's look as the way Paul gave himself to the Thessalonians.

1. *"Like a mother caring for her little children" (v. 7).* Paul knew the people under his care, focused on their needs and carried them along a path of growth. He was gentle because his disciples were like babies—tender and undeveloped. He is like a mother who acts in the role of a nurse to bring each child to health.

2. *"We . . . share with you not only the gos-*

pel of God but our lives as well" (v. 8). Paul was not an untouchable authority figure who kept himself at a distance. He got involved in the lives of the Thessalonians to the extent that his humanity was showing. Paul gave his whole self. He shared his life with them. The people knew that their welfare had become his welfare. Discipling is a process of investing one's self in someone else for an extended period of time.

3. "As a father deals with his children" (v. 11). Again we see the emphasis on the uniqueness of the individual. No human being is the same, and no one is at the same point of growth and need. A father must foster the unique character of his children, and so must a discipler. A discipler encourages, comforts and urges his or her pupil toward more mature godliness.

PAUL'S STRATEGY OF MINISTRY VERSUS THE CHURCH'S
Paul's style is the opposite of what we often attempt in the church today. His ministry strategy could be prioritized in this way: disciples, fellowship, program. He didn't start with programs but let programs develop from the spontaneous context of disciplemaking and disciples' fellowship with each other. He proclaimed the gospel; those who responded became the object of his investment and were formed into a community of believers. From this foundation his ministry grew.

The church's ministry today is often the opposite of Paul's. We have a different order of priorities that often looks like this: organization, program, disciples. We think that making disciples must be done through programs, defined here as a spectator-performer relationship. In other words, a few people plan the activities that are spoon-fed to the many. So

often what occurs is that the bureaucrats (committees, session, boards, etc.) devise a system that people are herded through, and disciples are expected to be mass produced. But programs by their nature are task-centered and not people-centered. They cannot respond to the unique character of the individuals involved. Programs are the quick-fix approach to disciplemaking.

PAUL FOCUSED ON INDIVIDUALS
In the opening line of Paul's first letter to the Thessalonians he writes, "Paul, Silas and Timothy . . ." Paul's mention of two companions gives us insight into his strategy. He was very conscious of his responsibility to pass on the faith. He chose people to be with him so that faith could be imparted in the context of real life. And the investment in people's lives was over a long period. Paul was faithful to Christ. He knew the character of God and the content of the gospel, which he painstakingly transmitted to his people.

Coupled with this focus on individuals was the self-assurance that his life was worthy of copying. Because of this, Paul can sound arrogant. Without apology he says, "You became imitators of us and of the Lord" (1 Thessalonians 1:6). Also, "You are witnesses, and so is God, of how holy, righteous and blameless we were among you who believed" (1 Thessalonians 2:10). Paul's attitude was "I represent Christ, and you should follow in my footsteps." Paul knew he had something to offer and did not drum up false humility to apologize for it. A discipler must feel he or she has something to give.

PAUL'S VISION FOR FUTURE GENERATIONS
Paul did not select Timothy because he could

help carry the luggage. He saw in Timothy the quality of faithfulness that would serve the future church. We gain an insight into Paul's long-range vision from 2 Timothy 2:1-2.

Paul transmitted his faith to Timothy before many witnesses. Timothy was trained in a public ministry, not as a member of a secret sect. Paul raised Timothy in the faith just as a father would his child, teaching him his trade. Paul addresses Timothy as his son in the faith.

Timothy is to continue to pass the faith on to reliable people. A faithful person is one who is loyal, faithful and dependable. Timothy stood as a link between the apostolic age and the next generation. William Barclay has said, "Every Christian must look on himself as a link between two generations."[1]

Paul was not concerned to pass on structure, organization or program. The test of his ministry was whether disciples were being produced for future generations. Paul identifies his motivating passion when he says, "We proclaim him, admonishing and teaching everyone with all wisdom, so that we may present everyone perfect in Christ. To this end I labor, struggling with all his energy, which so powerfully works in me" (Colossians 1:28-29).

---

[1]William Barclay, *The Letters to Timothy* (Philadelphia: Westminster Press, 1956), p. 131.

Reading Study Guide

1. As you examine Paul's model, what aspects of his character impress you?

2. Summarize Paul's method.

3. How does Paul's strategy of ministry contrast with the way we often operate in the church?

4. Paul puts himself forth as an intentional model. What was it he wanted others to imitate?

How can we follow his model?

5. Every Christian must look on him- or herself as a link between two generations. What must occur within you in order for this to be true?

6. What is your prayer as you look toward investing in others?

7. What questions do you have about the reading?

8. Does the reading convict, challenge or comfort you? Why?

Going Deeper

Coleman, Robert. *The Master Plan of Evangelism*. Old Tappan, N.J.: Revell, 1963.

BONUS SECTION

25 / Money

LOOKING AHEAD

MEMORY VERSE: Matthew 6:24
BIBLE STUDY: Selected verses on the tithe
READING: "Living with Cheerful Abandon"

 **Core Truth**

What attitude and practice should disciples have regarding money?

Disciples live with a healthy fear of the money god (mammon), knowing that it has the power to command devotion. A way to put limits on our greed and to laugh in the face of mammon is to begin our practice of giving with a minimum of a tithe of our resources to the Lord's work.

1. Identify key words or phrases in the question and answer above, and state their meaning in your own words.

2. Restate the core truth in your own words.

3. What questions or issues does the core truth raise for you?

Memory Verse Study Guide

Jesus was quite skeptical about the ability of humans to handle the allure of money. We tend to view money as simply a neutral means of exchange. It is the currency we use to transact business. Conversely, Jesus viewed money as having the power to secure devotion. The pursuit of "mammon," the money god, can lead to idolatry. Our memory verse places us on notice and issues a strong warning of this danger.

1. *Putting it in context:* Read Matthew 6:19-34. How does the teaching before and after our memory verse, set up the choice that Jesus puts before us?

2. The memory verse is *Matthew 6:24*. Copy the verse verbatim.

3. What is the choice that Jesus puts before us?

4. Why can't we serve two masters?

5. What is there about money that it has the power to become a god?

6. Where do you see evidence of money's drawing power in your own life? Where are you susceptible to money becoming a god?

7. Does the power of money to become a god frighten you? Why or why not?

8. How has this verse spoken to you this week?

Inductive Bible Study Guide

Though giving a tithe to the Lord is largely an Old Testament practice, mentioned only sparingly by Jesus in the New Testament (Matthew 23:23-24), it is still the foundational starting point to guide our obedience in giving. The tithe has never been set aside and, in fact, Jesus supports its continued practice, as long as the more important matters of justice, mercy and faithfulness take precedence. Therefore, this study will introduce us to the meaning and importance of the tithe in three key Old Testament passages.

1. *Read Leviticus 27:30-33.* To what does the tithe apply and to whom does it belong?

2. Note the process for the selection of the animals to be tithed. Why do you suppose the Lord chose such a "mechanical" approach?

3. How might we fall into the practice of not giving our best to the Lord?

4. *Read Deuteronomy 14:22-29.* What are the various uses for the tithe identified in these instructions of Moses?

5. Who are the Levites and why are they singled out for special provision?

6. Why might the "aliens, fatherless and widows" be selected as beneficiaries of the tithe?

7. *Read Malachi 3:7-12.* The Lord through Malachi calls upon the people to return to him. In what way does the Lord require the people to "return"?

8. The Lord asked to be "tested." What does the Lord promise for those who tithe?

9. Find yourself in this text: Place a check in the box(es) that applies and explain.
   ☐ Robbed God: must honestly admit that I have withheld my giving
   ☐ Ready to trust God: I am ready to tithe and in faith watch God provide
   ☐ Am trusting God: living on the stretch in trust and have watched God come through

👓 Reading: Giving with Cheerful Abandon

There is a stewardship principle built into God's economy: *You get back, what you give.* This phrase summarizes well the Apostle Paul's motivational message in 2 Corinthians 9:6-15.

Paul illustrates this principle through the practice of farming. "He who sows sparingly will also reap sparingly, and whoever sows generously will also reap generously" (2 Cor 9:6). It is common knowledge among farmers that if you plant few seeds you will yield a meager crop; but if you sow seeds with abandon you will have a much greater chance of an abundant harvest.

The Scripture unashamedly appeals to personal reward as an incentive for living out the Christian life. Sow to your own joy. Out of sheer self interest, the best way to live is to give. Some purists might find this appeal to personal reward to be troubling. One commentator wrote, "Nowhere does Scripture propose the gaining of rewards as a motive for goodness." Many of us were taught this as children. However, Scripture consistently tells us to seek our own pleasure and how to find it. So, if you are at all concerned for your own happiness, give; if you care about your quality of life, give. Principle: *The extent you give will be the extent to which you get back.*

Please don't misunderstand. This is not at all promoting the pursuit of financial reward as an end in itself, as some "health and wealth" preachers would. Their teaching is that the size of one's faith is equal to the growth of one's financial capacity. The more faith you have the more material rewards you will attain. One such preacher told how his faith had grown from believing that God could provide an inexpensive car, to paying cash for a Cadillac, to where he could believe God for a Rolls Royce, which was given to him as a gift. The Scripture does not teach that faith equals riches. In fact, you could make a case from the New Testament that faith will actually lead to hardship, but that is another lesson.

An implication of the principle of sowing and reaping is that some people struggle financially because they have not yet learned to give. We read in Proverbs 11:24, "One man gives freely, yet grows all the richer; another withholds what he should give, and only suffers want."

THE PLAN

A first step to getting one's financial house in order is develop the practice of giving. Bill Hybels proposes a simple plan for sound financial management: (1) pay God; (2) pay yourself (save); (3) pay your bills.

Hybels begins his discussion of motive by honoring the individual choice that each person must make regarding their financial resources. "Each man should give what he has decided in his heart to give" (2 Cor. 9:7). In other words, we should each pause and thoughtfully consider before God what should be our practice for financial giving. This implies planned giving, versus a haphazard approach. We should not come to the end of the month and then say to ourselves, "What do I have left over to give?" We don't wait until the offering plate is passed down the aisle, then to pull out our check book or wallet to see what we can afford to throw in. At the conclusion of this article you will be given a process that you can go through to evaluate and plan your giving with forethought.

Paul undergirds the principle—*you get*

back what you give—with the appropriate mindset. Let's turn our attention to the attitude that will lead us to financial freedom. Before Paul asserts the positive, he identifies two attitudes that must be rejected if we are to find our way to joy.

First, "Each man should give what he has decided in his heart to give, *not reluctantly.*" Literally, this word means "to give without grief or regret." Do not mourn the loss of money. If there is a phenomenon called "buyer's remorse," then there may be "giver's remorse" as well.

Why might we be reluctant to give? In order to give we might have to cut back on our wants. Giving and greed cannot co-exist. Giving means that there are things I might want that I won't be able to have. Greed is the insatiable desire for more. Greed is fueled by the spirit of the age; it is the air that we breathe. In a myriad of ways every day we are told, "We are what we have." This is why Jesus called money, mammon, the money god. Money is not just a neutral means of exchange, it has the power to inspire devotion. Charlie Sheen, the Oscar winning actor, captured this truth in the common vernacular, when he honestly said, "Money is energy, man."

The way to loose the grip of greed is to give. In his book *Money, Sex, and Power*, Richard Foster tells us how to dethrone money, "The powers that energize money cannot abide that most unnatural of acts, giving. Money is made for taking, for bargaining, for manipulating, but not for giving. This is exactly why giving has such an ability to defeat the powers of money."

In addition to greed being a reason for reluctance to give, we are also stymied by fear. Money becomes a god when we find our security in what we accumulate. John D. Rocke-feller was asked, "How much is enough?" His answer: "A little bit more." Enough is never enough if anxiety is the underlying tension and we seek our security in how much we have. I am not arguing here against prudent planning. Remember our formula: (1) pay God; (2) pay yourself (save); (3) pay your bills. There is a difference between prudent planning for the contingencies of life and being obsessed and driven by anxiety over what might be. The only way to financial freedom, even if you are following the above principles, is to find our security in the Lord. The only protection we have against the future is the God who rules the future. Stock markets rise and fall, only Jesus is the same yesterday, today and forever.

We are reluctant to give because we bow before the twin gods of greed and security.

Paul identifies a second attitude that can keep us from financial freedom.

"Each man should give what he has decided in his heart to give, not reluctantly *nor under compulsion*" (2 Cor 9:7). Under compulsion means "to give out of necessity, duty or under pressure."

We can be compelled to give out of guilt. Appeals to give in order to absolve of a guilty conscience are commonplace. For example, we are told that we wealthy Westerners absentmindedly misplace about $100 a year, which is more in per capita income of many third world countries. I was at gathering where the speaker asked us to look at the manufacturer's label inside our shirt collar. Where was it made? We were then told that we live well off of meagerly paid sweat workers who produce in expensive goods. Message: Give because you are an exploitive Western consumer. The trouble with manipulating giving out of guilt is that it does not cultivate a spirit of generosity.

Another motivation that derives from compulsion is to give in order to look good in comparison to others. This was the sin of the infamous Ananias and Sapphira recorded in the fifth chapter of the book of Acts. When they saw the generosity of others they too wanted to have their faces on the Givers Hall of Fame. Ananias and Sapphira had sold a piece of property and gave part of the proceeds to the apostles to be given to those in need. Their sin was deception. They acted as if they had given the whole amount. They wanted to look more generous than they were. Peter made it crystal clear that there were not *under compulsion* to give any more than their faith permitted. They could give whatever they were led to give from the sale. It was their deception of false generosity that led to the judgment of God upon them.

Neither reluctance nor compulsion are motives that are honoring to God. What is the attitude that leads to financial freedom? "Each man should give what he has decided in his heart to give, not reluctantly nor under compulsion, *for God loves a cheerful giver*" (2 Cor 9:7). The word translated "cheerful" in the original Greek has the meaning "hilarious." God loves a "hilarious" giver. This implies that the most joyful moment in our worship services should be when the offering plate is passed. We give not out of reluctance or any sense of "have-to," just out of the overflow of joy that we can be a conduit of the Lord's generosity.

But what is the wellspring from which cheerfulness comes? How do we get the attitude that is the foundation for financial freedom? There is only one thing that produces hilarity in life. Gratitude. The words "grace," "gift" and "thanksgiving" dominate Paul's thought in the rest of our text. Read 2 Corin-

thians 9:8-15 and circle these words and note the spirit of generosity and abundance that marks Paul's thought. Paul concludes this section with, "Thanks be to God for his indescribable gift!" (2 Cor 9:15).

Of what gift is Paul speaking here? The gift of His Son Jesus Christ. Cheerful givers are those who hearts have been overwhelmed and captured by undeserved grace. There is no greater feeling in the world that gratitude.

Dr. Lewis Smedes, like only he can do, put into words the feelings of gratitude. Doris, Lewis's wife, had found him lying on the floor, as he wrote, "looking quite dead." He lay in the hospital for a couple of days, tilting heavily in death's direction, lungs filled with blood clots as if they were buckshot. On the fourth day, his physician of Norwegian extraction leaned over his bed and congratulated him on surviving the twenty-to-one odds that medical statistics had stacked up against him.

Lewis responded matter-of-factly, "Oh yeah? That's terrific, doctor."

In retrospect, he said, his heart was not awash with gratitude, for until the doctor informed him, it never occurred to him that he might die. He closed his eyes and went back to sleep.

But here is what happened two nights later in Smedes' own words, "In the moody hush that settles on a hospital room at two o'clock in the morning, alone, with no drugs inside of me to set me up for it—I was seized with a frenzy of gratitude. Possessed! My arms rose straight up by themselves, a hundred-pound weight could not have held them at my side. My hands open, my fingers spread, waving, twisting, while I blessed the Lord for the almost unbearable goodness of being alive on this good earth in this good body at this present time."

"I was flying outside of myself, high, held in weightless lightness, as if my earthly existence need no ground to rest in, but was hung in space with only love to keep it aloft."

"It was then I learned that gratitude is the best feeling I would ever have, the ultimate joy of living. It was better than sex, better than winning the lottery, better than watching your daughter graduate from college, better and deeper than any other feeling . . . I am sure that nothing in life can ever match the feeling of being held in being by a gracious energy percolating from the abyss where beats the loving heart of God."

Once gratitude gets a hold of us, rooted in undeserved grace, giving will not be an issue ever again.

STEPS TO FREEDOM

Here's a very practical picture of the steps to financial freedom.

Step 1—Give Cheerfully

All giving begins with attitude, not the amount. Giving has nothing to do with how much you have. There is no correlation in God's economy between means and munificence. The first step to financial freedom is to ask the Lord to show you how outrageously lavish is his grace toward you.

Step 2—Give Regularly, Not Haphazardly

Giving that is honoring to God has a thoughtful faith goal that is translated into a plan. What can you believe God for this year? Giving is not just reactive or sporadic, but done with forethought. Plan your giving in the same way that you would an addition to your house.

Step 3—Give Your First Fruits

Pay God. Pay yourself (save). Pay your bills. It was the practice in the Old Testament that people gave the first fruits of the harvest or the best of their flock to the Lord. Make the first checks you write each month to further the Lord's work.

Step 4—Give When It's Tight

Giving is an act of faith in the ability of God to provide, whatever the circumstances. The beauty of stepping out in faith in regards our money is that it gives the Lord an opportunity to demonstrate his faithfulness to us in very tangible ways. How often do we get to see the Lord's hand clearly at work? When we trust God even in the lean times, and watch him provide, we have clear evidence that he is real.

Step 5—Give Sacrificially

C. S. Lewis has said it best: "I do not believe one can settle how much we ought to give. I am afraid the only safe rule is to give more than we can spare. In other words, if our expenditure on comforts, luxuries, amusements, etc., is up to the standard common among those with the same income as our own, we are probably giving too little. If our charities do not at all pinch or hamper us, I should say they are too small. There ought to be things we should like to do and cannot because our charitable expenditures exclude them."

Step 6—Give a Tithe

There is no more exact guideline for obedience that to give a tenth of our income to the Lord's work. Write down your annual or monthly income and multiply by 10%. Here is your goal and starting point. Build from there.

Step 7—Give in Faith

Giving should always contain the element of the risk of faith. In the realm of stewardship, this is called making a "faith promise." In other words, the goal of giving is set to the level that the Lord must provide in faith. You reach at least a little beyond where you know the resources will come from. For those who have been practicing tithing for some time, the edge of adventure may have been lost. Giving has simply become a financial transaction. Consider what it would be to move beyond the routine, to a place of cheerful adventure.

Giving that is honoring to God is motivated by gratitude. Cheerfulness and the awareness of undeserved grace are inseparable. When we know what we have been given, we give. And then the cycle repeats itself. We get back, what we give.

Reading Study Guide

1. Put in your own words the key principle of this reading: *You get back what you give.*

2. Paul tells us to not give "reluctantly" nor "under compulsion." Where do you see evidence of *reluctance* or *compulsion* in your own motives?

3. According to the reading, what is gratitude? What is gratitude's connection to cheerful giving?

4. Since being a "cheerful giver" is the motivation that is honoring to God, on a scale of 1-5, 1 being *grim* and 5 being *hilarious*, how would you rate yourself and why?

5. Look at the steps for financial freedom. State where you are in regards to each:

   Step 1—Give Cheerfully

   Step 2—Give Regularly, Not Haphazardly

   Step 3—Give Your First Fruits

   Step 4—Give When It's Tight

   Step 5—Give Sacrificially

   Step 6—Give a Tithe

   Step 7—Give in Faith

6. What is one commitment that you are being led by God to make in order to be a more faithful steward of the Lord's resources?

7. What questions do you have about the reading?

8. Does this reading convict, challenge or comfort you? Why?

Going Deeper

Sider, Ronald J. *Rich Christians in an Age of Hunger: Moving from Affluence to Generosity*. Nashville: Thomas Nelson, 2005.

Appendix

BUILDING A DISCIPLESHIP MINISTRY

My vision is to see disciples made and churches empowered through the multiplication of small, reproducible discipleship groups. It has been my joy as pastor to witness the transformation of two churches through this expanding network. Since this material was self-published for ten years prior to its current form, it has been gratifying to receive continuous reports about the value of this tool in implementing a strategy of disciplemaking.

After years of trial and error in attempting to disciple others, I have arrived at the following five criteria as essential to any program of discipleship. These criteria then serve as the basis upon which this tool has been designed.

LIFE INVESTMENT

Discipling is not a six-week program. We are geared to herding people in mass through a program, and once completed we expect mature disciples to pop out at the other end. Classroom models are necessarily focused on mastering content at the same pace for all, with standardized requirements. Disciplemaking should be viewed in terms of a parent's investment in a child who is nurtured through the stages of infancy, childhood, adolescence and finally into adulthood. Making disciples will only occur when we change our thinking from a quick fix to a long-term life investment. In the long run the results are both deeper and numerically greater.

It may be three to five years before the effects of this approach on the quality and vitality of a church will be seen. Those selected for leadership of the church will be those who have been discipled and in turn can disciple others. The leadership base will be expanded, and spontaneous ministry will begin as "self-starters" energize the body of Christ. Mission groups will crop up because qualified leaders have a passion to meet a heart-felt need.

TRANSFERABILITY

In my discipling efforts I had been frustrated by my inability to move the discipling process beyond the first generation. Those in whom I had invested either did not catch the vision or did not feel equipped to do for others what I had been attempting to do for them. Yet, inherent in anything called discipling must be the ability to transfer life to life to life. When Paul wrote Timothy, he looked four generations down the road (2 Timothy 2:2).

One of the obstacles to transferability is dependency. In a one to one relationship an authoritarian model of discipler over disciple can lead to an unhealthy reliance upon the "mature" believer. This is especially true when pastors disciple "laity." For transferability to occur one must move out of a hierarchical view to one of mutual dependency. Instead of parent-child, teacher-student images for discipleship, I much prefer a relational model of partners walking together toward maturity in Christ. The discipler in this process is not so much a teacher as a guide, facilitator or partner along the way.

From the beginning of the discipling relationship the new disciple is asked to give serious consideration to continuing the discipling chain by committing to the next generation. The order of the chapters also places the next generation in clear focus so that the disciples from the beginning are thinking and praying about whom they can give themselves to. The process of weaning disciples away from the discipler is supported by sharing the leadership of the discipleship sessions among the group members. This allows disciples to practice in a safe environment what they will be asked to do in their next discipleship unit.

PURPOSEFULNESS
Spiritual maturity is difficult to quantify. However if disciplines are being practiced, if content is being learned and applied, and if lifestyle changes are taking place, then progress is experienced. For example, Paul apparently felt mature disciples should know their spiritual gifts and be using them. They also should be reproducing themselves in the next generation.

This approach to discipling is designed to give participants a sense of growth toward maturity. The sequential format gives a sense of movement, working through the essentials of the Christian character, content and call. Simply progressing through the numerical sequence gives a sense of direction.

I do not mean to imply that if you master this content, you automatically become a mature disciple, as if it is the tool that transforms. But entering the discipline of this process creates a context for the Holy Spirit to do his work.

FLEXIBILITY
If you are discipling more than one group at a time, there is a need to be at a different point with each. Discipling is by design individualized instruction. There is content to be absorbed, there are tools to be practiced, and there are personal lifestyle changes to be made. No two people do this in the same way or at the same speed. Therefore an approach to discipling will take into account that Christ is formed in each person on a timetable unique to them.

This can put a strain on disciplers who are investing themselves in a number of people who are at very different points of spiritual development. One of the advantages of *Discipleship Essentials* is the sequential nature of the teaching design. This means you can be studying a different chapter with each person you are discipling. You can go as fast or as slow as needed, without worrying that you are at the same point with each person.

PREPARATION

Once you get into a multiple discipling situation, the time you will have to prepare for each appointment will be limited. This is especially true if the discipler is pastor. Given the preparation for weekly teaching and preaching events, a pastor will have neither the time nor the emotional energy to prepare two or three different lessons a week for discipling.

Discipleship Essentials is a tool which disciplers can use to convey their vast experience and knowledge. The core truth brings to focus their life experience and theological training. Initially, preparation time is required for the discipler to master the lessons, but once the lessons are mastered the material can be used in multiple discipling appointments with a minimum of preparation. Since the format is so simple, the only preparation needed to cover the same material with other disciples is a brief review along with prayer for the disciples.

May we be empowered to do God's work in God's way so that the whole world may know the good news of Jesus Christ.

FOR FURTHER TRAINING

In order to pass on the vision and skills necessary for a church- or ministry-based discipleship strategy, I have developed a five-hour training workshop. I am available on request to train your leaders in the criteria and methods for a discipleship program. I can be reached at the following:

Dr. Greg Ogden
Executive Pastor of Discipleship
Christ Church of Oak Brook, IL
31st and York Rd.
Oak Brook, IL 60523
Office: (630) 321-3902
E-mail: gogdencc-ob.org
Website: www.gregogden.com

Praise for *Discipleship Essentials*

"I have long admired Greg Ogden's rare ability to distill the complex down to the essential. *Discipleship Essentials* has become a modern classic in the field of discipleship because it does just this. If you've ever looked for a tool to help people you care about understand the core principles and practices of the Christian life, look no further than this book. I have seen it help absolute beginners and advanced disciples alike mature in their walk with Christ in a life-changing way. The book is interactive, thought-provoking, enjoyable and deep. I use it weekly myself."

DANIEL MEYER, SENIOR PASTOR, CHRIST CHURCH OF OAK BROOK, ILLINOIS

"Greg Ogden's engaging book sets the expectation that every follower of Jesus has the joyful responsibility to invest into two or three regularly and purposefully for the kingdom. For the past ten years, *Discipleship Essentials* has provided an engaging and balanced approach to the task of raising up mature believers who will then invest in others. I can only imagine that in the next ten years thousands more will be shaped toward maturity because of his important work that gives each believer the inspiration and the framework to do what they were made to do: advance the kingdom by making mature disciples."

REV. TIMOTHY J. YEE, MINISTER OF YOUNG ADULTS, ST. ANDREWS PRESBYTERIAN CHURCH, NEWPORT BEACH, CALIFORNIA

"I am currently leading my fourth group. The study is a Spirit-inspired study of the skeletal structure of our Christian faith upon which individuals can flesh out the shape of their individual walk with our Lord. If taken seriously and followed as a spiritual discipline, the truths it contains will change the follower's life, and lives that come in contact with the disciple will be touched by God's love. It's a powerful tool in a group for learning to practice confession and being accountable. It is never old for me. The Spirit speaks to me through the Word in the study. I am refreshed every time we meet as a group."

HUDSON STAFFIELD, PRESIDENT, CHI RHO MINISTRY

"Our entire congregation used *Discipleship Essentials* as the template for a yearlong sermon and small group series. It served as a life-changing tool that united our church family and deepened our faith as a community. Ogden's work is thorough, organized and challenging—a great resource for churches and small groups who desire to grow in their love for the Lord and their commitment to following him."

REV. JANE FILKIN, ASSOCIATE PASTOR OF COMMUNITY LIFE, FIRST PRESBYTERIAN CHURCH, BOULDER, COLORADO

"If you're looking for a shortcut to the likeness of Christ, stop looking because there isn't one. No program or structure can replace the hard, time-consuming, rewarding and utterly fulfilling process of discipleship. *Discipleship Essentials* is revolutionizing the lives of the people in our church. Everyone can and should use this effective tool! Stop talking about it and start doing it. Today!"

JAN DEN OUDEN, MINISTER-AT-LARGE, OM INTERNATIONAL, ROTTERDAM, NETHERLANDS

ALSO AVAILABLE

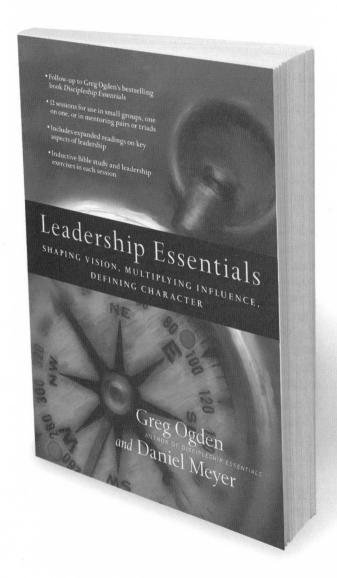

• Follow-up to Greg Ogden's bestselling book *Discipleship Essentials*

• 12 sessions for use in small groups, one on one, or in mentoring pairs or triads

• Includes expanded readings on key aspects of leadership

• Inductive Bible study and leadership exercises in each session

Leadership Essentials

SHAPING VISION, MULTIPLYING INFLUENCE, DEFINING CHARACTER

Greg Ogden

AUTHOR OF DISCIPLESHIP ESSENTIALS

and Daniel Meyer

978-0-8308-1097-0, paper, 175 pages